THE ECONOMETRICS OF INFLATIONARY EXPECTATIONS

Studies in Monetary Economics

Editor

KARL BRUNNER

Associate Editors

RUDIGER DORNBUSCH
PIETER KORTEWEG
THOMAS MAYER

Volume 7

NORTH-HOLLAND PUBLISHING COMPANY
AMSTERDAM • NEW YORK • OXFORD

The Econometrics of Inflationary Expectations

KAJAL LAHIRI

Department of Economics
State University of New York at Albany
Albany, New York, U.S.A.

1931 N·H 1981
P C

NORTH-HOLLAND PUBLISHING COMPANY
AMSTERDAM • NEW YORK • OXFORD

ISBN: 0 444 86208 0

Publishers

NORTH-HOLLAND PUBLISHING COMPANY
AMSTERDAM · NEW YORK · OXFORD

Distributors for the U.S.A. and Canada

ELSEVIER/NORTH-HOLLAND, INC.
52 VANDERBILT AVENUE
NEW YORK, N.Y. 10017

Library of Congress Cataloging in Publication Data

Lahiri, Kajal.
The econometrics of inflationary expectations.

(Studies in monetary economics ; v. 7)
Includes bibliographical references and index.
1. Inflation (Finance)--Mathematical models.
I. Title. II. Title: Inflationary expectations.
III. Series.
HG229.L18 332.4'1'028 81-11292
ISBN 0-444-86208-0 AACR2

PRINTED IN THE NETHERLANDS

To my parents

INTRODUCTION TO THE SERIES

This new series will publish books of interest to students and researchers working in the fields of macroeconomics, monetary theory and policy, banking and the operation of financial markets. It is intended that works of empirical emphasis will be included in the series along with theoretical contributions. Publications will include research monographs and the proceedings of significant conferences. The editor welcomes submissions of manuscripts for inclusion in the series.

PREFACE

This study develops a systematic approach to analyze inflationary expectations in the context of macroeconomic models. It emphasizes the role of structural models involving unobservables which often yield over-identifying restrictions across reduced form equations. When valid, these restrictions can supply important information on the nature of inflationary expectations implied by the structure. Based on certain *a priori* theoretical speculations that expectations may be heterogenous across markets, we have studied their role in standard macroeconomic models and in the market for treasury bills separately. To examine the contrasting estimates one obtains by using different proxy measures for inflationary expectations, we have used certain survey data and the rational expectations hypothesis as two alternative ways to model expectations. Thus, the study breaks away from the old tradition of modeling price expectations as a distributed lag of past inflation rates and utilizes the fact that rational forecasts embody stochastic specifications on the evolution of all predetermined variables together with other structural details in terms of over-identifying restrictions.

I am indebted to Professor G.S. Maddala for his constant encouragement and advice. This work began at Rochester under his guidance and without his active interest it would have never been completed. Whatever positive fragments there may be in the present study, I share with him. The first draft was written while I was visiting the University of Florida during 1980. I acknowledge the National Science Foundation (under grant SOC 78-09473) and the Center for Econometrics and Decision Sciences for generous research support.

In the course of the study, I had the privilege of getting useful comments and suggestions from Karl Brunner, John Carlson, Michael

Connolly, Alex Cukierman, Jacob Frenkel, Arthur Goldberger, Robert Gordon, Edward Kane, Bennett McCallum, Timothy McGuire, Charles Nelson, Christopher Sims, and an anonymous referee. Professors Carlson, Gordon and McCallum were kind enough to supply some of the data used in this study at an early stage. I have benefited from the collaborative research with Raymond Fishe, Jung Soo Lee, Hwang Lee and Professor Peter Schmidt; some of these results can be found in the chapters to follow. Three Albany graduate students, Kenneth Gold, Christie Teigland and Mark Zaporowski have provided able research assistance. However, the responsibility for any errors and omissions remains entirely with me. I owe special thanks to Betty Serra and Tammy Coviello for typing the manuscript promptly and efficiently.

I am deeply indebted, of course, to my wife Nandini for her everlasting patience and for correcting many typographical errors, and to our son Indraneil who is six months old at the time the manuscript goes to the press.

CONTENTS

Introduction to the series vi

Preface vii

List of Tables xiii

Introduction xv

PART I: INFLATIONARY EXPECTATIONS IN MACROECONOMIC MODELS

Chapter 1. Models of expectations and the Phillips curve 3
1.1. Wage inflation and formation of expectations 5
1.2. Estimation procedure 10
1.3. Empirical results 11
1.4. Summary of results 14

Chapter 2. Simultaneity in wages, prices, and unobservable price expectations 21
2.1. Structural model 23
2.2. Estimation of the measurement error variance by using the overidentifying restrictions 26
2.3. A general method of estimation 30
2.4. Empirical results 34
2.5. Tests of error-in-variables 36
2.6. Effects of Wage-Price Controls 39
2.7. Conclusions 42

Chapter 3. Rational expectations in macro models 51
3.1. Estimation methods with a general covariance structure 54
3.2. Empirical results 57
3.3. Real effects of unanticipated inflation 64
3.4. Tests of the rational expectations hypothesis (REH) and the implications of different information availability assumptions 67
3.5. Further tests of REH using data-based distributed lag representations 72
3.6. McCallum's model and some limited-information estimates 76
3.7. FIML estimation of the structured model 80
3.8. Further implications of REH in McCallum's model 81
3.9. Conclusions 89

PART II: INFLATIONARY EXPECTATIONS IN FINANCIAL MARKETS

Chapter 4. Inflationary Expectations: Their formation and interest rate effects 109
4.1. Interest rates and models of expectations 112
4.2. The results 113
4.3. Structural change around 1960 117
4.4. Conclusions 119

Chapter 5. Rational expectations and the Fisher effect 125
5.1. Search for a full Fisher effect 125
5.2. Maximum likelihood estimates 128
5.3. Three-indicator models: systematic errors in measurement 139
5.4. Conclusions 144

Chapter 6. Variability of real interest rates and the efficient market hypothesis 151
6.1. A structural model of <u>ex-ante</u> real rate 153
6.2. Estimation of covariance between <u>ex-ante</u> real rate and anticipated inflation 155
6.3. Rationality of Livingston's survey data 158
6.4. An estimated real rate series 161
6.5. Conclusions 166

Chapter 7. Concluding Remarks 175

Appendix A: Full-information maximum-likelihood estimation in triangular models 185

Appendix B: The maximum likelihood framework for generating price forecasts from SRC data 197

Appendix C: Sources and description of variables 211

Footnotes 223

References 229

Index 245

LIST OF TABLES

1.1. OLS to explain the formation of expectations 16
1.2. OLS estimates of the wage equation 17
1.3. 2SLS estimates of the wage equation 18
1.4. FIML estimates of the structural parameters 19
2.1. Estimated reduced form coefficients before and after the correction for measurement errors 45
2.2. Auxiliary regressions used in simultaneous wage-price models 46
2.3. Efficient estimation of the simultaneous wage-price model 47
2.4. Efficient estimation of the wage-price model without time trend in price equation 48
2.5. Efficient estimation of the simultaneous wage-price model with price expectations appearing in both equations 49
2.6. Effect of Wage-Price Controls 50
3.1. Maximum likelihood estimation of wage price-models with survey data on price expectations 93
3.2. Test of existence of observational error in survey data 94
3.3. Instrumental variable estimation of wage equation 95
3.4. Estimation of short-run Phillips curve under rational expectations hypothesis 96
3.5. Tests of rational expectations hypothesis 97
3.6. Tests of rational expectations hypothesis with specific information-availability assumptions 98
3.7. A joint test on the survey data and rational expectations hypothesis 99
3.8. ML estimation of reduced form parameters with and without restrictions implied by the REH 100

3.9. Explanatory variables in First-Stage Regression used to Create Instruments for $\Delta \log P_{t+1}$ 101
3.10. Two-Stage Least Squares Estimates of Wage Equation: U.S. Quaterly Data, 1952-70 102
3.11. 3SLS estimates of McCallum's entire model 103
3.12. Coefficient estimates with and without restrictions imposed by REH 104
4.1. OLS to explain the formation of expectations 121
4.2. Two-stage least squares estimates of the interest rate equation 122
4.3. Three-stage least squares estimates of the structural parameters 123
4.4. Estimates of the error variances of the structural model 124
5.1. FIML estimates of the Fisher coefficient 146
5.2. 2SLS estimates of the Fisher equation with GNP gap 147
5.3. Alternative estimates of the three-indicator model 148
5.4. Parameter estimates of the three-indicator model 149
5.5. Estimates of υ and α_1 for different values of β 150
6.1. IV estimates of the structural parameters and other statistics 168
6.2. Estimates of structural parameters in the three-indicator model 169
6.3. Test for "no Mundell effect" where expectations are rational 170
6.4. In-sample predictive efficiency of different Fisherian real rate models 171
6.5. Estimates EARR and the price expectations 172
B.1. Estimates of price expectations and their uncertainty from SRC data 207
B.2. Estimates of the uncertainty-augmented Phillips curve 208

INTRODUCTION

In recent years, an increased attention is being devoted to analyzing the role and the nature of inflationary expectations in macroeconomic models. An appreciably sustained rate of inflation during the last two decades and the consequent build up of expectations have led economists to study its impact on every sector of the economy. Historically, a rudimentary analysis of interest rate effects of expectations can be found in the writings of Henry Thornton (1760-1815), whose ideas were taken up later, independently, by Irving Fisher (1867-1947) and before that by Alfred Marshall (1842-1924). Expectations played a central role in Keynes' General Theory; however, they were analyzed in psychological terms determined by the "animal spirits" of businessmen, by waves of optimism and pessimism and regressivity. Moreover, due to his primary preoccupation with underemployment equilibria and sticky prices, the neo-Keynesian economists have given inflationary expectations only a very limited role to play in macroeconomic relationships. As a result, much of the recent research dealing with inflationary expectations has proliferated around two seemingly unrelated topics. On the one hand, expectation was introduced in wage-price models to study the effects of demand-pull and cost-push factors. On the other hand, with new econometric tools to analyze distributed lag models, researchers reopended Irving Fisher's old problem of estimation to study the basic Fisherian proposition that interest rates fully adjust to changes in inflationary expectations.

The rationale behind the Fisher hypothesis, though remarkably robust, is rather simple. For a given nominal rate, a rise in expected rate of inflation lowers the real rate which should stimulate both investment expenditures and aggregate demand. With output set at full-employment, this excess demand will push prices up, thereby raising the nominal rate via the demand for money equation. A state of excess aggregate demand will continue to exist until the nominal rate fully adjusts to expected inflation. With the same full-employment assumption, Robert Mundell [1963], however, has demonstrated how the full adjustment may not prevail due to possible real balance effect. Based on the assumption that interest elasticity of demand for money is not zero, he derived an inverse relationship between real rate and anticipated inflation. Though demand management policies are still ineffective in fine-tuning the equilibrium output, the IS and LM curves shift independently in such a way that the nominal rate of interest rises by less than the anticipated inflation. Mundell's analysis has been criticized on the ground that he utilized essentially short-run disequilibrium factors to explain a long-run equilibrium phenomenon. In fact, Sargent [1973] has shown, without full-employment assumption, that the full impact of inflationary expectations over a sufficiently long period of time is unity. Sargent's result, however, holds only if there is no real balance effect on expenditures (see Visco [1975]).

Further implications of anticipated inflation on real interest rates can be studied once the labor market is also introduced in the standard IS-LM framework. (See Turnovsky [1974], and Levi and Makin [1978]). Apart from the real balance effect and the effect of interest on demand for money, the induced change in income and employment due to unanticipated inflation can now affect savings further, thereby increasing the effect of a change in expected inflation on real rate. In this integrated framework, one clearly sees the intimate relationship between the existence of short-run Phillips curve and the Fisher relationship, that systematic money illusion on part of labor suppliers will tend to produce a Fisher relation in which interest rates adjusts only partially to movements in price expectations. However, once the effect of unanticipated inflation on credit market is considered, it can be argued that there may be compensating impact on the real rate. Thus, the sources, nature and the relative importance of these effects in the context of an extended Fisher equation becomes an empirical issue.

One problem with the above framework is that expectation is treated as exogenous, determined from outside the model. In recent years, using the concept of rationality due to Muth [1961], a considerable emphasis is being placed on models with endogenous expectations. The rational expectations hypothesis (REH) assumes that "expectations, since they are informed predictions of future events, are essentially the same as the predictions of the relevant economic theory," and hence depend "specifically on the structure of the relevant system describing the economy." (Muth [1961, p. 316]). Lucas, Jr. [1972], Sargent [1973] and others have developed models using this concept of rationality in which the short-run Phillips curve is a result only of expectational errors. Indeed, these models eliminate the distinction between short-run and long-run altogether. Rational expectations then imply that there is no way for the government stabilization policies to depress unemployment rate below the natural rate, even in the short-run. A key macro implication of the hypothesis is also that nominal rates adjust immediately and fully in response to new information (cf, Fama [1975]).

The rational expectations hypothesis also presents itself with a promising approach to model the unobservable price expectations variable. In its weak form, it states that expected price is related to the actual price in a classical errors-in-variables framework. Early econometric implementation of the hypothesis by Sargent [1976] and McCallum [1977] used the approach. This was distinctly different from the early approach (e.g. Fisher) where a distributed lag of past prices was used to model expectations. The problem with the latter procedure is that, apart from being totally ad hoc, it failed to identify all the structural parameters of interest. However, the full force of the implications of REH in macro models is yet to be felt. Given the drastic policy implications that emerge from this hypothesis, it is equally important to examine the consistency of these restrictions in the context of specific macroeconomic models.

Another approach to estimate price expectations is through direct surveys. Two such surveys -- one by Mr. Joseph Livingston of *Philadelphia Inquirer* and another by the Survey Research Center of the University of Michigan -- have been collecting data on price expectations for more than thiry years now. These data can be used directly in structural relationships as a proxy for the true underlying variable, and also can be used to test competing hypotheses on the formation of expectations. However, since the survey responses did not result from actual market transactions, their usefulness should be studied with due care.

In this study we have used the survey data, the rational expectations hypothesis and other conventional models of expectations to supplement one another as a measure of true price expectations. Also, to obtain structural information on inflationary expectations, we have used standard macroeconomic models and the Fisher equation as our basic economic framework. However, to allow for the possibility that the basic nature of price expectations imbedded in nominal interest rates may be different from that in macro models with labor market, we have treated them separately in Parts I and II. Lucas [1975] has emphasized the need to specify informationally disjoint markets in macro models.

The basic econometric approach followed in both parts of the book is the same: corresponding to a reduced form relationship involving only observables, there exists an underlying structure containing both observables and unobservables which typically implies certain overidentifying restrictions across equations. These overidentifying restrictions can be used fruitfully to study the nature and consequences of inflationary expectations. However, before this additional source of information is used, the validity of these restrictions should be carefully studied.

In Chapter 1, we illustrate these points in the context of a standard wage equation developed by Gordon [1971] and Eckstein and Brinner [1972]. We included Livingston's original data and a stochastic distributed lag of past inflation rates as indicators for the underlying price expectations variable. Our calculations suggest that the survey data, indeed, contains substantial errors in measurement. This explains why earlier studies using the survey data found very low values for the price expectations coefficient in wage equations. In addition we have tested a new theory on the formation of expectations recently developed by Frenkel [1975]. He has proposed a unified theory on the formation of short-term expectations which is consistent with the empirical evidence on the effects of monetary expansion in the short-run as well as in the intermediate- and long-run. Cagan's model of inflationary process does not explain the transitory period between two long-run equilibrium situations. In Frenkel's formulation, short-term expectations are determined by both regressive and adaptive elements. We found that the hypothesis explains the available data better than certain other conventional models.

In Chapter 2 we extended our analysis by considering a simultaneous wage-price model without modeling price expectations as a distributed lag function of past prices. The instability of many of the estimated wage-price models may partially be traced back to the restrictive nature of these deterministic proxies. By using the overidentifying restrictions due to simultaneity in wage- and inflation rates, we estimated all the structural parameters. For a wide range of model specifications, our estimates support the Natural Rate Hypothesis (NRH). We also evaluated the Wage-Price Controls Program in terms of counterfactual predictions of the model. It failed to indicate any restraining effect on wages; however, it showed large effects on price increases during the early phase of the Freeze, with a partial rebound in 1973.

In Chapter 3, we studied certain derivable implications of the rational expectations hypothesis in the context of two standard macroeconomic models. These models allowed us to distinguish between NRH, which posits that the government can persistently depress the unemployment rate below the natural rate only at the cost of an ever accelerating inflation, and REH which implies that there may be no way that the government can expect to have some control over counter-cyclical policies. The empirical evidence indicates that implementation of the REH in the context of these models do tend to wipe out the conventional short-run Phillips curves, and the assumption that public expectations of future rates of inflation are true conditional mathematical expectations based on all available information is indeed borne out quite well against its alternative. These results were obtained without explicitly introducing the orthogonality assumption between expectations errors and the conditioning variables.

Part II contains similar calculations in the context of the Fisher equation. This relationship has been subjected to extensive econometric tests including those by Fisher [1930] himself, utilizing a distributed lag of past prices as observable proxy for the price expectations variable. However, the success of these proxies, rather than the one-period-ahead rate of inflation (subsequently observed) is inconsistent with a well-functioning capital market. We tested the validity of REH and the Fisher hypothesis as two disjoint hypotheses. Evidence suggests that the basic Fisherian framework can still be used for descriptive purposes. However, models which allow the ex ante real rate to vary and be correlated with price expectation appear to be more consistent with the efficient market hypothesis.

To highlight the contrasting implications that one obtains by utilizing different proxy measures for inflationary expectations, we also used the Livingston series as adjusted by Carlson [1977] side by side with REH. The variance and mean for Carlson's data are nearly 40 percent less than those for the rate of inflation based on C.P.I. Our evidence in part II shows that the survey data consistently underestimated the true price expectations implicit in the market for treasury bills. The wage-price models, however, did not indicate such significant underestimation. Thus, it appears that expectations may as well be qualitatively heterogeneous across these markets and hence, should be treated as such.

In addition to the main text, there are three appendices. Appendix A contains further technical details on the properties of triangular structural models which we have used in earlier chapters. An analysis of the responses on price expectations collected by the Survey Research Center has been presented in Appendix B. By using an appropriate maximum likelihood procedure, we generated two series on price expectation and the associated variability over 1966:2 - 1975:4. It is shown that these two variables have very significant compensating effects on the employment growth. This is Friedman's [1977] Phillips curve in its third stage. Finally, a detailed description of the data utilized in the study are given in Appendix C. This includes the Livingston data together with a description of the nature of corrections made by Carlson [1977].

PART I

INFLATIONARY EXPECTATIONS IN MACROECONOMIC MODELS

CHAPTER 1

MODELS OF EXPECTATIONS AND THE PHILLIPS CURVE

The implications of alternative theories of formation of inflationary expectations in the context of shifting Phillips curves have been extensively studied in recent years.[1] A substantive econometric problem, however, is that the inflationary expectations are not directly observable. As a result, the treatment has been essentially ad hoc for a long time. In two important studies, Perry [1970] and Lipsey-Parkin [1970] have taken the lagged one-period rate of change in consumer prices as an observable proxy for the price expectations variable. Eckstein and Brinner's [1972] chosen proxy is a moving four-quarter average of actual rates of change in consumer prices plus the positive excess of the accumulated price inflation rates over 5 percent for two years. Gordon [1971] takes a distributed lag of actual rates of inflation to represent price expectations. These formulations imply modeling expectations in a deterministic fashion which may be quite restrictive in diverse periods. More properly, expectations should be modeled with an error. This would then result in a reduced form wage equation, where one of the explanatory variables is correlated with the composite error term. Secondly, the coefficient corresponding to the price change expectations can be identified only if some assumption is made on the distributed lag coefficients. Typically, the sum of these coefficients is assumed to be unity, which in turn means that a sustained inflation would eventually be fully anticipated. Since, during the periods used in estimation, inflation has never been so sustained, it may not be a reasonable identifying restriction to impose [see Sargent (1971]. Lastly, the distributed lag of past prices may very well reflect a catching up or adjustment of current wages to past inflation.

To avoid these problems, Turnovsky and Wachter [1972] used Livingston's survey data on price expectations to test the Accelerationist Hypothesis. The data in question are based on consensus forecasts from a semi-annual survey of economists and financial analysts by Joseph Livingston, a financial columnist now with the Philadelphia Inquirer. They found that: (i) though the observed data on price expectations are important in explaining wage changes, the coefficient is only around 0.20; (ii) the size of the response of the actual wage change to this expectations variable is largely invariant with respect to the specification of the wage equation; and (iii) the coefficient on the error adjustment term is significantly different from zero (nearly 0.40). They, however, noted that errors in the measurement of the expectations variable might have underestimated the true coefficient. The same was pointed out by Gibson [1972] and Pyle [1972] in the context of their studies on Fisher effect. Gordon [1971] also used the Livingston data in his wage equation; the estimated coefficient on price expectations was only 0.215 and the error-adjustment term was insignificant.

Turnovsky [1970] used this survey data to test three well-known models of the formation of expectations: adaptive, extrapolative and unrestricted distributed lag. The 'extrapolative' hypothesis showed the expectations to be regressive. In two recent papers, Frenkel [1975, 1976] has presented a theory of the formation of short-term expectations that combines both regressive and adaptive elements. To study the implications of these four different hypotheses in the context of the Phillips curve, we have estimated a structural model of the following form:

$$\bar{p}^e_t = p^e_t + u_{1t}, \tag{1.1}$$

$$W_t = \alpha + \beta_1 U^{-1}_t + \beta_2 p^e_t + a \cdot X_t + u_{2t}, \tag{1.2}$$

$$p^e_t = \sum_{i=0}^{m} w_i P_{t-i} + u_{3t} \tag{1.3}$$

where W_t = percentage rate of change in wages, $\bar{p}^e_t$ = percentage rate of change in observed expectations, p^e_t = the unobservable price expectations variable, P_t = actual rate of inflation, U_t = rate of unemployment, $a \cdot X_t$ represents the other variables multiplied by their respective coefficients, and u_1, u_2 and u_3 are random error terms.

Apart from analyzing the formation of price expectations and their impact on actual wage change in a unified framework, the model would take into account one of the simplest types of errors that might have 'blurred' the observed price expectations variable. In the process, we will also reexamine the apparently anomalous results obtained by Gordon [1971] and Turnovsky and Wachter [1972].

1.1 Wage inflation and formation of expectations

The structural model (1.1)-(1.3) can be rewritten in the following alternative form:

$$\bar{p}^e_t = \sum_{i=0}^{m} w_i P_{t-i} + v_{1t}, \tag{1.4}$$

$$W_t = \alpha + \beta_1 U^{-1}_t + \beta_2 \bar{p}^e_t + a. X_t + v_{2t}, \tag{1.5}$$

where $v_{1t} = u_{1t} + u_{3t}$, and $v_{2t} = u_{2t} - \beta_2 u_{1t}$.

The contemporaneous variance-covariance matrix of the $v_i(t)$'s can be written (under the assumption that $cov(u_{it}, u_{jt}) = 0 \;\; i \neq j;\; i, j = 1, 2)$ as:

$$\Sigma = E \begin{bmatrix} v_1(t) \\ v_2(t) \end{bmatrix} [v_1(t) \;\; v_2(t)]$$

$$= \begin{bmatrix} \sigma_1^2 + \sigma_3^2 & -\beta_2\sigma_1^2 \\ -\beta_2\sigma_1^2 & \sigma_2^2 + \beta_2^2\sigma_1^2 \end{bmatrix}, \tag{1.6}$$

where $var(u_i) = \sigma_i^2$: $i = 1, 2, 3$. This alternative structural form serves to point out the bias in the structural parameters that would result from an application of ordinary least squares to eq. (1.5).

Turnovsky [1970] tested three most popular and widely used hypotheses concerning the formation of expectations: adaptive, extrapolative, and unrestricted distributed lag. The adaptive expectations formula used by Cagan [1956] and Nerlove [1958] is given by

$$P_t^e = w_o + w_1 P_{t-1}^e + w_2 P_t \,, \tag{1.7}$$

where $w_1 + w_2 = 1$ and $w_o = 0$ will give the original version of adaptive expectations, viz.

$$P_t^e - P_{t-1}^e = w_2 \, (P_t - P_{t-1}^e) \quad ; \; 0 \leq w_2 \leq 1. \tag{1.7a}$$

This says that expectations are revised upward or downward based on the most recent error. One problem with this formulation is that it implies systematic underestimation in the presence of a trend in price inflation.

The extrapolative hypothesis, originally suggested by Farber [1953] and studied extensively by Hirsch and Lovell [1969], can be written as:

$$P_t^e = w_o + w_1 (P_t - P_{t-1}) + w_2 P_t, \tag{1.8}$$

where the original version of the extrapolative hypothesis stipulated that $w_o = 0$ and $w_2 = 1$ in (1.8). One major point in (1.8) is the regressivity of expectations. If $w_1 > 0$, the forecaster is extrapolating the past trend, expecting to continue. On the other hand, $w_1 < 0$ will imply a regressive expectation, expecting past trend to reverse itself.

It is well-known that both the extrapolative and the adaptive hypotheses are special cases of a general distributed lag model; viz.

$$P_t^e = \sum_{i=0}^{m} w_i P_{t-i} . \tag{1.9}$$

As we have indicated earlier, $\sum_{i=1}^{m} w_i = 1$ is one identifying restriction that has sometimes been used to identify the coefficient of price expectations in the wage equation.

Frenkel [1975, 1976] has proposed an alternative theory of the formation of expectations which tries to explain the impact of money supply on nominal interest rates in the short-run as well as in the intermediate and the long-run.[2] Specifically, he hypothesized that short-term expectations are influenced by two factors: (i) a regressive element, which is determined by the discrepancy between the actual rate of inflation, P_t, and an average long-term expected rate; and (ii) the usual adaptive element which is determined by the discrepancy between P_t and the expected short-term rate.

Frenkel gives a numerical example to explain the first element: consider a steady state in which all expectations are realized, and the actual and expected rates of inflation are 10 percent per unit of time. Now, consider a sudden jump in the rate of inflation to 15 percent per unit of time. Since individuals believe on the basis of past history that the average normal rate of inflation is 10 percent, they will expect the rate of inflation for the next unit of time to be below 10 percent, say 5 percent, so as to average out to the normal mean rate of 10 percent and thus to conform with their expectations on future price level. They might, in addition, revise their expected path of prices and thus their average long-term expectation slightly upwards, in which case they will expect the rate of inflation for the immediate next period to be above 5 percent but still below 10 percent. Regarding the second element, it is assumed that whenever the actual rate of inflation exceeds the expected short-term rate, individuals will revise their short-term expectations upwards by some constant multiple of the discrepancy.

The discrete time version of the hypothesis can be written as:

$$p_t^e = w_1 P_t + w_2 p_{t-1}^e + w_3 p_{12}^e(t),\ w_2 < 1,\ w_2 > 0 \ldots \qquad (1.10)$$

where $p_{12}^e(t)$, the expected percentage price change at time t for next 12 months, stands for the long-term price expectations.

The coefficient w_3 gives the coefficient corresponding to the regressive element and $(1 - w_2)$ would give the coefficient corresponding to the adaptive element. w_1 is $(1 - w_2 - w_3)$, i.e., the difference between the coefficients corresponding to the adaptive and regressive elements respectively. It may be noted that to make the theory consistent with the empirical finding that a rise in the rate of monetary expansion induces initially a rise in the real quantity of money [see Frenkel (1976)], the coefficient w_3 should be greater than $(1 - w_2)$. On the basis of the above hypothesis on the formation of price expectations, Frenkel [1976] has also elaborated on some aspects of the welfare cost of inflation in a dynamic context.

We have used $\bar{p}^e_{12}(t)$, the 12-month ahead prediction from the Livingston surveys to serve as a proxy for $p^e_{12}(t)$, and the variable $\bar{p}^e_{12}(t)$ has been defined in the same way as $\bar{p}^e_t$ is defined in Appendix C.

The wage variable we use in the calculations is based on Gordon's [1971] fixed weight wage index which is adjusted for overtime and interindustry employment shifts. Thus, we do not use the series on compensation per manhour utilized in many econometric studies. The compensation per manhour series tends to overestimate the slope of the short-run Phillips curve because procyclical changes in overtime and in the industry mix will be erroneously treated as representing changes in actual wage rates.

Three labor market variables have been used: the conventional unemployment rate (1/U), disguised unemployment rate (U^D) and unemployment dispersion index (DU). Disguised unemployment (U^D), originally used by Gordon [1971], estimates the number of individuals not in the labor force, and, therfore, not officially counted as unemployed individuals, who would accept jobs if they were available. Since workers in different subgroups are not perfect substitutes, Perry [1970] has constructed a dispersion measure along the age-sex dimension of the labor force, which basically hypothesizes that for any given unemployment rate (1/U), the labor market has become tighter and tighter, especially after 1963-64. Following the recent literature in wage determination, we have also tested the significance of a dummy variable (DG) to represent the effect of the Kennedy-Johnson wage-price guideposts. [See Perry (1967, 1969), Sheahan (1967) and Eckstein and Brinner (1972)].

1.2 Estimation Procedure

The alternative structural model (1.4)-(1.5) is a special type of simultaneous equations model -- it is triangular. A recursive model is a special type of traiangular model which is characterized by the additional requirement that the disturbance covariance matrix, Σ, is diagonal. Recursive models have been widely studied and are of considerable theoretical interest because of their unusual statistical properties. Most notably, it is well known that in a recursive model, the ordinary least squares (OLS) estimates are consistent and in fact are identical to the full information maximum likelihood (FIML) estimates. However, in triangular models, the non-diagonality of Σ makes OLS inappropriate for equations containing endogenous variables. Thus, a conventional solution is to apply the two-stage least squares procedure (2SLS) to (1.4). To implement the 2SLS procedure, we have generated the instrumental variables by regressing $\bar{p}_t^e$ on all the exogenous variables of the model. For example, with adaptive expectations formulation, we regress $\bar{p}_t^e$ on $\bar{p}_{t-1}^e$, P_t, U_t^{-1} and DG_t to obtain least squares prediction for $\bar{p}_t^e$, which is then used in place of $\bar{p}_t^e$ in (1.5) for 2SLS procedure. In what follows, we did not report these first stage regressions; introduction of U^{-1} and DG in equations (1.7)-(1.9) improved the $\bar{R}^2$ by merely 1-2 percent.

The three-stage least squares (3SLS) procedure can be applied to improve upon the efficiency of the estimates. We have, however, obtained the FIML estimates of all the structural parameters by an iterative generalized least squares (IGLS) procedure. An alternative proof of the result [Lahiri and Schmidt (1978)] that IGLS (with no allowance for the endogeneity of the right hand side endogenous variables) is, in fact, the FIML estimator in triangular models is given in Appendix A.

1.3 Empirical Results

Regression results concerning the four hypotheses to explain the formation of expectations are given in Table 1-1. The estimates largely confirm the results obtained by Turnovsky [1970]. All three hypotheses considered by him are equally good in explaining Livingston's data for 1953-70. The negative coefficient on the trend term suggests regressivity. The lower values for the D.W. statistic is possibly due to the particular aggregation involved in the definition of $\bar{p}^e_t$. It may be noted that the values of the D.W. statistics corresponding to the adaptive and the Frenkel hypotheses are likely to be biased towards 2.0 because a lagged endogenous variable is present on the right-hand side of both the equations [see Durbin (1970)].

The hypothesis proposed by Frenkel is clearly superior to the other three well-known theories on the formation of inflationary expectations. The variable $\bar{p}^e_{12}(t)$ is highly significant and the positive coefficient value suggests regressivity corresponding to longer-term expectations. The coefficient of $\bar{p}^e_{t-1}$ has appeared with the expected sign. In addition, the fact that we find $w_3 > (1 - w_2)$ implies that Livingston's data on price expectations are consistent with Frenkel's [1975] theoretical speculations. The low value for the coefficient of P_t is only expected since it measures the difference between the coefficients corresponding to short-term and long-term adjustments. $\bar{R}^2$ was significantly higher and the value of D.W. was very close to two. Thus, it seems that Frenkel's [1975, 1976] hypothesis best explains the observed data on price expectations.[3]

Ordinary least squares estimates of wage equations, with Livingston's measure of expected inflation as one of the explanatory variables, have been presented in Table 1-2. Precise variable definitions and data sources can be found in Appendix C. Looking at the third column, we find that the contemporaneous price expectations variable appears with a coefficient value of around 0.40.[4] It was only around 0.20 in the experiments reported by Turnovsky and Wachter [1972]. Also, a catch-up term $(P_t - \bar{P}^e_{t-1})$ was never found to be significant when introduced directly into the wage equation.[5] Two other variables - a guidepost dummy (DG) and the disguised unemployment rate (U^D) - were always significant.

In equation (V) Perry's Unemployment Dispersion Index, DU, has been introduced. We find that Livingston's price expectations variable loses all its capacity to explain wage variation. The result confirms an earlier finding by Gordon [1972] and Wachter [1976] that there exists an important trade-off relationship between DU and p^e_t in a standard wage model. Thus, though Livingston's measure by itself is quite important in explaining the behavior of wages, the size of the response of actual wage changes to the expectation variable is not invariant with respect to the specification of the wage equation.

We have used wage equation I to implement the 2SLS procedure.[6] The 2SLS estimates of the wage equation have been given in Table 1-3, where we find that the estimated coefficient of the price expectations has risen from

0.40 on the average to around 0.512 on the average. Thus it seems that there exist substantial errors in the observed price expectations coefficient. Still, the estimated coefficient is significantly below unity -- which is the value it should take according to the accelerationist hypothesis. Thus, our finding supports the conjecture of Turnovsky and Wachter [1972] that taking into account the possible errors in the variable may not be sufficient to support the neoclassical expectations hypothesis.

As expected, the loss in efficiency in the process of computing the 2SLS estimates is noticeable since the standard errors of estimates have increased uniformly. Since a consistent estimate of the variance-covariance matrix of residuals showed a rather high negative value for the covariance term, we computed the FIML estimates of all the structural parameters. They are reported in Table 1-4. The standad errors for all the coefficients have decreased considerably. The FIML estimate of the parameter corresponding to $\bar{p}_t^c$ has maintained an estimated value which is much higher than that of the OLS estimate. By comparing equations in Table 1-2 and Table 1-4, we find that more precise estimates of the lag structure in the formation of price expectations have been obtained. We also calculated the correlation coefficient between the instrument variable for p_t^e and the residuals of the Phillips curve. In all four cases, its significance was resoundingly rejected.

It may be noted that consistent estimates of error variances of the original structural model (1-1)-(1-3) can be obtained from estimates of Σ as given in (1-6), if we assume that cov $(u_i, u_j) = 0$ for $i \neq j$; $i, j = 1, 2, 3$. Though there is no way to test these assumptions, there is some indirect evidence which suggests that they may be roughly correct. We may note that the assumption, cov $(u_i, u_j) = 0$ for $i \neq j$, $i, j = 1, 2, 3$, would imply the following three independent restrictions:

$$\text{var}\ (v_1) = E[v_1^2(t)] = \sigma_1^2 + \sigma_3^2\ , \tag{1.11}$$

$$\text{var}\ (v_2) = E[v_2^2(t)] = \sigma_2^2 + \hat{\beta}_2^2\sigma_1^2\ , \tag{1.12}$$

$$\text{cov}\ [v_1(t),\ v_2(t)] = -\hat{\beta}_2\sigma_1^2\ . \tag{1.13}$$

Thus, the cov (v_1, v_2) must have a sign opposite to that of β_2. Since in our case β_2 is always positive, eq. (1.13) implies that cov (v_1, v_2) should assume negative values. This, then, would give a positive σ_1^2. Similarly, given that σ_2^2 and σ_3^2 are positive quantities, we get two additional restrictions. In all our experiments, these restrictions were always satsified.

To the extent we can rely on these estimates, calculations suggest that the variance of the measurement error is quite large. It would be nearly 25% of the total variation in the observed price expectations series.

1.4 Summary of Results

To avoid certain problems associated with the use of a deterministic distributed lag function as an observable proxy for price expectations, Gordon [1971] and Turnovsky and Wachter [1972] used Livingston's data on price expectations in their wage equations. To substantiate the speculation that the data may contain error, we proposed an 'unobservable variable model,' which accommodates not only some errors in measurement, but also the presence of a stochastic term in the distributed lag function determining the unobservable variable.

The results of this chapter can be summarized as follows: (i) Our calculations suggest that the survey data on short-term expectations may contain substantial error in measurement. This partially explains why Turnovsky and Wachter [1972] and Gordon [1971] found such low values for the coefficient corresponding to the price expectations variable in their wage equations. (ii) The size of the response of actual wage changes to the expectations variable is not invariant with respect to the specification of the wage equation. In particular, it is very sensitive to the presence of Perry's [1970] unemployment dispesion index. (iii) A 'catch-up' or an error adjustment term was insignificant when introduced directly into the wage equations. The model, however, posits error adjustment in the price expectations variable itself, which, in turn, affects the actual wage changes.

Frenkel [1975, 1976] has proposed a unified theory on the formation of short-term expectations which is consistent with the empirical evidence on the effects of monetary expansion in the short-run as well as in the intermediate- and long-run. Cagan's model of inflationary process does not explain the transitory period between two long-run equilibrium situations. In Frenkel's formulation, short-term expectations are determined by both regressive and adaptive elements. We found that the hypothesis explains the available data better than the other three hypotheses considered by Turnovsky.

Table 1.1 OLS to Explain the Formation of Expectations 1953-1970[a]

Expectations Hypothesis	$\bar{R}^2$	D.W.
(a) Adaptive:		
$\bar{P}^e_t = \underset{(0.115)}{0.370P_t} + \underset{(0.131)}{0.593\bar{P}^e_{t-1}}$	0.694	1.988
(b) Extrapolative:		
$\bar{P}^e_t = \underset{(0.336)}{-0.446} + \underset{(0.134)}{0.985P_t} - \underset{(.005)}{0.184}(P_t - P_{t-1})$	0.606	0.681
(c) Weighted:		
$\bar{P}^e_t = \underset{(0.371)}{-0.478} + \underset{(0.333)}{0.378P_t} + \underset{(0.381)}{0.003P_{t-1}} + \underset{(216)}{0.606P_{t-2}}$	0.632	0.612
(d) Frenkel's:		
$\bar{P}^e_t = \underset{(0.144)}{-0.047P_t} + \underset{(0.133)}{0.390\bar{P}^e_{t-1}} + \underset{(0.280)}{1.085\bar{P}^e_{12(t)}}$	0.785	1.718

[a]Standard errors are in brackets, $\bar{R}^2$ is adjusted R^2 and D.W. stands for Durbin-Watson statistic. Observations are semiannual.

Table 1.2 OLS Estimates of the Wage Equation, 1953-1970[a].

Variable	Equation I	Equation II	Equation III	Equation IV	Equation V
Constant Term	1.780 (0.586)	2.217 (0.670)	2.611 (0.653)	1.784 (0.651)	0.886 (0.745)
Inverse of Conventional Unemployment Rate, 1/U	10.265 (2.799)	8.565 (3.063)	6.750 (2.982)	9.929 (3.227)	
Livingston's Measure of Expected Inflation, $\bar{P}_t^e$	0.403 (0.006)	0.373 (0.006)	0.336 (0.006)	0.418 (0.007)	0.006 (0.010)
Catch-up Variable, $P_t - \bar{P}_{t-1}^e$				0.005 (0.009)	
Guidepost Dummy, DG	-1.318 (0.279)	-0.829 (0.467)		-1.286 (0.294)	-1.312 (0.444)
Disguised Unemployment Rate, U^D		-0.361 (0.278)	-0.758 (0.169)		-0.360 (0.235)
Unemployment Dispersion Index, D^U					10.829 (2.513)
R^2	0.751	0.757	0.740	0.743	0.809
DW	1.278	1.485	1.643	1.228	1.888

[a]Observations are semiannual. Standard errors are in parentheses. The dependent variable, W, is rate of change in hourly earnings corrected for changes in overtime and interindustry employment shifts. DG was set equal to 0.575 in 1962: I, 0.875 in 1962: II, 1.0 in 1963: I to 1966: II, 0.625 in 1967: I, 0.125 in 1967: II, and 0.0 in other periods. The wage equation being estimates is of the form (1.5).

Table 1.3 2SLS Estimates of the Wage Equation, 1953-1970.[a]

Expectations Hypothesis	$\bar{R}^2$	D.W.
(a) Adaptive: $W_t = \underset{(0.927)}{2.196} + \underset{(3.254)}{7.157}\, U_t^{-1} + \underset{(0.185)}{0.533}\bar{p}_t^e - \underset{(0.488)}{1.318}\, DG_t$	0.781	1.821
(b) Extrapolative: $W_t = \underset{(0.933)}{2.224} + \underset{(3.339)}{6.943}\, U_t^{-1} + \underset{(0.192)}{0.542}\bar{p}_t^e - \underset{(0.485)}{1.319}\, DG_t$	0.749	1.488
(c) Weighted: $W_t = \underset{(0.871)}{1.964} + \underset{(2.816)}{8.673}\, U_t^{-1} + \underset{(0.188)}{0.493}\bar{p}_t^e - \underset{(0.500)}{1.337}\, DG_t$	0.748	1.369
(d) Frenkel's: $W_t = \underset{(0.919)}{2.104} + \underset{(3.093)}{7.856}\, U_t^{-1} + \underset{(0.187)}{0.502}\bar{p}_t^e - \underset{(0.497)}{1.317}\, DG_t$	0.817	1.755

[a]Standard errors are in parentheses. $\bar{R}^2$ is adjusted R^2 and D.W. stands for the Durbin-Watson statistic. Observations are semiannual.

Table 1.4 FIML Estimates of the Structural Parameters, 1952-1970[a]

Expectations Hypothesis	w_0	w_1	w_2	w_3	Constant	U_t^{-1}	P_t^e	D_G
(a) Weighted:	-0.470	0.410	-0.055	0.707	1.710	9.505	0.490	-1.133
	(0.455)	(0.298)	(0.322)	(0.170)	(0.560)	(2.700)	(0.008)	(0.250)
(b) Adaptive:		0.448	0.510		2.045	7.518	0.543	-1.120
		(0.105)	(0.110)		(0.591)	(3.122)	(0.071)	(0.280)
(c) Extrapolative:	-0.479	0.992	0.417		2.344	5.838	0.569	-1.090
	(0.301)	(0.134)	(0.165)		(0.628)	(3.220)	(0.088)	(0.262)
(d) Frenkel's:		0.062	0.434	0.972	1.718	8.729	0.540	-1.058
		(0.130)	(0.101)	(0.241)	(0.596)	(3.055)	(0.070)	(0.254)

[a]The Structural model is given in (1.1) - (1.3). Standard errors are in parentheses.

CHAPTER 2

SIMULTANEITY IN WAGES, PRICES, AND UNOBSERVABLE PRICE EXPECTATIONS

In the last chapter we studied the role of inflationary expectations in the determination of wage inflation without bringing in a price formation equation. However, a common theoretical framework shared by many important studies on domestic inflation in recent years is a simultaneous wage-price model with the unobservable price expectations variable occurring in the structural equations. Since the price expectations variable is not directly observable, for actual estimation of it, researchers have typically used a deterministic proxy, such as a weighted average of past inflation rates. The instability of many of the estimated wage-price models may partially be traced back to the restrictive nature of these deterministic proxies. The so-called Natural Rate hypothesis (NRH) posits that there is no way for the government stabilization policies to keep the unemployment rate permanently below the natural rate. This means that there is no long-run trade-off between inflation and unemployment, which in turn implies that the coefficients of expected inflation variable in the reduced form wage and price equations will be unity. Thus, estimation of simultaneous wage-price models without modeling price expectations can have important implications with regard to earlier studies. It may be noted that in the last chapter, the price expectations coefficient was estimated to be only around 0.50.

In addition, a distributed lag of past prices produces reduced-form parameters which may involve rather complicated ratios of polynomials in the lag operators. To avoid the resulting complications of non-linear estimation, almost all the studies concentrated on simple-equation estimation, grossly neglecting the simultaneity in estimation. (Oi, 1976, p. 39).

In a pioneering study, McGuire [1976a] estimated a wage-price model without modeling the price-expectations variable. His approach is that of multiple equations and in one set of equations he used Livingston's survey data we used in the last chapter. However, he did not incorporate the simultaneity and, as he himself pointed out, time constrants precluded a full-blown unobserved variables econometric treatment of the data. Another possible limitation of the approach, pointed out by Gordon [1976] in his comments on McGuire's approach, is that he brought in the Fisher equation as an additional indicator for the _same_ price expectations variable. Though the counterfactual predictions on the basis of his estimated models were quite different from those due to Gordon [1972, 1973], the coefficients of price expectations in his structural equations were very close to unity - an estimate obtained in most studies using the data of late 60's.

So far as providing serious evidence against the 'no trade-off in the long-run hypothesis' is concerned, one study, viz. Cukierman [1974] stands out in recent years. He explicitly treated the simultaneity, however, using a deterministic adaptive expectations hypothesis. Some of the estimates of the speeds of adjustment were so implausible that in conclusion he pointed out that adaptive expectations formulation might have been too restrictive for the model under consideration.

The purpose of the present chapter is the following: We estimate a set of simultaneous wage-price models without modeling the price-expectations variable. However, like McGuire [1976a] we use the survey data on price expectations as the observable proxy, after taking care of possible measurement errors. This study can thus be considered as a generalization of our model of chapter 1 and that of McGuire [1976a] in the sense that now we need not incorporate any hypothesis on the expectations formation and that the interest rate equation can be omitted. We also incorporate some of the relevant exogenous variables that appear in the works of Perry [1970], Gordon [1971] and Eckstein and Brinner [1972]. The estimated simultaneous model can then allow us to test the Accelerationist hypothesis in the context of the two reduced form equations. As Cukierman [1974] has demonstrated, Solow's [1969] and Gordon's [1971] conditions are neither necessary nor sufficient once simultaneity is recognized.

Also, we looked at the counterfactual predictions in our model to judge the usefulness of Nixon's wage-price controls. Since McGuire's results are strickingly different from those of Gordon's, it will certainly be useful to have a closer look at them.

Since the observed data on price expectations are based on sample surveys, procedures to deal with measurement errors in the true variable are called for. Goldberger [1972] has demonstrated that a simultaneous equation model with measurement error in some of the exogenous variables can be identified provided the model is otherwise overidentified. Our approach, however, is that of treating the error-ridden exogenous variable as another endogenous variable in the model. This was suggested earlier by Anderson and Hurwicz [1949], Sargan [1958] and Durbin [1953]; and has recently been treated more rigorously by Hausman [1978] and Hsiao [1976]. We also developed certain statistical tests to ascertain the significance of the hypothesized errors in the context of well specified structural models.

2.1 Structural Model

We consider a series of simultaneous wage-price models of the following form:

$$W_t = a_o + a_1 \cdot P_t + a_2 \cdot U_t^{-1} + a_3 \cdot p_t^e + a_4 \cdot GD_t + U_{1t} \quad (2.1)$$

$$P_t = b_o + b_1 \cdot W_t + b_2 \cdot PR_t + b_3 \cdot p_t^e + b_4 \cdot UFK_t + U_{2t} \quad (2.2)$$

where W = the annual percentage change in standard unit labor cost, U^{-1} = the inverse of the official unemployment rate to represent any disequilibrium in the labor market, P = the annual percentage change in the Consumer Price Index (CPI), p^e = our unobservable expected inflation rate, GD = the dummy variable used in the last chapter, to capture the impact of the informal guideposts of the mid 1960's, PR = the percentage change in the ratio of actual to trend productivity, UFK = the percentage change in the ratio of unfilled orders to capacity, and (U_1, U_2) are random disturbance terms.

In the above formulation of the wage-price dynamics, we do not specify a priori whether inflation is of a cost push and/or a demand pull variety. One of the reasons for the lack of agreement as to the type of inflation present at any given time is the lack of precise method of identifying the different types due to the simultaneity in wage-price inflation. The variable PR is introduced with an expected negative coefficient ($b_2 < 0$); if actual productivity increases faster than the long-run trend rate, the percentage change in the ratio of actual to trend productivity should exert a downward pressure on prices. The rate of change in the ratio of unfilled orders to capacity (UFK) in the manufacturing sector is brought in as a measure of disequilibrium in the product market. An increase in UFK signals a rise in the relative excess demand for products leading to a price increase.[7] The variable P tries to catch the increases in wages caused by increases in prices through the equalization of the wage rate to its marginal revenue product.[8] We also include p^e in the price equation primarily because there are fixed administrative and legal costs associated with price changes. Cukierman [1974] argues that each firm tries to minimize the number of times it changes prices. As a result, the more it expects the general level of prices to change, the more it will adjust its own price level, causing higher inflation. In a recent study, Maccini [1979] justified a direct role of price expectations in the price equations: "If in making price decisions firms take into account the prices that their competitors are charging, both now and in the future, then their expectations will directly affect the prices that they set".

We used Livingston's survey data ($\bar{p}^e$), which have been recently adjusted by Carlson [1977], as a proxy for p_t^e:

$$\bar{p}_t^e = p_t^e + U_{3t} , \tag{2.3}$$

where U_{3t} is the random error in measurement. Thus, even though $\bar{p}^e$ may contain significant random errors, we believe that over diverse time periods, such survey data may often be more flexible to 'track' the true price expectations. As Friedman [1968] and Gordon [1973] have both stressed, price forecasts right after World War II were influenced more by the behavior of prices following World War I than by price changes in the immediately preceeding years; thus, in the late 40's, a distributed lag on recent inflation would not have performed better than the consensus forecasts.

Also, as Anderson [1979] has demonstrated in the context of the St. Louis and the FRB-MIT-PENN econometric models, the fixed-coefficient distributed lag models for price expectations are quite inadequate for policy evaluation purposes. [See Lucas (1972]. The use of survey data, in principle, can circumvent this problem.

2.2 Estimation of the measurement error variance by using the overidentifying restrictions.

The advantages of survey data as a measure of price expectations are many; it reflects all recent developments in the economy no matter how abrupt they might have been. However, in estimating structural models using the data, one has to carefully allow for any possible measurement errors, that might have contaminated the data. We shall now illustrate how the over-identifying restrictions due to the simultaneity between wages and prices can be "traded-off" against the underidentification introduced by the measurement errors associated with the survey data. This idea was first introduced by Goldberger [1972, 1974] using Tintner's [1952] meat market data.

Specifically, the result is based on the relationship:

$$\Pi^{*} = (\phi - \Theta)^{-1} \phi \Pi \tag{2.4}$$

where Π^{*} is the reduced form coefficient matrix in standard simultaneous equation model with the reduced form:

$$Y' = X^{*\prime}\Pi^{*} + v'. \tag{2.5}$$

The matrix of exogenous variables X^{*} is not observable; we observe X which is related to X^{*} in the usual errors-in-the variables fashion:

$$X = X^{*} + \varepsilon \tag{2.6}$$

with $\mathrm{Cov}(X\ \varepsilon) = \mathrm{Cov}(\varepsilon\ v) = 0$. The variance-covariance matrix of ε is a diagonal matrix Θ with a few non-zero elements. Also

$$\Phi = E(XX') = E[X^* + \varepsilon)(X^{*\prime} + \varepsilon')] = E(X^* X^{*\prime}) + \Omega \tag{2.7}$$

defines the covariance matrix of observed X in terms of $E(X^* X^{*\prime})$ and measurement error variances. Now, if we define $\Pi = E(XX')^{-1}\, E(XY')$, we get

$$\begin{aligned} \Pi = \phi^{-1}\, E(XY') &= \phi^{-1}\, E[X^* + \varepsilon)(X^{*\prime}\Pi^* + v')] \\ &= \phi^{-1}\, E[X^* X^{*\prime})\, \Pi^* \end{aligned} \tag{2.8}$$

Thus,

$$\begin{aligned} \phi\Pi &= E(X^* X^{*\prime})\, \Pi^* \\ &= (\phi - \Omega)\quad \Pi^*\ , \end{aligned} \tag{2.9}$$

yielding the relation (2.4), which connects the observable moments and the coefficients ϕ and Π to the parameters Π^* and Ω . This relationship in conjunction with the zeros in Ω and the overidentifying restrictions on Π^* may be enough to identify all the structural parameters.

For our purposes, then, consider a simultaneous wage-price model in which the wage equation is overidentified by one degree and the price equation is just identified:

$$W_t = a_1 P_t + a_2 p_t^e + a_3 U_t^{-1} + U_{1t} \tag{2.10}$$

$$P_t = b_1 W_t + b_2 \cdot p_t^e + b_3 \cdot PR_t + b_4 UFK_t + V_{2t}, \tag{2.11}$$

where, in the present context, the variables are defined from their respective means. We also use (2.3) where $\mathrm{var}(U_3) = \theta$. The reduced form of the model is:

$$W_t = \pi_{11}^{*} P_t^e + \pi_{21}^{*} U_t^{-1} + \pi_{31}^{*} PR_t + \pi_{41}^{*} UFK_t + V_{1t} \quad (2.12)$$

$$P_t = \pi_{12} P_t^e + \pi_{22}^{*} U_t^{-1} + \pi_{32} PR_t + \pi_{42}^{*} UFK_t + V_{2t} \quad (2.13)$$

The reduced form coefficients can be expressed in terms of structural coefficients as:

$$\begin{bmatrix} \pi_{11}^{*} & \pi_{12}^{*} \\ \pi_{21}^{*} & \pi_{22}^{*} \\ \pi_{31}^{*} & \pi_{32}^{*} \\ \pi_{41}^{*} & \pi_{42}^{*} \end{bmatrix} = \begin{bmatrix} (a_2 + a_1 b_2)/\delta & (a_2 b_1 + b_2)/\delta \\ a_3/\delta & a_3 b_1/\delta \\ a_1 b_3/\delta & b_3/\delta \\ a_1 b_4/\delta & b_4/\delta \end{bmatrix} \quad (2.14)$$

where $\delta = 1 - a_1 b_1$

Hence the overidentifying restriction is given by

$$(\pi_{31}^{*}/\pi_{32}^{*}) = (\pi_{41}^{*}/\pi_{42}^{*}) = a_1 \quad (2.15)$$

After some algebra, (2.4) gives us the following formula which relates the true reduced form coefficient with the estimable moments and error variances:

$$\begin{bmatrix} \pi^*_{11} & \pi^*_{12} \\ \pi^*_{21} & \pi^*_{22} \\ \pi^*_{31} & \pi^*_{32} \\ \pi^*_{41} & \pi^*_{42} \end{bmatrix} = \begin{bmatrix} \frac{1}{1-\theta\phi^{11}}\pi_{11} & \frac{1}{1-\theta\phi^{11}}\pi_{12} \\ \frac{\theta\phi^{12}}{1-\theta\phi^{11}}\pi_{11}+\pi_{21} & \frac{\theta\phi^{12}}{1-\theta\phi^{11}}\pi_{12}+\pi_{22} \\ \frac{\theta\phi^{13}}{1-\theta\phi^{11}}\pi_{11}+\pi_{31} & \frac{\theta\phi^{13}}{1-\theta\phi^{11}}\pi_{12}+\pi_{32} \\ \frac{\theta\phi^{14}}{1-\theta\phi^{11}}\pi_{11}+\pi_{41} & \frac{\theta\phi^{14}}{1-\theta\phi^{11}}\pi_{12}+\pi_{42} \end{bmatrix} \tag{2.16}$$

where ϕ^{ij} denotes "ij"th element of ϕ^{-1}.

From (2.15) and (2.16) we have

$$\theta = \frac{\pi_{41}\pi_{32} - \pi_{31}\pi_{42}}{\phi^{11}(\pi_{41}\pi_{32}-\pi_{31}\pi_{42})+\phi^{13}(\pi_{11}\pi_{41})+\phi^{14}(\pi_{12}\pi_{31}-\pi_{11}\pi_{32})} \tag{2.17}$$

By substituting the estimable moments and coefficients in (2.17), we have $\hat{\theta}$ = .0188, which is nearly 1% of total variance of survey data. Also by substituting $\hat{\theta}$ into (2.16), we can now get the estimates for the true reduced form coefficients (Table 2.1). In this example, the only overidentifying restriction has been successfully traded off against the measurement error variance. However, these preliminary calculations indicate that the measurement errors are possibly not very serious in the present context. The coefficient estimates before and after correction (in Table 2.1) also reveal this. Nevertheless, the procedure can handle the possibility of measurement errors without any ad hoc modeling of inflationary expectations. However, depending on the location and the number of overidentifying restrictions, one can obtain multiple estimates of θ. We now turn to a more general estimation procedure which avoids such problems.

2.3 A general method of estimation.

The G equations of a conventional simultaneous equation model can compactly be written as

$$y = Z.\delta + U, \tag{2.18}$$

where $y = \begin{bmatrix} y_1 \\ y_2 \\ \vdots \\ y_G \end{bmatrix}$, $Z = \begin{bmatrix} Z_1 & 0 & \cdots & 0 \\ 0 & Z_2 & \cdots & 0 \\ \vdots & & & \\ 0 & 0 & \cdots & Z_G \end{bmatrix}$, $\delta = \begin{bmatrix} \delta_1 \\ \delta_2 \\ \vdots \\ \delta_G \end{bmatrix}$,

$U = \begin{bmatrix} U_1 \\ U_2 \\ \vdots \\ U_G \end{bmatrix}$, $Z_i = [Y_i \; X_i]$ and $\delta_i = \begin{bmatrix} \beta_i \\ \nu_i \end{bmatrix}$,

Here y_i is the vector of observations on the ith endogenous variable; Y_i and X_i are matrices of observations on the endogenous and predetermined variables that actually appear in the ith equation; and β_i and ν_i are appropriate vectors of parameters.

To simplify the exposition, suppose the first exogenous variable in the first structural equation, denoted by x_1^*, is unobservable. Instead of x_1^*, we have a proxy $\tilde{x}_1$ such that

$$\tilde{x}_i = x_1^* + \varepsilon_1 , \tag{2.19}$$

where ε_1 is IID(0, $\sigma^2_{\varepsilon_1}$) and independent of x_1^*. We can write the first equation as

$$y_1 = Z_1^* \delta_1 + U_1 \tag{2.20}$$

where $Z_1^* = [Y_1\ x_1^*\ \tilde{X}_1]$; $\tilde{X}_1$ is the matrix X_1 with the first column deleted. Replacing the unobservable x_1^* by its proxy $\tilde{x}_1$, equation (2.20) becomes:

$$y_1 = Y_1\beta_1 + \tilde{x}_1\gamma_{11} + \tilde{x}_1\tilde{\nu}_1 + U_1 - \nu_{11}\varepsilon_1\ , \tag{2.21}$$

where $\tilde{\nu}_1$ is the vector ν_1 with the first element removed. Now, apart from the variables in Y_1, $\tilde{x}_1$ is also contemporaneously correlated with the composite disturbance term. Thus, provided sufficient number of instrumental variables are available for both Y_1 and $\tilde{x}_1$, equation (2.21) can be identified and consistently estimated.

Full-information estimation procedures can be designed by treating $\tilde{x}_1$ as another endogenous variable and bringing in explicitly the auxiliary regression relating $\tilde{x}_1$ to other exogenous variables in the system:

$$\tilde{x}_1 = \tilde{X}\alpha + \varepsilon_2, \tag{2.22}$$

where $\tilde{x}$ stands for <u>all</u> predetermined variables in the model with the first column deleted. ε_2 is some random error term containing ε_1. Under the assumption that all the exogenous variables follow a multi-variate normal distribution, equation (2.22) can be interpreted as the conditional expectation of x_1^* given $\tilde{x}$. Thus, in situations where the normality assumption is untenable, reformulating the unobservable variable as a stochastic linear function of other exogenous variables can be more meaningful (Goldberger 1972). Also, under the usual assumptions of a simultaneous equation model where the predetermined variables are not necessarily correlated, $\bar{R}^2$ in the auxiliary regression (2.22) may not be significant. In that case, the 3SLS applied to the augmented system would not work. In such a situation again, a stochastic multiple cause function for the unobservable variable will be necessary. One can then bring in one or more endogenous variables in the equation determining the unobservable variable (provided the model is otherwise identified). The augmented structural model with (G + 1) equation can now be written as:

$$y_1 = Y_1\beta_1 + \tilde{x}_1\nu_{11} + \tilde{x}_1\tilde{\nu}_1 + U_1 - \nu_{11}\varepsilon_1 \qquad (2.23)$$

$$y_i = Y_i\beta_i + X_i\nu_i + U_i \qquad i = 2, \ldots, G. \qquad (2.24)$$

$$\tilde{x}_1 = \tilde{X}\alpha + \varepsilon_2 \qquad (2.25)$$

Equations (2.23)-(2.25) can be rewritten in stacked form as:

$$y_* = Z_*\delta_* + V \qquad (2.26)$$

where now there are (G+1) equations, and δ_* contains the unknown β_i's, ν_i's and α. Under the assumption of unrestricted covariances between the errors in the (G+1) equations, an application of three-stage least squares (3 SLS) will produce asymptotically efficient estimates.

The system of equations (2.23)-(2.26) is now altered to reflect the presence of x_1^* in the second structural equation:

$$y_1 = Y_1\beta_1 + \tilde{x}_1\nu_{11} + \tilde{X}_1\tilde{\nu}_1 + U_1 - \nu_{11}\varepsilon_1 \tag{2.27}$$

$$y_2 = Y_2\beta_2 + \tilde{x}_1\gamma_{21} + \tilde{X}_2\tilde{\nu}_2 + U_2 - \nu_{21}\varepsilon_1 \tag{2.28}$$

$$y_i = Y_i\beta_i + X_i\nu_i + U_i \qquad i = 3, \ldots, G. \tag{2.29}$$

$$\tilde{x}_1 = \tilde{X}\,\alpha + \varepsilon_2 \tag{2.30}$$

where $\tilde{X}_2$ contains the exogenous variables in the second equation with x_1^* removed. Equations (2.27) - (2.30) can also be written in the form (2.26). A necessary and sufficient condition for identification of the simultaneous equation model with measurement error in some of the exogenous variables can be stated in terms of the augmented structural system by utilizing the counting rule proposed by Koopmans, Rubin and Leipnik [1950]:

An equation in a linear model of G equations containing an unobservable variable with a proxy is identified if and only if at least one non-zero determinant of G rows and columns is contained in the array of coefficients formed from the system (2.26) as follows: strating with the row-and-column array of coefficients in the model (2.26), omit all columns not having a prescribed zero in the equation in question and omit the row of coefficients of that equation.

This simple counting rule is equivalent to the rank condition obtained by Geraci [1976] for such contemporaneous shock-error models with unrestricted variance-Covariance matrix of structural disturbances.

The augmented system (2.26) can also be used to derive an expression for the asymptotic bias involved in an application of OLS to equation (2.23), by directly using the result given in Dhrymes [1970, p. 176]. Note that in the context of a simultaneous equation model, errors-in-measurement may even overestimate the coefficient of the error-ridden variable, cf. section 3.6.

The 3 SLS estimator as applied to (2.26) can be defined as

$$\hat{\delta}_{3SLS} = (Z_*' \tilde{P}_{\Sigma Z_*} Z_*)^{-1} Z_*' \tilde{P}_{\Sigma Z_*} y_* \tag{2.31}$$

where $\tilde{P}_{\Sigma Z_*} = \hat{\Sigma}^{-1} \otimes \tilde{X} (\tilde{X}'\tilde{X})^{-1} \tilde{X}'$ and Σ is the variance - covariance matrix of the (G+1) disturbances in (2.26).

2.4 Empirical results

Equations (2.1) - (2.3) can alternatively be written as:

$$W_t = a_o + a_1 P_t + a_2 U_t^{-1} + a_3 \bar{P}_t^e + a_4 GD_t + U_{1t} - a_3 U_{3t} \tag{2.32}$$

$$P_t = b_o + b_1 W_t + b_2 PR_t + b_3 \bar{P}_t^e + b_4 UFK_t + U_{2t} - b_3 U_{3t} \tag{2.33}$$

To obtain efficient estimates of all the structural parameters, we applied the 3 SLS procedure to (2.32) - (2.33) augmented by the auxiliary regression:

$$\bar{P}_t^e = c_o + C_1 U_t^{-1} + C_i GD_t + C_3 UFK_t + C_4 PR_t + \varepsilon_t . \tag{2.34}$$

Computations were performed using the program ECOMP-3 (Richardson and Rohr 1975) on UNIVAC 1110 at the State University of New York (Albany) computer center.

Since the R^2 in the auxiliary regression (2.34) was very close to zero (see Table 2.2 option 0), the 3SLS procedure utilizing the internal instrumental variables U^{-1}, GD, UFK and PR did not yield meaningful estimates. To overcome this problem, we used three other options. For Option 1, we included a time trend (T) variable in the price equation such that the regression (2.34) used T as another internal instrument. We also experimented with 1/T, $\sqrt{T}$ and log T as alternatives to T without much difference. McCallum [1976] justified the inclusion of T as a variable to reflect technical progress. As expected, the $\bar{R}^2$ in option I (Table 2.2) increased to .898 yielding sensible estimates of the structural parameters. For option II we assume that true price expectations follow an extrapolative scheme, i.e., $p^e = w_o + w_1 (P_t - P_{t-1}) + w_2 P_t$. A value of $w_1 < 0$ would imply a regressive expectation. For option III, expected prices are determined by past rates of change in money supply narrowly defined. It is interesting to note that with extrapolative expectations, we obtain a three-equation structural model with three endogenous variables W_t, P_t and p_t^e where p_t^e is determined also by P_t. The $\bar{R}_2$ for these two cases are .421 and .722 respectively. The residuals calculated from these auxiliary regressions were analyzed to study whether U_3, the error term associated with $\bar{p}^e$, is (i) serially correlated, and (ii) heteroscedastic with respect to the level of p_t^e. By plotting the square of the residuals against the estimated values of $\bar{p}_t^e$, we found no evidence in support of heteroscedasticity. The Durbin-Watson statistic was significantly different from 2 for all the options at even the 5% level, indicating that U_3 may indeed be serially correlated. We may note, however, that serially correlated disturbances would not affect the consistency property of our estimator [Wickens 1969].

In Table 2.3, we have reported the estimates of the wage-price model with time trend, T, in the price equation. The OLS estimates ignore both the measurement errors in $\bar{p}^e$ and the simultaneiry; the 3SLS estimates of the two-equation system (2.32) - (2.32) with p^e replaced by $\bar{p}^e$ take care of the simultaneity only. Finally, the 3SLS as applied to the three-equation system adjusts for both possible measurement error in $\bar{p}^e$ and also the simultaneity between wages and prices. The estimated coefficients were all statistically significant with the expected signs. Even though the price expectations variable was statistically significant at the one percent level, the 95 percent confidence interval did not include the value $a_3=1$. Thus, one would have rejected the Natural Rate hypothesis if the inference were based solely on the single structural equation. The 3SLS estimates of the three-equation and two-equation models did not differ greatly. The same general pattern persisted when the model was estimated with options II and III. The results are given in Table 2.4, where we find that the estimated coefficients are strikingly similar even though the $\bar{R}^2$ in the different auxiliary regressions varied from .421 to .898 (cf. McCallum 1976).

We also included the price expectations variable in the price equation, primarily because there are fixed administrative and legal costs associated with price changes. The model has been estimated with the help of options II and III and the results are given in Table 2.5. We find that p^e is significant at the one percent confidence level in both the equations. Maccini [1979] could not capture this effect in his empirical work. However, now the importance of contemporaneous wage is substantially less in determining prices.

2.5 Tests of errors-in-variables.

The rather small difference between the two-equation and the three-equation model estimates suggests that the measurement error in $\bar{p}^e$ may not be very serious. We utilized a rather novel statistical test to ascertain if the measurement error variance was significant.

Consider a regression equation with one error-ridden exogenous variable. Under the null hypothesis (H_o) of no errors-in-the variable, OLS estimate ($\hat{\beta}_o$) is known to be unbiased and efficient. To construct a test of error-in-variables, one has to find an instrumental variable estimator ($\hat{\beta}_1$) which is not adversely affected under the alternative hypothesis (H_1), but not as efficient under H_o. An appropriate test statistic, due to Wu [1974], and Hausman [1978] is:

$$M = \hat{q}' \, V(\hat{q})^{-1} \hat{q} \sim \chi^2_k , \tag{4.1}$$

where $\hat{q} = \hat{\beta}_1 - \hat{\beta}_o$, $V(\hat{q}) = V(\hat{\beta}_1) - V(\hat{\beta}_o)$, and k is the number of parameters estimated.

We have generalized the test procedure in the context of simultaneous equation models. For such models one error-ridden exogenous variable will contaminate all the parameter estimates. To test for errors-in-variables, then, M can be calculated with $\hat{\beta}_1$ being the 3SLS estimator of the augmented system and $\hat{\beta}_o$ the 3SLS estimator as applied to the two-equation model, ignoring possible errors-in-measurement. To keep the dimensionality of the estimator vectors the same, we calculated the χ^2 statistic for the model with the time-trend in the price equation. The calculated χ^2 value was 10.615. Since the critical χ^2_{10} at even the 10% level of significance is 15.99, we cannot reject the null hypothesis of no error-in-measurement. Thus, it seems we should depend on the 3SLS estimates of the two-equation system to obtain the structural parameters.

It is interesting that the Livingston's survey data after the adjustment made by Carlson [1977] reveal no significant measurement errors. We pointed out earlier that Livingston's published "Consensus" forecasts were first used by Turnovsky [1970], Turnovsky and Watcher [1972], Gilson [1972], Pyle [1972] and others; and our evidence in the last chapter indicated a substantial amount of measurement error in these data. Carlson [1977] carefully analyzed two specific problems with the 'consensus' forecasts: (i) these data implicitly assumed that the December and June price indexes were known at the time these six-monthly forecasts were made. However, when the forecasts are made, September and April data are usually most current. Thus, the 6-month ahead and the 12-month ahead forecasts really cover an 8-month span from October to June and a 14-month span from October to December. (ii) The second related problem is that Livingston, as a journalist, has occasioanlly made some adjustments himself in order to avoid some inconsistencies in the face of substantial (and possiblly unexpected) changes in the price indexes in the two months just before June and December each year.[9] Carlson recalculated the implied expected inflation rates which avoided these problems. His specific adjustments have been described in appendix C. Our empirical evidence in this chapter clearly indicate that Carlson's adjustments, indeed, improved upon the original "Consensus" data as a measure of inflationary expectation.

Even though the numerical differences between the OLS and 3SLS estimates are small, the wage-price simultaneity has a very important implication for the 'no trade-off in the long-run' hypothesis. An implication of this hypothesis is that the coefficient of the price expectations variable is unity in the <u>reduced form</u> wage and price equations. Although the 3SLS estimates of the coefficients of $\bar{p}_t^e$ in the structural wage equations in Tables 2.2, 2.3 and 2.4 are all less than one at the one percent level of significance, the reduced form regressions yielded a totally different conclusion with respect to the

Natural Rate hypothesis. The coefficients of price expectations variable in the reduced form regressions (not reported here) of W and P on $\{\bar{p}^e, U^{-1}$, GD, UFK, PR$\}$ were .837 (with standard error .099) and 1.215 (with s.e. = .144) respectively. When T was also included in the above regressions, the coefficient estimates were .852 (s.e.=.29) and 1.722 (s.e.=.48) respectively. In none of the above cases, we could reject the null hypothesis of a unitary price expectations coefficient even at a 1% level of significance.

2.6 Effects of Wage and Price Controls

To judge the effects of Price and Wage Controls, we compared the actual performance of the rate of price and wage changes with the counterfactual predictions generated by the estimated reduced forms. Gordon [1973] reached the conclusion that Phases I and II had achieved a slight reduction in the advancement of wages and a marked decline in the rise in prices between 1971:3 and 1972:2 as compared with econometric simulation to his equations in the absence of controls. Thus, according to Gordon, short-run effects of controls worked not by moderating the behavior of wages relative to prices, but rather by squeezing the profit-margins sufficiently to hold the price level below its free market value. McGuire [1976b], on the other hand, reached strikingly different conclusions; his model predictions were such that the controls program could claim no credit for the slow down which actually occurred.

Before one attempts to evaluate the effectiveness of controls program in terms of counter-factual model predictions, the stability of the parameter estimates should be tested. We applied the usual Chow test to the reduced form equations with different points of sample separation. Dividing the total sample period between 1951:1 - 1962:1 and 1962:2 - 1973:2, the calculated F-statistics were 1.151 and .323 in the wage and price equations respectively.

accepting the null hypothesis of no parameter drift at 5% level of significance. Thus, the Chow Test, when applied to the reduced form equations, indicates no parameter instability over rather a long sample period 1951-1973. We also tested whether the observations during the controls period (1972:2 - 1973:2) basically belong to the same pre-control regression (1951:1-1971:1). The F-test statistics were found out to be .943 in the reduced form wage equation and .868 in the reduced form price equation - supporting the homogeneity hypothesis at the 5% level of significance, cf. Lucas [1972].

At this point we may test the specification of the structural wage-price model itself. The zero-nonzero restrictions on the structure ruled out any direct effect of GD and U^{-1} on P and that of PR and UFK on W. These specifications in turn, implied certain overidentifying restrictions on the reduced form coefficients. Let us write the reduced for equations for (2.32) and (2.33) as

$$W = \pi_{10} + \pi_{11} U^{-1} + \pi_{12} GD + \pi_{13} UFK + \pi_{14} PR + \pi_{15} \bar{P}^{e} + V_1 \quad (2.35)$$

$$P = \pi_{20} + \pi_{21} U^{-1} + \pi_{22} GD + \pi_{23} UFK + \pi_{24} PR + \pi_{25} \bar{P}^{e} + V_2 \quad (2.36)$$

The zero-nonzero restrictions when $\bar{P}^{e}$ appears only in the wage equation are:

$$\pi_{21}/\pi_{11} = \pi_{22}/\pi_{12} = \pi_{23}/\pi_{13} = b_1 \text{ , and}$$

$$\pi_{14}/\pi_{24} = \pi_{15}/\pi_{25} = a_1 \text{ .}$$

Thus, we can impose the restrictions

$$\pi_{21} = (\pi_{11}/\pi_{12})\pi_{22};\ \pi_{23} = (\pi_{13}/\pi_{12})/\pi_{22} \text{ and } \pi_{14} = (\pi_{15}/\pi_{25})\cdot\pi_{25}$$

on the reduced form equations. The two equations (2.35)-(2.36) were estimated using Zellner's seemingly unrelated regression procedure (using the TSP program), with and without the restrictions. The log-likelihood values were respectively -130.8 and -127.06, giving the χ^2 (Likelihood Ratio) statistic to be only 6.04. Since the critical value for a χ^2 with three degress of freedom is 6.25 even at the 10% level of significance, we could not reject the null hypothesis. When $\bar{p}^e$ also appeared in the structural price equation, we had one less restriction to impose. In this case, the χ^2 statistic turned out to be only 0.04. The generalized least squares estimates converged in 5/6 iterations and the restricted estimates were very close to their unrestricted counterparts. We also tested the overidentifying restrictions in the context of the model with time trend in the price equation. The results were again overwhelmingly in favor of the overidentifying restrictions.

Our evaluation of the Controls program is based on unrestricted reduced form wage and price equations of the 2-equation structural model given in Table 2.4. The effect of the controls program on price and wage changes is shown in Table 2.6. Even though the dependent variable in the price equation has been constructed on the basis of the CPI, the results are very similar to those obtained by Gordon [1973]. There was a significant reduction (at 5 percent level) in the price increases during 1971:2-1972:2 with a partial rebound during 1973; this reaffirms the widely held view that the short-run success of the controls program would imply its long-run failure. We find no significant dampening effect on wage inflation during 1971:2-1973:2. On the contrary, during 1972:1 and 1973:1, the controls seem to have actually caused wages to increase more rapidly than would have been the case in the absence of controls. Only during the last half of 1973 did the effectiveness of the program show up at a 1% level of significance. The failure of the program to control wage inflation can be explained in view of the fact that there are easy ways to evade the guidelines of the Pay Board. For example, subcontracting of work, changed working conditions, higher overtime rates, spurious promotion and similar other means can easily be recorded as reducing productivity and/or increasing materials cost instead of increasing wages. Apart from having very little enforcement efforts to prevent evasion, the low-wage and small-firm exemptions covered nearly 56% of the private non-farm labor force by the end of July 1972. Enforcement efforts were concentrated primarily on union labor contracts. But the Pay Board can influence only newly negotiated agreements; many actual wage increases were deferred increases from previously negotiated wage-agreements. Thus, it is not surprising that our model did not indicate any dampening effect of the wage-price freeze on the wage increases during the early control period.

2.7 Conclusions

We estimated a set of simultaneous wage-price models without any explicit modeling of the unobservable inflationary expectations. In addition to the Livingston's survey measure of price-expectations, McGuire [1976] utilized an interest rate equation to estimate the wage and price equations. Gordon [1976] has pointed out certain difficulties of utilizing the Fisher equation in the context of wage-price models. Instead of using the interest rate equation, we exploited the overidentifying restrictions obtained by explicitly bringing in the simultaneity between wages and prices. We also tested statistically the significance of the hypothesized measurement error in the survey data in the context of the simultaneous model. The test failed to reject the null hypothesis of no significant errors in measurement. The empirical results can be summarized as follows:

(i) The parameter estimates of the wage and price equations were found to be quite stable over the sample period 1951-73 when the Chow tests were applied to the reduced form equations. Thus, it seems that the widely found (cf. Gordon 1972) parameter instability in the wage-price equations can partly be explained on the basis of a failure to take care of simultaneity, together with the deterministic modeling of the price expectations variable.

(ii) A dynamic implication of the Natural Rate hypothesis would predict the price expectations coefficients in the reduced form wage and price equations to be unity. For a wide range of models, our estimates support the Natural Rate hypothesis. This also highlights Cukierman's [1974] view that tests based on ordinary least squares estimates of structural wage-price equations may produce misleading conclusions.

(iii) We evaluated the Wage-Price Controls Program in terms of the counter-factual predictions of the model. It failed to indicate any restraining effect on wages; however, it showed large effects on price increases during the early phase of the Freeze, with a partial refound in 1973. These conclusions are very similar to those reached by Gordon [1973].

Our structural model generated significant short-run Phillips curves primarily because the survey data that we have used as a proxy for true price expectations contain significant amount of unanticipated inflation. However, this aspect of the wage-price dunamics will be studied in the next chapter in further details.

Table 2.1 Estimated Reduced Form Coefficients Before and After the Correction for Measurement Errors*

Exogenous Variables	Before the Correction		After the Correction	
	Wage Equation**	Price Equation***	Wage Equation	Price Equation
p^e	.859 (7.168)	1.218 (8.351)	.868	1.231
U^{-1}	10.096 (3.206)	3.916 (1.022)	10.124	3.956
PR	- .075 (-1.888)	- .255 (-2.486)	- .074	- .254
UFK	.003 (1.428)	.017 (1.925)	.003	.017

*Figures in the parentheses are t-ratios. The measurement error variance was .0188.

**R^2 = .650, DW = 1.162

***R^2 = .724, DW = 1.451.

Table 2-2 Auxilliary regressions used in simultaneous wage-price models, 1951-1973[a]

	OPTIONS			
	0	I	II	III
Constant	2.189 (2.36)	-1.577 (-4.81)	1.948 (2.41)	1.331 (2.86)
U^{-1}	-3.157 (-.776)	3.572 (2.92)	-1.990 (- .56)	-9.19 (-4.28)
GD	- .224 (-.439)	-1.08 (-6.53)	- .309 (- .62)	- .33 (-1.24)
UFK	.015 (1.655)	.025 (8.75)	.015 (1.70)	.013 (2.37)
PR	- .085 (-.776)	.043 (1.22)	- .074 (- .72)	- .024 (- .35)
T		.103 (19.22)	---	---
P_{-1}			.247 (2.23)	---
MG		---	---	.148 (2.77)
MG_1		---	---	.199 (4.14)
MG_2		---	---	.139 (2.71)
MG_3		---	---	.111 (2.28)
MG_4		---	---	.014 (.294)
$\bar{R}^2$	.035	.898	.421	.722
DW	.129	.890	.701	.686

[a] Option I uses internal instruments only. t ratios are in brackets. MG is rate of change in money supply, narrowly defined. The dependent variable is $\bar{P}_t^e$ in all the options.

Table 2-3 Efficient-estimation of the simultaneous wage-price model, 1951-73[a]

		OLS	Three-Stage Least Squares: Two Equation Model	Three-Stage Least Squares: Three Equation Model
Wage Equation	p^e	.524 (3.60)	.471 (2.99)	.507 (2.07)
	P	.242 (2.73)	.293 (1.73)	.264 (1.46)
	U^{-1}	8.130 (3.57)	7.243 (2.99)	7.715 (3.07)
	GD	-1.373 (-4.39)	-1.304 (-4.23)	-1.377 (-4.35)
	Const.	- .465 (-.871)	- .341 (-.667)	- .406 (-.781)
	$\bar{R}^2$	.801	---	---
Price Equation	W	.762 (5.66)	.891 (5.71)	.750 (5.06)
	UFK	.026 (2.88)	.023 (2.64)	.027 (3.34)
	PR	- .182 (-1.81)	- .145 (-1.54)	- .176 (-2.04)
	T	.054 (3.28)	.047 (2.87)	.055 (3.66)
	Const.	-1.073 (-2.04)	- .766 (-1.79)	- .622 (-1.61)
	$\bar{R}^2$	.728	---	---

[a]The instrument used in this model for p^e is obtained from option I in Table 2.2 t-ratios are in brackets.

Table 2-4 Efficient estimation of the wage-price model without time trend in price equation: 1951-73[a]

		OLS	3 SLS Estimation of the 2-Equation Model	3 SLS Est. of the 3- Eqn. Model: Option II[b]	3 SLS Est. of the 3- Eqn. Model: Option III
Wage Equation	p^e	.524 (3.60)	.536 (2.85)	.561 (1.27)	.566 (2.48)
	P	.242 (2.73)	.288 (1.36)	.281 (1.11)	.273 (2.48)
	U^{-1}	8.130 (3.57)	6.319 (2.32)	5.347 (1.78)	7.308 (2.72)
	GD	-1.373 (-4.33)	-1.106 (-3.24)	-1.096 (-3.28)	-1.268 (-3.64)
	Const.	- .465 (-.870)	- .264 (-.568)	- .069 (-.103)	- .455 (-.791)
Price Equation	W	.951 (7.03)	1.101 (7.22)	1.057 (6.18)	.882 (5.57)
	UFK	.015 (1.60)	.012 (1.41)	.013 (1.48)	.017 (1.96)
	PR	- .169 (-1.52)	- .126 (-1.19)	- .141 (-1.37)	- .177 (-1.76)
	Const.	.223 (.580)	- .151 (-.359)	- .024 (-.053)	.385 (.942)
	$\bar{R}^2$	.657	---	---	---

[a] t-ratios are in brackets.

[b] The 3 SLS estimate of the auxiliary equation was $\bar{p}^e = \underset{(.11)}{.022} + \underset{(5.95)}{.428}\, P^e + \underset{(2.19)}{.160}\, P_{-1}$

Table 2-5 Efficient estimation of the simultaneous wage-price model with price expectations appearing in both equations[a]

		OLS	3 SLS Est. of the 2-Eqn. Model	3 SLS Est. of the 3-Eqn. Model Option II	3 SLS Est. of the 3-Eqn. Model Option III
Wage Equation	P^e	.524 (3.60)	.499 (1.88)	.457 (1.11)	.550 (2.62)
	P	.242 (2.73)	.261 (1.36)	.274 (1.15)	.258 (1.66)
	U^{-1}	8.130 (3.57)	7.963 (3.01)	7.695 (2.65)	7.957 (3.20)
	GD	-1.373 (-4.33)	-1.362 (-4.19)	-1.382 (-4.17)	-1.350 (-4.20)
	Const.	- .465 (- .87)	- .444 (-.812)	- .349 (-.541)	- .516 (-9.58)
Price Equation	P^e	.814 (4.49)	.855 (4.02)	1.421 (6.82)	.651 (2.97)
	W	.472 (3.04)	.424 (2.01)	.174 (1.03)	.442 (2.24)
	UFK	.015 (1.91)	.015 (2.05)	.012 (1.96)	.017 (2.36)
	PR	- .213 (-2.29)	- .219 (-2.41)	- .215 (-2.56)	- .228 (-2.55)
	Const.	.165 (.51)	.223 (.634)	.005 (.013)	.475 (1.33)
	$\bar{R}^2$	.769	---	---	---

[a]Option II incorporates extrapolative formation of price-expectations hypothesis, and Option III used money supply as additional external instruments.

Table 2-6 Effect of Wage-Price Controls (actual minus predicted values)[a]

Period	Wages			Prices		
	Actual	Predicted	Error	Actual	Predicted	Error
1971:2	3.752	3.788	- .036	3.696	5.036	-1.34[b]
1972:1	5.276	3.816	1.46[b]	3.047	5.041	-1.99[b]
1972:2	3.420	3.939	- .519	3.492	4.820	-1.33[b]
1973:1	5.284	4.554	.730[b]	6.024	6.109	- .085
1973:2	4.755	5.603	- .847	9.276	8.095	1.18

[a]Counterfactual predictions are based on unrestricted reduced form equations of the model given in Table 2.4.

[b]Significantly different from zero at the 5% level of significance.

CHAPTER 3

RATIONAL EXPECTATIONS IN MACRO MODELS

In a series of influential papers, Lucas, Jr. [1972, 1973, 1975], Sargent and Wallace [1975, 1976], and others have developed macroeconomic models incorporating the concept of rationality due to Muth [1960, 1961], in which the short-run Phillips curve is a result only of expectational errors. Rational expectations in such models can then imply that there is no way for the government stabilization policies to depress the unemployment rate below the natural rate, even in the short-run. This rather dramatic attack on policy activism has aroused a number of strong reactions. It has been argued (cf. Poole [1976], Fisher [1972] and Arrow [1978]) that the *rational expectations hypothesis* (REH) *per se*, which says only that individuals make the best use of the information that is available, is entirely unexceptional; but to hypothesize that price expectation in each period is an unbiased prediction of the actual inflation may be too restrictive in the context of macroeconomic models. A second line of argument (see Barro and Fischer [1976]) is that even with REH, stabilization policies might not be entirely ineffective if there is short-run wage-price inflexibility and limited information in the economy. Friedman [1979] has questioned the specific information availability assumption in Muth's rational expectations hypothesis. It states that the information available to economic agents is such that it permits them to form expectations characterized by conditional subjective distribution of outcomes that are equivalent to the conditional objective distribution of outcomes implied by the relevant economic theory. He argues that this particular information availability assumption plays a crucial role in establishing the policy-ineffectiveness result in Sargent-Wallace's [1975] model.

The purpose of the present chapter is to study certain derivable implications of the REH in the context of two different macroeconomic models and to subject the REH to statistical tests. The first one is our wage-price model discussed in previous chapters and the second one is McCallum's [1976] three-equation macromodel. These models will allow us to distinguish between the NRH, which posits that the government can persistently depress the unemployment rate below the natural rate at the cost of an ever accelerating inflation, and the REH which implies that there may be no way that the government can expect to have some handle over counter-cyclical policies. Friedman [1979] is critical of the role of the specific information-availability assumption in obtaining the markedly classical results - such as a vertical Phillips Curve, or independent of real economic activity and the real rate of interest from central bank policies - even in the short-run. To examine the implications of a persistent unanticipated inflation on the existence of conventional short-run Phillips curve and to test the NRH in the context of our simultaneous wage-price model, we have also used the Livingston series on anticipated inflation as developed by Carlson [1977a]. There is enough evidence now which indicates that the Livingston series does not satisfy the so-called efficiency and consistency properties of rational expectations in the sense of Muth [1961]. [See section 6.3] For our purposes, this series together with the REH will hopefully yeild the contradistinction in policy implications due to different information-availability assumptions in the context of the wage-price model.

Our aim here is not to construct a macroeconomic model with built-in "monetarist properties, but rather to test certain derivable implications of the REH in the context of a widely discussed models which are known to have Keynesian policy implications. In this sense, our aim here is quite different from those in Anderson [1979] and Fair [1979]. The importance of empirical research on the short-run dynamics of wage-price behavior in a rational expectations model has been emphasized by Gordon [1976a].

This chapter is organized as follows: In section 3.1 we present a short description of the estimation procedures used. Fortunately, both the approaches -- use of survey data and the REH -- give a unified framework of a simultaneous equations model with random errors in one of the exogenous variables. Sections 3.3 - 3.5 are devoted to our wage-price models, whereas sections 3.6 - 3.9 deal with McCallum's macroeconomic model. Section 3.2 contains the structural estimates of the wage-price model including some tests on the significance of errors that might have blurred the survey data. In section 3.3, we examine the implied short-run Phillips curves which relates unemployment to unanticipated inflation. Sections 3.4 and 3.5 presents the statistical tests on REH in the context of wage-price models already estimated. Sections 3.6 - 3.9 contains basically, the same type of analysis in the context of McCallum's model. Finally, conclusions have been summarized in section 3.10.

The empirical evidence indicates that implementation of the REH in the context of these models tend to wipe out the conventional short-run Phillips curves, and the assumption that public expectations of future rates of inflation are true conditional mathematical expectations based on all available information is indeed borne out quite well against its alternative. These results were obtained without explicitly introducing the orthogonality assumption between expectational errors and the conditioning variables.

3.1 Estimation Methods

Consider a triangular structural model in the sense that there exists an ordering of endogenous variables and equations such that the ith equation contains the ith endogenous variable, and may also contain endogenous variables whose position in the ordering is less than i, but does not contain endogenous variables whose position in the ordering is greater than i. To be more explicit, let us write the model as

$$YB + XC + U = 0 \tag{3.1}$$

where Y is a T x G matrix containing T observations on the G endogenous variables; X is a T x K matrix containing observations on the K predetermined variables; U is a T x G matrix of disturbance with unrestricted covariance matrix ; and B and C are G x G and K x G matrices of unknown parameters. The model is triangular if the matrix B is upper triangular; that is, if $B_{ij} = 0$ for i > j.

We can write the ith equation as

$$y_i = Y_i\beta_i + X_i\gamma_i + u_i = Z_i\alpha_i + u_i \tag{3.2}$$

where $Z_i = (Y_iX_i)$, $\alpha_i = \binom{\beta_i}{\gamma_i}$.

Here y_i is the vector of observations on the ith endogenous variable; Y_i and X_i are matrices of observations on the endogenous and predetermined variables that actually appear in the ith equation; and β_i and γ_i are appropriate vectors of parameters. Consider the first equation:

$$y_1 = X_1\gamma_1 + u_1 \tag{3.3}$$

Suppose the first exogenous variable in the first structural equation, denoted x_1^*, is unobservable. Instead of x_1^*, we have a proxy $\tilde{x}_1$ such that

$$\tilde{x}_1 = x_1^* + \varepsilon_1 \tag{3.4}$$

where ε_1 is IID(0, $\sigma^2_{\varepsilon_1}$) and independent of x_1^*. Then, the equation (3.3) can be written as

$$y_1 = \tilde{x}_1\gamma_{11} + \tilde{X}_1\tilde{\gamma}_1 + u_1 - \gamma_{11}\varepsilon_1 \tag{3.5}$$

where $\tilde{X}_1$ = the matrix X_1 with the first column deleted, and $\tilde{\gamma}_1$ = the vector γ_1 with the first element removed.

Since $\tilde{x}_1$ is contemporaneously correlated with the composite error term and also because the covariance matrix of disturbances in a triangular model is unrestricted, ordinary least squares would yield inconsistent estimates.

Estimation With Survey Data:

Let us denote the covariance matrices of X and U by Φ and ψ respectively. Also denote the covariance matrix of measurement error in X by Θ_δ:

$$\Theta_\delta = \begin{bmatrix} \sigma^2_{\varepsilon_1} & 0 & \cdots\cdots & 0 \\ 0 & 0 & \cdots\cdots & 0 \\ \\ \cdot \\ \cdot \\ 0 & 0 & \cdots\cdots & 0 \end{bmatrix} \tag{3.6}$$

Then the covariance matrix $\underset{\sim}{\Sigma}$ of $Z = (Y:\tilde{X})$ is

$$\underset{\sim}{\Sigma} = \begin{bmatrix} B'^{-1}C'\phi CB^{-1} + B'^{-1}\psi B^{-1} & -B'^{-1}C'\phi \\ \\ -\phi CB^{-1} & \phi+\Theta_\delta \end{bmatrix} \tag{3.7}$$

where $\tilde{X}$ = the matrix X with the first column replaced by $\tilde{x}_1$.

Given the proper specification of the model and the initial starting values for each parameter, the FIML procedure minimizes the function

$$F = \log|\underset{\sim}{\Sigma}| + \mathrm{tr.}(\underset{\sim}{S}\,\underset{\sim}{\Sigma}^{-1}) - \log|\underset{\sim}{S}| - (G + K), \tag{3.8}$$

where $\underset{\sim}{S}$ is the sample covariance matrix of Z. The estimation problem is essentially that of fitting the matrix $\underset{\sim}{\Sigma}$ imposed by the model to the sample covariance matrix $\underset{\sim}{S}$. Under the usual normality assumption, the procedure yields asymptotically efficient parameter estimates.

Estimation Under Rational Expectations Hypothesis:

Suppose the unobservable variable (x_1^*) represents the anticipated values of x_{t+1}. Now x_{t+1} is equivalent, in our notation of $\tilde{x}_1$. REH specifies that

$$x_1^* = E(\tilde{x}_1/I) \tag{3.9}$$

where I denotes the relevant public information available as of time "t" for the prediction of x_{t+1}.

To take care of the correlation between x_1 and the composite error term in equation (3.5), instrumental variable (IV) technique can be utilized to obtain consistent estimates of γ_{11} and $\tilde{\gamma}_1$.[10] An appropriate <u>internal</u> instrument for x_1^* can be obtained from

$$\hat{\tilde{x}}_1 = (w'w)^{-1}w'\tilde{x}_1, \tag{3.10}$$

where w is the appropriate matrix of instrmental variables. The IV method then has the solution:

$$\begin{bmatrix} \gamma_{11} \\ \\ \tilde{\gamma}_1 \end{bmatrix} = \begin{bmatrix} \hat{\tilde{x}}_1'\tilde{x}_1 & \hat{\tilde{x}}_1'\tilde{X}_1 & \tilde{x}_1'y_1 \\ \\ \tilde{X}_1'\tilde{x}_1 & \tilde{X}_1'\tilde{X}_1 & \tilde{X}_1'y_1 \end{bmatrix}^{-1} \tag{3.11}$$

It is well-known that though the IV estimates are not asymptotically efficient, they are consistent, cf.: McCallum [1976a].

3.2 <u>Empirical Results</u>

As stated earlier, one of the main purposes of the present paper is to test an important implication of the REH that changes in output depend on "surprises", i.e. random deviations between actual and expected prices only. Thus the short-run stabilization policies are rather unnecessary since the conventional short-run Phillips curves no longer exist. To test the proposition we have implemented the REH in the context of our wage-price model of the U. S. economy where the inflationary process can be described by a system of two simultaneous equations - a wage equation and a price equation:

$$W_t = a_0 + a_1 p_t^e + a_2 U_t^{-1} + a_3 GD_t + a_4 SG_t + u_{1t} \qquad (3.12)$$

$$P_t = b_0 + b_1 W_t + b_2 PR_t + b_3 UFK_t + b_4 CMW + u_{2t} \qquad (3.13)$$

where we have introduced two additional exogenous variables, SG and CMW, in the determination of wage-price inflation. SG is the percentage change in Social Security tax paid by employers. The rate of change in the ratio of compensation per manhour to wage rate (CMW) is introduced in the price equation to correct for the fact that our fixed-weight wage index does not include earnings paid as sales commissions, tips and executive bonuses for lack of separate data. Actual price is now excluded from the wage equation because as indicated before, over 1954-1973 P_t was no longer statistically significant.

Models With Survey Data:

We assume that the Livingston's survey data can represent the true price expectations with some random errors:

$$\bar{p}_t^e = p_t^e + u_{3t} \qquad (3.14)$$

where $\bar{p}^e$, the proxy for p_t^e, is given by the survey data and u_3 is the random disturbance.

Since observed price expectations data are available semi-annually only, we constructed six-monthly indices from the monthly and/or quarterly data, and then calculated the compounded annual percentage changes up to the first half of 1973. Since Livingston's survey was on the C.P.I., we used percentage change in C.P.I. as our inflation variable.

With the existing FIML estimation procedure, the model using equation (3.12)-(3.14) did not yield reasonable results. The reason is an econometric one. In the process of experimentation, we have found out that to obtain meaningful FIML estimates it is necessary that the proxy for the unobservable price expectations variable be correlated significantly with at least some of the exogenous variables of the model. Thus, we added percentage changes in the money supply narrowly defined (MG), time trend (T) and percentage changes in lagged price (P_{t-1}) as separate options. In similar contexts these variables have been justified by McCallum [1976a], Rutledge [1974] and others. The FIML estimates for options I, II and III are given in Table 3.1. It may be noted that UFK and CMW in the price equation do not occur simultaneously because they are highly correlated. Otherwise all the variables in the wage equation came up significantly with the right signs. In options I and II, the coefficient of price expectations came out to be less than that in the OLS estimation. On the other hand, option III gave us an estimate greater than the OLS estimate. It is interesting to note that in simultaneous equation models with errors-in-variables in one of the exogenous variables, OLS need not bias the estimated coefficient of the error-ridden variable towards zero in absolute value. Also, it may be noted that the models utilizing the unadjusted Livingston's survey data produced an estimated price-expectations coefficient which was less than 0.60 (cf. Turnovsky-Watcher [1972] and our evidence in Chapter 1). The sum of the coefficients of W_t and P_{t-1} in the price equation is very close to unity - a condition necessary for static and steady stage neutrality of real variables, with respect to nominal variables. (See deMenil and Enzler [1972] and McCallum [1979]).

Since Livingston's data on price expectations are based on sample survey, statistical tests to ascertain the seriousness of the hypothesized errors are desirable.[11] To accomplish this in the context of our simultaneous equations model we have again utilized the novel test procedure due to Hausman [1976]. The theory behind the test procedure is based on the idea that under the null hypothesis of no 'error-in-variables' there will exist an unbiased and efficient estimator which, under the alternative hypothesis, will be inconsistent. To construct an appropriate test it is necessary to find another estimator which is not adversely affected by the errors in the survey measure; but this estimator will not be efficient under the correct specification. A consideration of the difference between these two estimates will then lead to the required test.

The robust estimator is generally based on some instrumental variables (IV). The IV test for errors in variables is not new in the econometric literature, but an alternative formulation due to Hausman [1976] leads to easier implementation. Using (3.14) the wage equation can be written as:

$$W_t = a_0+a_1\cdot \bar{p}_t^e+a_2\cdot U_t^{-1}+a_3\cdot GD_t+a_4\cdot SG_t+u_{4t} \,, \tag{3.12a}$$

where $u_{4t} = u_{1t} - a_1u_{3t}$. Since $\bar{p}_t^e$ will be correlated with u_{4t}, application of ordinary least squares to (3.12a) will yield inconsistent parameter estimates. Letting $\hat{p}_t^e = w(w'w)^{-1}w'\bar{p}_t^e$ where w is a matrix of appropriate instruments we can write (3.12a) alternatively as:

$$W_t = a_0+a_1\cdot \bar{p}_t^e+a_2\cdot U_t^{-1}+a_3\cdot GD_t+a_4\cdot SG_t+\alpha\cdot \hat{p}_t^e+u_{5t} \,, \tag{3.12b}$$

where u_{5t} is another random disturbance term. Hausman has shown that a test of $\alpha = 0$ is a test for errors in variables. However, since our wage equation is only a part of the simultaneous model, the matrix w should include all predetermined variables which can possibly be important in the determination of W and P in (3.12) = (3.13).

We have applied the above test to the wage equation with five alternative sets of instrumental variables (see Table 3.2). In one case, α came out to be significant at 5% level of significance while in four other cases it came out to be insignificant. Thus, we are inclined again to believe that the random errors in the survey data are not serious, at least in the context of these models. This is consistent with our evidence in the last chapter.

Models With Rational Expectations Hypothesis:

In order to incorporate the REH, we assume that people expect inflation based on the information available at time "t" and their expectation is essentially the same as the predictions of the relevant economic theory (see Muth [1961]). In particular, we assume that the information is based on past values of variables which enter the reduced form of price equations, i.e.,

$$p_t^e = E(p_t \;/ U_{t-1}^{-1}.., GD_{t-1}..., SG_{t-1}..., PR_{t-1}.., UFK_{t-1}..., CMW_{t-1}...,) \tag{3.15}$$

Since we are not constrained by the survey data, we used the percentage change in the deflators on personal consumption expenditures as our price variable, cf. Gordon [1971]. Now, equations (3.12), (3.13) and (3.15) constitute our model. Application of IV method using the three options mentioned before yielded results which are given in Table 3.3. The DW statistics in the auxiliary regressions did not show any significant autocorrelation in the residuals. In all the options the coefficients of price expectations variable came out very close to unity with the coefficients of SG and U_t^{-1} being statistically insignificant. The latter finding, which is rather striking, was remarkably typical in all the experiments we conducted. However, since it is sometimes argued that the official unemployment rate may not measure the tightness of the labor market variable appropriately, we replaced our unemployment variable by total unemployment rate (TE) which is defined as

$$TE_t = 100 - (U_t + UD_t) ,$$

where UD_t is the disguised unemployment rate in percentage terms (see, Gordon [1971]). TE was more significant than U_t^{-1} in the OLS regression, but it was also found out to be insignificant in all the three options when we implemented the REH.

In some formulations, percentage change in current price is utilized as a proxy for price expectations. In that case equation (3.15) becomes:

$$p^e = E(P_t/U_{t-1}^{-1}, GD_{t-1}, \ldots\ldots). \tag{3.15'}$$

The instrumental variable estimation of the wage equation with the above formulation produced estimates which were very similar to those presented in Table 3.3.

Partly rational expectations hypothesis utilizes only the information contained in past inflation rates, i.e.,

$$p^e = E(P_{t+1}/P_t, P_{t-1}, \ldots). \tag{3.16}$$

Model estimates using 6-8 lags of price inflation were so similar that we have reported (in Table 3.3) only the results with 6 lags. We also introduced six lagged values of MG in addition to six past inflation rates as another option, cf. Rutledge [1974]. The result is also given in Table 3.3.

Thus, whether we use the survey data or implement the REH, our empirical evidence so far supports the NRH at a very high level of significance. However, the important contradistinction is that models with survey data reveal a rather strong relationship between wage inflation and unemployment. This can be explained by the fact that Livingston's series is characterized by significant amount of unanticipated inflation (see Carlson [1977]). But, in models with REH we no longer find any observable relationship between wages and unemployment. The latter result is true even when we used some additional labor market variables and treated U_t^{-1} as an endogenous variable.[12] It is worth noting that this finding is consistent with a rather drastic version of the REH; i.e., while NRH implies that the Phillips curve is vertical in the long-run, the application of REH makes the Phillips curve vertical even in the short-run, cf. Anderson [1979].

It may be argued that the statistical insignificance of the unemployment variable is an econometric artifact as a result of the conventional instrumental variable procedure. To generate the instruments for price expectations, one regresses prices on a number of lagged values of all the exogenous variables including the unemployment rates. This is justified under the presumption that in a RE model, people generally do not waste information, and the information includes lagged values of U_t^{-1}. But since U_t has a very strong autoregressive representation, it is not surprising that U_t^{-1} no longer offers any direct aid in predicting the wage inflation. We, however, feel that the disappearance of the conventional short-run Phillips curves in our models with REH can not simply be explained by the IV procedure utilized. First, prices are not regressed on current values of the exogenous variables to generate the instruments, and hence, even if U_t is autoregressive, it is entirely possible for the U_t^{-1} term to remain statistically significant. Secondly, models with partly rational expectations came up with the same result. Finally, the results reported in Section 3.4, where the RE models were estimated quite independent of the auxiliary regressions, revealed the same general regularity.

3.3 Real effects of unanticipated inflation: Are they expolitable?

According to the Accelerationist hypothesis, the temporary trade-off between unemployment and inflation comes not from inflation *per se*, but from unanticipated inflation (see Friedman 1968). Fully anticipated inflation merely gets *absorbed* in prices and wages without any real effects. Similarly, the application of REH implies that the changes in output and employment are caused by the random prediction errors of firms and workers regarding prices and wages (see Poole 1976).

Sargent [1973] gives a clear explanation of this possibility:

> "Unexpected rises in the price level thus boost aggregate supply, because suppliers mistakenly interpret surprise increases in the aggregate price level as increases in the relative prices of labor or goods they are supplying. This mistake occurs because suppliers receive information about the price of their own goods faster than they receive information about the aggregate price level."

In these situations, the short-run Phillips curves under the Accelerationist hypothesis can be written as (cf. Gordon 1976a):

$$U_t = U_t^N - \gamma(P_t - E_{t-1}P_t) + \varepsilon_t^s \tag{3.17}$$

where U_t^N = the natural rate of unemployment; and ε_t^s = exogenous supply shocks with zero expectation, beyond the control of the policy maker.

It is important to identify the monetarists' Phillips curves because, as Barro and Fischer [1976] have pointed out, too much information in a REH framework can clearly wipe out any such relationship, and the analysis then degenerates to that of a "perfect foresight" model. Assuming that the natural rate of unemployment was roughly constant during our sample period, we estimated (3.17) using the implied unanticipated inflation series obtained under options I, II, III and also under partly rational expectations schemes. All the coefficients came out with the right signs. Except in option I, the coefficients of unanticipated inflation were significant at 5% level of significance, suggesting the validity of these short-run Phillips curves. The results are given in Table 3.4. It should be pointed out that the insignificance of the correlation between unanticipated inflation and unemployment in option I can not be explained by arguing that option I used too much information[13] in generating the forecasts. In fact the $\bar{R}^2$ in the auxiliary regression of option I was lowest of the three options. However, it is consistent with the fact that our tests of REH (reported in Section 3.4) in the context of option I were not too encouraging.

It is interesting to note that our models estimated the natural rate of unemployment to be around 5%, which is simply the mean of the unemployment rate during our sample periods.

Even though we find substantial evidence in support of a systematic relationship between unanticipated inflation and unemployment, an important issue still remains to be resolved. Is it possible for the monetary authority to make the unemployment rate temporarily deviate from the natural rate through a systematic stabilization policy?

If the economic agents can make unbiased predictions of the future course of monetary policy, the feedback effects of money are fully taken into account in the formation of price expectation. Hence government's counter-cyclical policies loose their effectiveness. In this case, although a Phillips curve exists, it is not exploitable by monetary policy. Sargent and Wallace [1975] consider this kind of a situation. However, if the policy maker has superior information about the economy, Barro [1976] shows that countercyclical monetary policy can be effective. Also if the monetary authority has superior information about its own actions and they are willing to undertake a deceptive policy, Taylor [1975] argues that it is possible to have desirable real effects in the transition period during which new information is combined with old. Fischer [1977] constructed a rational expectations model with longterm wage contracts. He demonstrated that shortrun wage stickiness due to the longterm contracts enables the monetary policy to affect the behavior of real output.

McCallum [1977] and Barro [1977] have responded to this kind of criticism. As pointed out by Fischer [1977] himself, the existence of the fixed period contracts are taken as exogenous to the model. Rational expectations argues that it pays the economic agents to anticipate the effect of policy changes. Any systematic attempt to expolit the fixed contracts will eventually be discovered and will form a part of the information upon which economic plans are based. By assuming that firms choose to set their prices and wages one period in advance of the period over which they will apply, Phelps and Taylor [1977] showed that monetary policy can stabilize fluctuations in output and employment.[14]

In relation to the exploitability of short-term Phillips curves, Sargent [1976] stands on the one extreme end by claiming that "there is no way that the government can operate so that it can expect to depress the unemployment rate below the natural rate even in the shortrun."

In order to test the hypothesis, he proposed an F-test (Granger [1969] causality) on the following equation (see Sargent 1976)

$$U_t = \sum_{j=1}^{k_1} \alpha_1 U_{t-j} + \sum_{j=1}^{k_2} \beta_j Y_{t-j} + \varepsilon_t \tag{3.18}$$

where Y = policy variables subject to test; k_1, k_2 = number of lagged variables in U_t and Y_t; $\varepsilon_t \sim$ IID $(0, \sigma_{\varepsilon\varepsilon})$.
Testing the null hypothesis H_0: $\beta = (\beta_1 \ldots\ldots \beta_{k_2}) = 0$ is equivalent to the test of Sargent's version of NRH. In order to see the effectiveness of stabilization policy, we added 6 lags of percentage changes in narrowly defined money supply (MG_t) and 6 lags of percentage changes in government purchases of goods and services (G_t) both separately and jointly.

F-statistics($F_{6,28}$) associated with the lagged values of MG_t and G_t came out to be 1.879 and 2.242 respectively. They are not significant at a 5% level of significance. However, it is interesting to note that the F statistic ($F_{12,22}$) associated with both the lagged values of MG_t and that of G_t came out to be 2.506, which is significant at the 1% level of significance. However, this latter result should not suggest that a suitable policy mix between monetary and fiscal policy can have some role in affecting the unemployment rate to deviate from the natural rate in the short-run. Nelson [1979] has shown that the causality test is a predictive concept which can not be used to test the NRH in this framework.

3.4 Tests of rational expectations hypothesis and the implications of different information - availability assumptions.

Direct statistical tests of the rational expectations hypothesis implemented in this section were motivated by the fact that REH in the context of econometric models with unobservable variables is an alternative source of identifying restrictions. Given the wage-price model (3.12) - (3.13) and noting that (3.15) implies

$$P_{t+1} = P_t^e + v_t, \; v_t \sim \text{IID}\,(0, \sigma_{vv}) \,, \tag{3.19}$$

it is possible to show that the overidentifying restrictions implied by the simultaneity in (3.12) - (3.13) can be traded off with the underidentification introduced by (3.19).[15] Thus, to estimate the model (3.12) - (3.13) and (3.19), it is not necessary to bring in auxiliary regressions explicitly. The estimates, then, would have the obvious advantage of being robust with respect to the widely varying $\bar{R}^2$ associated with different auxiliary regressions. The problem of obtaining widely different estimates for the price expectation coefficient corresponding to different auxiliary regressions having widely different $\bar{R}^2$ is well illustrated in McCallum [1976a].

To test the REH, we propose to estimate

$$P_{t+1} = \lambda_1 P^e + v_t \tag{3.20}$$

together with (3.12) - (3.13) and test whether the restrictions $\lambda_1 = 1$ is a reasonable restriction to impose. A value of λ_1 greater than one would imply that actual price changes are on the average underestimated. Unfortunately, the model (viz. (3.12), (3.13) and (3.20)) is not fully identified without further restrictions. Since there is no longer any serious debate on the validity of the NRH (see Gordon 1976, p. 193), and because we found an overwhelming evidence of favour of the hypothesis in all the experiments, we normalized a_1 in (3.12) to be unity. This condition is imposed in the M.I.T.-Penn.-S.S.R.C. (MPS 1975) model also. Thus, we test the validity of the REH conditional upon the NRH.

The FIML estimates of the model are given in Table 3.5.[16] Using the standard t-test, we can not reject the null hypothesis that $\lambda_1 = 1$ in all the three options. Only in option I, however, λ_1 was a little greater than one, lying beyond one estimated standard error of unity (but within two standard errors).

The corresponding results with partly rational expectations are given in Table 3.6. With partly rational expectations, since we did not consider the simultaneity, the covariance terms between the error terms of the first two equations were set equal to zero. In both the options, we find λ_1 to be very close to unity - supporting the basic implications of the REH. Except in the partly rational model with lagged prices only, the unemployment inverse never showed up significantly. This result is worth noting because we did not use any auxiliary regression to estimate the parameters. The statistical insignificance of U_t^{-1} in the partly rational model with only six lagged prices can be explained in view of Rutledge's [1974] demonstration that the use of lagged rates of money supply growth is necessary to specify adequately a partly rational expectations model. (See also Brunner and Meltzer [1972]). This particular option had the lowest $\bar{R}^2$ (.353) in the auxiliary regression. Thus, it seems that at least in the context of the wage-price models under consideration, the implied $\bar{R}^2$ in the auxiliary regressions should at least be around .50 to obtain the drastic implications of the REH. All the coefficients including the estimated variances of the error terms came up with proper and reasonable magnitudes.

Friedman [1979] has argued that the 'policy-neutrality' results of Sargent and Wallace [1975] follows as a result of the strong information availability assumption of REH, viz. people's expectations of P_{t+1} conditional on information available as of time t, differ from P_{t+1} itself only by a purely random error term. The prediction error $(P_{t+1} - p_t^e)$ implied by the REH is orthogonal to all the conditioning variables including the money supply. Thus, it is not surprising that the deviation of output from its 'natural' level is also independent of moentary policy. The tests of REH that we are reporting here are however, not specific to any information availability assumption. We are rather, testing a very specific requirement of the Muthian rationality, viz. $P_{t+1} = p_t^e + v_t$, without imposing the error-orthogonality property on the estimation procedure. The null hypothesis is consistent with Muth [1960, p. 317] where he writes, "It (the hypothesis) does not assert that the scratch work of entrepreneurs resembles the system of equations in any way, nor does it state that predictions of entrepreneurs are perfect or that their expectations are all the same." Koopmans [1957, p. 139] had made a similar point about the 'scratch work of entrepreneurs' earlier in his example of an expert billiard player. The player may not know all the complicated dynamics of the shots but may behave rationally in the sense that he makes the shots as if he does know it. As Kantor [1979] has pointed out, the fundamental issue is whether actual market prices can be regarded as serviceable "knowledge-surrogates." A somewhat discouraging evidence against the REH was obtained when we conducted another test which considers the survey data and version (3.20) of the REH jointly. Wage equation (3.12) and the following two equations constitute our model:

$$P_{t+1} = \lambda_1 p_t^e + v_t$$

$$\bar{p}_t^e = \lambda_2 p_t^e + \omega_t, \quad \omega_t \sim \text{IID } (0, \sigma_{\omega\omega}) \tag{3.21}$$

We want to test whether λ_1 and/or λ_2 are/is significantly different from unity. The maximum likelihood estimation under the constraint $a_1 = 1$ gave us $\lambda_1 = 1.478$ and $\lambda_2 = 1.003$ (see Table 3.7). This test apparently suggests that the survey data rather than the REH tracted the true price expectations more closely. In other others, when the survey measure is confronted with the REH, the wage equation seems to choose the former as a better proxy for the unobservable price expectations. Not surprisingly, the coefficient of U_t^{-1} comes back with a significant coefficient. However, we should realize that λ_1/λ_2 are estimated conditional on $a_1 = 1$. The FIML estimates of a_1 in Tables 3.1 and 3.3 were on the average a little less than unity. This by itself is not inconsistent with the NRH. Consider an increase in the rate of growth of the money supply, and assume everyone knows that this is occurring. Then expected inflation, actual inflation, and actual wage growth should also increase, and the coefficient of p^e in the wage equation will be unity. Now consider an exogenous increase in expectations, without a matching money growth. An Accelerationist will expect that prices and wages will rise somewhat, but by less than if monetary growth had occurred. The rise in expected inflation reduces the demand for money and thereby increases the price level - once and for all. Since there is no reason to think that anything has affected real wages, the nominal wage rate would presumably rise once-for-all also. This effect occurs with or without money growth. In this case expected inflation would result in a less than proportionate rise in actual price and wage growth. Thus, a_1 which is really a mixture of these two effects may turn out to be less than unity.[17] Constraining $a_1 = 1$ when in fact it is less than unity will correspondingly inflate the estimated value of λ_1. In this sense, an estimate of $\lambda_1 = 1.478$ with the standard error of estimate = .195 may not be inconsistent with the REH. In the next section, we present some additional evidence on the REH where no such normalization is needed. In any case, our econometric evidence so far overwhelmingly support one of the basic implications of Muth's rational expectations hypothesis that logically it precludes the existence of short-run Phillips curve in the conventional sense. The same result was obtained by Anderson (1979), utilizing a completely different approach. His simulation result with the original St. Louis model demonstrated an exploitable trade-off between inflation and unemployment partly due to the existence of systematically mistaken expectations of the inflation rate. However, when the rational expectations adjustment was made to the structure of the St. Louis model, the trade-off virtually disappeared, see also Fair [1979].

3.5 Further tests of the REH using data-based distributed lag models

So far our main emphasis was on efficient estimation of structural equation models with rational expectations and to test directly whether the subsequently observed actual rate of inflation could be taken as an unibased predictor for the true price expectations. In these tests we did not consider the nature of the predetermined variables of the model which may condition the price expectations variable. By introducing certain 'data-based' distributed lag models of the relevant exogenous variables, one may test a much broader set of testable restrictions implied by the REH without introducing any further identifying restriction. In recent years, several economists including Wallis [1979], Revankar [1979], and Hoffman and Schmidt [1978] have examined these testable restrictions in the reduced form equations of the structural model which are directly a function of the relevant information at the time the expectation is formed. In order to shed additional light on the issue, we shall now show that the restrictions implied by the REH in the context of our wage-price model are consistent with the available data at a confortable level of statistical confidence.

Derivation of Testable Restrictions:

Consider again the structural model:

$$W = a_1p^e + a_2U + a_3GD + a_4\ SG + U_1 \tag{3.22}$$

$$P = b_1W + b_2PR + b_3CMW + b_4T + U_2 \tag{3.23}$$

where W = the percentage change in standard unit labor cost, U = the inverse of official unemployment rate, p^e = the percentage rate of expected inflation, GD = guidepost dummies, SG = the percentage change in Social Security tax paid by employers, P = percentage change in the C.P.I., PR = the percentage change in the ratio of actual to trend productivity, CMW = the percentage change in the ratio of compensation per manhour to wage rate, and (U_1U_2) are random disturbances.

Treating p^e as an exogenous variable, we get the following reduced form equations:

$$W = a_1p^e + a_2U + a_3GD + a_4SG + U_1 \tag{3.24}$$

$$P = b_1(a_1p^e + a_2U + a_3GD + a_4SG) + b_2PR + B_3CMW +$$
$$b_4T + b_1U_1 + U_2 \tag{3.25}$$

The rationality criterion demands that p^e should be equal to the model's prediction , or

$$p^e = E[P|I_{t-1}]$$
$$= \pi\ [b_1a_2E(U) + b_1a_3GD + b_1a_4SG + b_2PR + b_3CMW + b_4T] \tag{3.26}$$

where $\pi = 1/(1 - a_1b_1)$. The reason the expectational operator E is attached to the unemployment variable only is purely econometric. Though the future values of the other exogenous variables with the exception of GD and T are unknown at the time expectations are formed (hence E should be applied to them), their autogressive processes turned out to have extremely low $\bar{R}^2$ values. Introducing the following auto-regressive process:[18]

$$U = \sum_{i=1}^{4} \alpha_i U_{-i} + \varepsilon, \ \varepsilon \text{ is IIN}(o, \sigma_\varepsilon^2) \tag{3.27}$$

we get the following "extended" reduced form equations if we substitute (3.27) for E(U) in (3.26) and (3.26) for p^e into (3.24) and (3.25):

$$W = a_1\pi b_1 a_2 \sum_{i=1}^{4} \alpha_i U_{-i} + a_2U + a_3\pi.GD + a_4\pi SG + a_1\pi b_2 PR$$

$$+ a_1\pi b_3.CMW + a_1\pi b_4.T + U_1 \tag{3.28}$$

$$P = b_1^2 a_1 \pi a_2 \sum_{i=1}^{4} \alpha_i U_{-i} + b_1b_2U + b_1a_3\pi.GD + b_1a_4\pi.SG$$

$$+ b_2\pi.PR + b_3\pi.CMW + b_4\pi.T + b_1U_1 + U_2 \tag{3.29}$$

Alternatively, (3.28) - (3.29) can be written more compactly as:

$$Y = \Pi.X + V \tag{3.30}$$

where $Y = (W,P)'$, $X = (U_{-1}, U_{-2}, U_{-3}, U_{-4}, U, GD, SG, PR, CMW, T)'$, with π_{ij} being the (ij) element of Π.

Then the following restrictions emerge. First, "type 1" restrictions according to Hoffman and Schmidt [1978], or the restrictions due entirely to the nature of the autoregressive process introduced:

$$\pi_{11}/\pi_{12} = \alpha_1/\alpha_2;\ \pi_{12}/\pi_{13} = \alpha_2/\alpha_3;\ \pi_{13}/\pi_{14} = \alpha_3/\alpha_4$$

$$\pi_{21}/\pi_{22} = \alpha_1/\alpha_2;\ \pi_{22}/\pi_{23} = \alpha_2/\alpha_3;\ \pi_{23}/\pi_{24} = \alpha_3/\alpha_4, \tag{3.31}$$

Consolidated together, the above restrictions would amount to constraining the parameter values across the equations in the following manner:

$$\pi_{11} = (\pi_{21}/\pi_{22})\cdot\pi_{12};\ \pi_{13} = (\pi_{23}/\pi_{22})\cdot\pi_{12};\ \pi_{14} = (\pi_{12}/\pi_{22})\pi_{24} \qquad (3.31)'$$

On the other hand, if we divide the coefficients across the equations by their counterparts, we get the following "type 2" restrictions due primarily to the over-identification of the structural model:

$$(\pi_{25}/\pi_{15}) = (\pi_{26}/\pi_{16}) = (\pi_{27}/\pi_{17}) = b_1$$

$$(\pi_{18}/\pi_{28}) = (\pi_{19}/\pi_{29}) = (\pi_{1,10}/\pi_{2,10}) = a_1 \tag{3.32}$$

Again, consolidated together, these restrictions can be written as:

$$\pi_{26} = (\pi_{25}/\pi_{15})\cdot\pi_{16};\ \pi_{17} = (\pi_{16}/\pi_{26})\cdot\pi_{27} = (\pi_{15}/\pi_{25})\cdot\pi_{27}$$

$$\pi_{29} = (\pi_{28}/\pi_{18})\ \pi_{19};\ \pi_{2,10} = (\pi_{29}/\pi_{19})\pi_{1,10}. \qquad (3.32)'$$

Test Results

We first estimated equations (3.28) - (3.29) without imposing any restrictions, and then constrained the parameters following (3.31)' and (3.31)' - (3.32)' separately. The equations are jointly estimated by using a non-linear maximum likelihood (ML) algorithm available through the Times Series Processor (TSP). The coefficient estimates together with the values of the DW statistic, R^2 and the maximized log-likelihood function have been reported in Table 3.8. The DW statistics indicate randomness in the residuals and all the statistically-significant parameter estimates are strikingly similar under constrained and unconstrained estimation.

We can now put the empirical results on a formal test. The χ^2 statistic for the 'type 1' restrictions is $-2x(-83.439+82.357) = 2.164$. With 3 degrees of freedom, the critical value for a χ^2 variate at the 95 percent level of confidence is 7.815. Thus, we fail to reject the 'type 1' restrictions in context of our model. When the two types of restrictions are imposed together, the statistic emerged as 10.22. With seven degrees of freedom, corresponding to the number of restrictions on the model, the critical values are 12.017 and 14.067 at the 10% and 5% levels of significance respectively. We, thus, cannot reject the null hypothesis of rational expectations at a confidence level of greater than 90 percent. We can, however, reject the REH at a low level of nearly 75% confidence: a χ^2 variate with seven degrees of freedom has a 25% probability of being larger than 9.035 by a pure chance.

3.6 McCallum's Model and Some 'Limited Information' Estimates

In a series of articles, McCallum [1976a, 1976b, 1977] has developed a three-equation macro model derived from othadox equilibrium theory. The structural equations of the model can be written as:

$$\Delta \log W_t = \gamma_0 + \gamma_1 \log(y/n)_{t-1} + \gamma_2 \log w_{t-1} + \gamma_3 \Delta \log P^e_{t+1} \tag{3.33}$$

$$\Delta \log y_t = \alpha_0 + \alpha_1 \Delta \log m_t + \alpha_2 \Delta \log G_t - (\alpha_1+\alpha_2) \Delta \log P_t + \alpha_3 \Delta \log C_{t-1} \tag{3.34}$$

$$\Delta \log P_t = \beta_0 + \beta_1 \log(y/q)_t + \beta_2 \log W_t + \beta_3 t + \beta_4 \log P_{t-1} \tag{3.35}$$

Equation (3.33) is the expectations-augmented Phillips curve; (3.34) is the aggregate demand function obtained as a solution of standard IS-LM relationships, and (3.35) describes short-run excess demand for output. Here $\Delta \log W_t$ represents the proportionate change of money wage rates from period t-1 to t; $\log(y/n)_{t-1}$ and $\log w_{t-1}$ together represent any excess demand for labor where y_t, n_t and w_t denote output of the employing sector, a population measure, and deflated wage rate (W/P) respectively. $\Delta \log P^e_{t+1}$ is the anticipated rate of price change expected at the beginning of period t. The symbols q, c, m, and G denote potential output, real consumption, the nominal money stock, and the nominal government spending. In this model, t is a simple trend variable designed to reflect technical progress. One advantage of the above model is that it explicitly considers the real and the monetary sectors of the economy.

To be comparable, we use the same data as was used by McCallum [1976], namely quarterly time-series data over 1952-1970. The wage variable is the Gordon-index which reflects hourly earnings in the entire private non-agricultural sector of the economy corrected for changes in fringe benefits including overtime and inter-industry employment shifts. Except for P and q, all variables were seasonally adjusted. Because P and q are seasonally unadjusted, seasonal dummies were introduced as additional variables.

McCallum [1976a] estimated the wage equation by first substituting the actual value of the variable (i.e., $\Delta \log P_{t+1}$) for $\Delta \log P^e_{t+1}$ and then using an instrumental variable estimator, the instruments being the information set in the auxiliary regression. We, however, estimated the equation by the conventional two-stage least squares procedure (2SLS) on efficiency grounds. The 2SLS estimates of the wage equation have been reported in Table 3.10. The instrument for $\Delta \log P_{t+1}$ was generated by eleven different first-stage regressions; four of these are so-called 'partly-rational' cases. To facilitate comparison, we have reporduced McCallum's [1976a] Table 1 (our Table 3.9) to list the explanatory variables used in different options. Our 2 SLS estimates are very close to those obrained by McCallum. The γ_3-estimates are, though, slightly higher possibly because of our use of 2SLS procedure. However, the associated standard errors are such that like McCallum, we also reject NRH (γ_3=1) at 5 percent level using options I-VII (except, of course, for option V which is ordinarily least squares) and accept the hypothesis using the partly rational options. Thus, one of the disturbing features of the estimates is that the validity of NRH crucially depends on the auxiliary regression one chooses to generate the instrument.

McCallum [1976a] has taken this logic one step further. Since the OLS option, (which estimated γ_3 to be only around .38), can be interpreted as having a first-stage regression with R^2=1, he concluded that inclusion of 'too many' first-stage regressors will lead to systematic underestimation of γ_3. McCallum further argued that this result is predictable on the basis of asymptotic theory: as the framework is equivalent to an errors-in-variables model, the OLS estimator of γ_3 is asymptotically biased toward zero. The point to note, however, is that an errors-in-variable problem in the context of simultaneous equations models need not bias the associated coefficient toward zero. The bias can go in any direction depending on the variance-covariance structure of the variables and the disturbances. (See section 2.3). Also, as Wallis [1980] has made it explicit, once the implications of rationality and the structure of the model are fully exploited, more information can only increase the efficiency of the structural estimates.

Indeed, in terms of the complete structural model, it is interesting to estimate the structural parameters by using the three-stage least squares procedure (3SLS). McCallum [1976] did not report these estimates. We have reported them in table 3.11. The 3SLS estimates of γ_3 is now less than the corresponding 2SLS estimates and NRH is now rejected even at the 10% level of significance. Option I estimated γ_3 to be only .713. The other structural parameters came up with expected signs and reasonable magnitudes. The output equation (3.34) was estimated after imposing the constraint that the coefficient of $\Delta \log P_t$ is $-(\alpha_1+\alpha_2)$. It is worth pointing out that for options I through IV, the unconstrained estimate of the coefficient of $\Delta \log M_t$ stayed around .863 (with standard error .235), the $\Delta \log G_t$ term was .175 (with standard error .055) while $\Delta \log P_t$ term was -1.712 (with a standard error .480). Thus, contrary to what McCallum [1973] hypothesized, the sum of the first two terms was not statistically the same as the last one, although the signs were consistent with *a priori* expectations.

It is interesting to note that γ_1 and γ_2 together represents the short-run Phillips curve in this model. As compared with the OLS estimates (i.e., option V), the absolute magnitude of these coefficients is reduced by nearly 50 percent once rationality is built into the model. This implies that while rationality does minimize the short-run 'trade-off' between excess demand for labor and inflation, it does not wipe out the relationship completely in the context of this model. This is consistent with the results of dynamic simulations in Gelfand, Lahiri and Osborne [1981] where the monetary and fiscal policies were not entirely ineffective as short-run income stabilizers.

The 2SLS estimates, however, are not the full information maximum-likelihood estimates for these kinds of models partly because it does not use the special structure of the variance-covariance matrix of the disturbances that rationality implies, cf. Wallis [1980]. Rational expectations should certainly use all the structural details, including any overidentifying restrictions from other equations.

3.7 FIML Estimation of the Structural Model

In this section we shall estimate the three-equation structural model after imposing the rationality and an appropriate information set conditioning the price forecasts. To compute the FIML estimates we have again used LISREL-IV, the computer algorithm developed by Joreskog and Sorbom [1979].

We estimated the structural model (3.33) - (3.35) after adding two more equations, viz. $\log\Delta P^*_{t+1} = E(\log\Delta P_{t+1}|\Phi) = \log\Delta P_{t+1} + \varepsilon_t$ and an appropriate auxiliary regression. Here ε_t is the random disturbance term and Φ is the relevant information set given by the auxiliary regression. The structure was estimated as follows (standard erros are given in the parantheses):

$$\Delta \log W_t = \underset{(.003)}{.0246} \log(y/n)_{t-1} + \underset{(.017)}{.0414} \log w_{t-1} + \underset{(.070)}{.920} \Delta \log P^e_{t+1}$$

$$\Delta \log y_t = \underset{(.339)}{.701} \Delta \log m_t + \underset{(.277)}{.202} \Delta \log G_t - \underset{(.010)}{.920} \Delta \log P_t + \underset{(.079)}{.067} \Delta \log C_{t-1}$$

$$\Delta \log P_t = \underset{(.004)}{.045} \log(y/q)_t + \underset{(.008)}{.200} \log W_t - \underset{(.004)}{.025}\, t - \underset{(.005)}{.111} \log P_{t-1}$$

$$\Delta \log P^e_{t+1} = \underset{(.002)}{.065} \log(y/n)_{t-1} + \underset{(.026)}{.080} W_{t-1} + \underset{(.048)}{.077} \Delta \log M_t + \underset{(.043)}{.032} \Delta \log G_t$$

$$- \underset{(.006)}{.016} \Delta \log C_{t-1} - \underset{(.006)}{.010} \log q_t - \underset{(.004)}{.023}\, t + \underset{(.014)}{.097} \log P_{t-1}$$

We have not reported the constant terms and the coefficients for dummy variables to save space. The most important feature of the above estimates is that now the coefficient of $\Delta \log P^e_{t+1}$ in the wage equation is .92 (standard error .070). Thus, we accept NRH at the 1% level of confidence. The other structural parameters have turned out to be very similar to those we have obtained before. These estimates were strikingly similar when we estimated the same model with auxiliary regressions (options II-IV) and hence have not been reported. Thus, once the complete structural details of the model is exploited in estimation, we obtain overwhelming evidence in favor of NRH, even using option I where McCallum's γ_3-estimate was decisively below unity.

3.8 Further Implications of REH in McCallum's Model

Following our analysis in section 3.5, here we shall derive further implications of REH and examine whether these implications are consistent with McCallum's model.

To make the notations less cumbersome for future purposes, let us rewrite our equations (3.33) - (3.35) as

$$DW = \gamma_1 YN1 + \gamma_2 WP1 + \gamma_3 DP^e + u_1 \tag{3.33'}$$

$$DY = \alpha_1 DM + \alpha_2 DG + \alpha_3 DP + \alpha_4 DC1 + u_2 \tag{3.34'}$$

$$DP = \beta_1 YQ + \beta_3 t + \beta_4 P1 + u_3 \tag{3.35'}$$

where DW $=\Delta\log W$ = W-W1, YQ = Y-Q, DY = Y-Y1, DP* = $\Delta \log P^e_{t-1}$, YN1 = $\log(y/n)_{t-1}$, etc. and u_i (i=1,2,3) are random disturbance terms. After writing (3.33') and (3.34') as

$$W = \gamma_1 YN1 + \gamma_2 WP1 + \gamma_3 DP^e + W1 + u_1 \tag{3.33''}$$

$$Y = \alpha_1 DM + \alpha_2 DG + \alpha_3 DP + \alpha_4 DC1 + Y1 + u_2 \tag{3.34''}$$

and by substituting the above equations for Y and W in (3.35'), we get

$$DP = \pi\beta_1(\alpha_1 DM + \alpha_2 DG - Q) + \pi\beta_2\gamma_3 DP^e + \theta_1 DC1 + \theta_2 Y1$$
$$- \theta_3 N1 + \theta_4 W1 + \theta_5 P1 + \theta_6 T + v_3 \tag{3.35''}$$

where

$\pi = (1-\beta_1\alpha_3)^{-1}$, $\theta_1 = \pi\beta_1\alpha_4$, $\theta_2 = \pi(\beta_1+\beta_2\gamma_1)$, $\theta_3 = \pi\beta_2\gamma_1$

$\theta_4 = \pi\beta_2(\gamma_2+1)$, $\theta_5 = \pi(\beta_4-\beta_2\gamma_2)$, $\theta_6 = \pi\beta_3$, v_3 is the composite disturbance term.

Then, by substituting (3.35") for DP in (3.34'), we get the reduced form equation for DY:

$$DY = (1+\alpha_3\pi\beta_1)(\alpha_1 DM + \alpha_2 DG) - \alpha_3\pi\beta_1 Q + \alpha_3\pi\beta_2\gamma_3 dP^e$$
$$+ (\alpha_3\theta_1 + \alpha_4) DC1 + \alpha_3\theta_2 Y1 - \alpha_3\theta_3 N1 + \alpha_3\theta_4 W1 + \alpha_3\theta_5 P1$$
$$+ \alpha_3\theta_6 T + v_2 \tag{3.36}$$

Since (3.33') does not involve any of the endogenous variables, it is recursive to the other structural equations and hence its reduced-form equation is the same as the structural one. This is because we have thus far treated

DP^e as an exogenous variable.

Rationality criterion specifies DP* should be equal to the model's prediction. Since the structural equation for DP involves all the endogenous variables in the system, it is appropriate to generate the model's prediction through its reduced-form. To be more specific, by taking the conditional expectation on (3.35") above, we get the model's prediction on DP^e:

$$DP^e = E(DP) = \pi\pi'\beta_1 \{\alpha_1 E(DM) + \alpha_2 E(DG) - Q\}$$
$$+ \pi' (\theta_1 DC1 + \theta_2 Y1 - \theta_3 N1 + \theta_4 W1 + \theta_5 P1 + \theta_6 t) \quad (3.37)$$

where $\pi' = (1 - \pi\beta_2\gamma_3)^{-1}$, $E(\cdot)$ is the expectation operator attached to the exogenous variable $(\cdot)$ whose values are unknown when the expectations are taken. Note that potential GNP is treated as predetermined because of severe autocorrelation in the series.

To make the model's prediction operational, we need to specify how the expectations on the exogenous variables DM and DG are formed. Empirically, the following autoregressive processes emerge to describe the evolvement of the exogenous variables:

$$DM = a_1 DM1 + e_1 \quad (3.38)$$
$$DG = b_1 DG2 + b_2 DG3 + e_2 \quad (3.39)$$

where DM1 is one-period lagged value of DM and similarly for others; e_is are the disturbance terms independntly distributed from the u_i in (3.33') - (3.35'). Each equation has a constant term and three seasonal dummies in addition. The type of the regressors and their lag structures in the autoregressive process are selected on empirical grounds: they render statistically significant coefficient estimates. Since the coefficients in the autoregressive process enter the restrictions to be tested later, it is important to have non-zero values on them.

Taking conditional expectations on the autoregressive process (3.38) - (3.39) and substituting them for E (DM) and E (DG) in (3.37), we get the operational version of the model's prediction:

$$E\ (DP) = \pi\pi'\beta_1\ (\alpha_1 a_1 DM1 + \alpha_2 b_1 DG2 + \alpha_2 b_2 DG3 - Q)$$
$$+ \pi'\ (\theta_1 DC1 + \theta_2 Y1 - \theta_3 N1 + \theta_4 W1 + \theta_5 P1 + \theta_6 T) \tag{3.40}$$

Now, by substituting (3.40) for DP* in the reduced-form equations (3.33'), (3.36) and (3.35"), we get the following "extended" reduced-form equations after some algebra:

$$DW = \gamma_3\ \{\pi\pi'\beta_1(\alpha_1 a_1\ DM1 + \alpha_2 b_1\ DG2 + \alpha_2 b_2\ DG3 - Q)$$
$$+ \gamma_3\pi'\ (\theta_1\ DC1 + \delta_2\ Y1 - \delta_3\ N1 + \delta_4\ W1 + \delta_5\ P1 + \theta_6\ T) + v_1 \tag{3.41}$$

where $\delta_2 = (\theta_2 + \gamma_1/\gamma_3\pi')$, $\delta_3 = (\theta_3 + \gamma_1/\gamma_3\pi')$, $\delta_4 = (\theta_4 + \gamma_2/\gamma_3\pi')$, $\delta_5 = (\theta_5 - \gamma_2/\gamma_3\pi')$;

$$DY = (1 + \alpha_3\pi\beta_1)\ \ (\alpha_1\ DM + \alpha_2\ DG) - \alpha_3\pi\beta_1\ Q$$
$$+ \alpha_3\pi\beta_2\gamma_3\ \{\pi\pi'\beta_1\ \ (\alpha_1 a_1\ DM1 + \alpha_2 b_1\ DG2 + \alpha_2 b_2\ DG3 - Q\}$$
$$+ \rho_1\ DC1 + \rho_2\ Y1 - \rho_3\ N1 + \rho_4\ W1 + \rho_5\ P1 + \rho_6\ T + v_2 \tag{3.42}$$

where $\rho_1 = \kappa\pi'\theta_1 + \alpha_3\theta_1 + \alpha_4$, $\rho_2 = \theta_2(\kappa\pi' + \alpha_3)$, $\rho_3 = \theta_3(\kappa\pi' + \alpha_3)$, $\rho_4 = \theta_4(\kappa\pi' + \alpha_3)$, $\rho_5 = \theta_5(\kappa\pi' + \alpha_3)$, $\rho_6 = \theta_6(\kappa\pi' + \alpha_3)$, $\kappa = \alpha_3\pi\beta_2\gamma_3$; and

$$DP = \pi\beta_1(\alpha_1 DM + \alpha_2 DG - Q) + \pi\beta_2\gamma_3\{\pi\pi'\beta_1(\alpha_1 a_1 DM1 + \alpha_2 b_1 DG2$$
$$+ \alpha_2 b_2 DG3 - Q) + \lambda_1 DC1 + \lambda_2 Y1 - \lambda_3 N1 + \lambda_4 W1 + \lambda_5 P1 + \lambda_6 T + v_3\ . \tag{3.43}$$

where $\lambda_1 = \theta_1(h\pi' + 1)$, $\lambda_2 = \theta_2(h\pi' + 1)$, $\lambda_3 = \theta_3(h\pi' + 1)$, $\lambda_4 = \theta_4(h\pi' + 1)$, $\lambda_5 = \theta_5(h\pi' + 1)$, $\lambda_6 = \theta_6(h\pi' + 1)$, $h = \pi\beta_2\gamma_3$.

Let us rewrite the "extended" reduced-form equations as follows:

$$y = \Pi x + V \tag{3.44}$$

where y = (DW, DY, DP)', Π = a parameter matrix for the "extended" reduced-form equations with π_{ij} in the i-th row and j-th column when the three equations are stacked together, x = (DM, DG, Q, DM1, DG2, DG3, DC1, Y1, N1, W1, P1, T)'. Then, the following emerge. First, the coefficients on the lagged autoregressive terms DG2 and DG3 in all the three equations are constrained as

$$(\Pi_{15}/b_1) = (\Pi_{16}/b_2); \quad (\Pi_{25}/b_1) = (\Pi_{26}/b_2); \quad (\Pi_{35}/b_1) = (\Pi_{36}/b_2). \tag{3.45}$$

These are our "type 1" restriction, which depends on the number of lags in the autoregressive processes introduced. Observe that "type 1" restriction involves only DG2 and DG3 terms. If we introduce more than one lagged terms on the DM process, it is not difficult to see similar restriction would emerge along the lagged DM coefficients.

Across the equations, if we divide (3.41) by (3.42), the coefficients on the lagged autoregressive terms are constrained as

$$(\Pi_{14}/\Pi_{24}) = (\Pi_{15}/\Pi_{25}) = (\Pi_{16}/\Pi_{26})$$

and between (3.42) and (3.43):

$$(\Pi_{24}/\Pi_{34}) = (\Pi_{25}/\Pi_{35}) = (\Pi_{26}/\Pi_{36}) \quad .$$

We can identify above as the "type 2" restrictions, which are due to the overidentification of the structural model. The above restrictions can be consolidated further as:

$$\Pi_{24} = (\Pi_{14}/\Pi_{15})\Pi_{25}; \qquad \Pi_{25} = (\Pi_{15}/\Pi_{16})\Pi_{26}$$

$$\Pi_{34} = (\Pi_{24}/\Pi_{25})\Pi_{35}; \qquad \Pi_{35} = (\Pi_{25}/\Pi_{26})\Pi_{36} \quad .$$

By substituting the expressions for Π_{25} and Π_{35}, we get

$$\Pi_{24} = (\Pi_{14}/\Pi_{16})\Pi_{26}; \qquad \Pi_{34} = (\Pi_{24}/\Pi_{26})\Pi_{36} \tag{3.46}$$

Meanwhile, the coefficients on the DM and DG terms in (3.42) and (3.43) are constrained as

$$(\Pi_{21}/\Pi_{31}) = (\Pi_{22}/\Pi_{32}) \tag{3.47}$$

Together with (3.47) above, therefore, we have only three "type 2" restrictions. Without consolidation among the restrictions, convergence is not achieved in the ML estimation procedure.

Testing procedure would be to estimate the "extended" reduced-form model (3.41)-(3.43) with and without restrictions (3.45)-(3.46) being imposed and compare the resulting values of the log likelihood functions. If the restrictions are valid, the value of the log likelihood function from the restricted version of the model should be close to that from the unrestricted one. Minus twice the difference between the two, the latter subtracted from the former, will then be distributed as X^2 statistic.

If the value of the X^2 statistic is too big, we must reject the null hypothesis that the restrictions are valid. The REH can be accepted as a maintained hypothesis if this X^2 statistic is significantly small.

To test the "type 1" restrictions (3.45) empirically, we need to have estimates on b_1 and b_2. Empirically, the following autoregressive processes emerge, from which the coefficient values $\hat{b}_1 = .1302$ and $\hat{b}_2 = .2312$ are taken:

OLS Estimates of Autoregressive Processes:
1952/1-1970/4, U.S. Quarterly

$$\underset{}{DM} = \underset{(.003)}{-.0126} + \underset{(.103)}{.4769}\,DM1 \qquad R^2 = .834 \qquad DW = 1.97$$

$$DG = \underset{(.009)}{-.0792} + \underset{(.114)}{.1302}\,DG2 + \underset{(.115)}{.2312}\,DG3$$

$$R^2 = .781 \qquad DW = 2.19$$

Standard errors are included in the parentheses. Though seasonal dummy variables were added to the regressions, we do not report their coefficients as they are irrelevant.

The above processes are chosen because they render coefficient estimates significantly different from zero. Since some of the coefficients generated by the autoregressive processes enter the testable restrictions as denominators, it is important not to have their values equal to zero: otherwise, the restriction would amount to making the respective reduced-form coefficients as infinite, "blowing up" the equations.

As was noted earlier, the number and the type of the testable restrictions critically depend on the nature of the autoregressive processes introduced. Naturally, we tried different sets of lag structures. When we introduced more than one lagged terms on the money supply process, we got the following results:

<u>Alternative Money Supply Process</u>

$$DM = \underset{(.003)}{-.012} + \underset{(.119)}{.453}\,DM1 + \underset{(.118)}{.047}\,DM2 \qquad R^2 = .835 \qquad DW = 1.91$$

$$DM = \underset{(.002)}{-.002} + \underset{(.129)}{.321}\,DM2 - \underset{(.129)}{.108}\,DM3 \qquad R^2 = .803 \qquad DW = 1.12$$

The coefficients on the DM2 and DM3 terms are not significantly different from zero. Besides, with more regressors added, the $\bar{R}^2$ does not improve substantially, or even deteriorates. Similarly, we tried different lag structures on DG and got the following results:

<u>Alternative Autoregressive Processes on DG</u>

$$DG = \underset{(.009)}{-.077} - \underset{(.117)}{.083}\,DG1 + \underset{(.114)}{.129}\,DG2 + \underset{(.099)}{.244}\,DG3 \qquad R^2 = .782 \qquad DW = 2.03$$

$$DG = \underset{(.011)}{-.072} + \underset{(.099)}{.221}\,DG3 + \underset{(.092)}{.059}\,DG4 \qquad R^2 = .778 \qquad DW = 2.21$$

Some of the coefficient estimates turned out to be not significantly different from zero, and the improvement in the $\bar{R}^2$ is negligible, if not negative.

Then, the "type 1" restrictions (3.45) are imposed by contraining the parameter values on the DG2 and DG3 terms in (3.41) - (3.43)

$$\pi_{15} = \pi_{16}(\hat{b}_1/\hat{b}_2); \; \pi_{25} = \pi_{26}(\hat{b}_1/\hat{b}_2); \; \pi_{35} = \pi_{36}(\hat{b}_1/\hat{b}_2) \tag{3.48}$$

where $\hat{b}_1$ and $\hat{b}_2$ are the coefficient estimates retrieved from the OLS regression on the autoregressive process on DG: namely, $\hat{b}_1$ = .1302, $\hat{b}_2$ = .2312.

As for the "type 2" restrictions they are imposed by constraining the reduced-form parameters are given in (3.45) - (3.47)

The above restrictions are non-linear, and the constrained model is estimated through a non-linear least square procedure provided by the Time Series Processor (TSP). Together with the unconstrained estimate on the "extended" reduced-form model (3.41)-(3.43), we report the contrained estimates with the two types of restrictions imposed separately in table 3.12. Furthermore, we impose the "type 1 and 2" restrictions simultaneously, and report the results in the last column.

With the "type 1" restrictions imposed, the coefficient estimates do not change substantially from the unrestricted version. A glance at table 3.12 would confirm this. If the restrictions are valid, the two should generate similar estimates. Though the two values of the log likelihood functions are also very close to each other, hence leading to the acceptance of the restriction and the REH, we put them for a formal test. The test statistic is -2x (956.321 - 956-652) = .662. Since there are three restrictions, the degrees of freedom associated with the X^2 statistic is three. At this degree of freedom, the 95 percent significance level to reject the null hypothesis is 7.815. Since our statistic .662 falls far below the significance level, we accept the restrictions due to data-based distributed lag models for the exogenous variables at the 10% level of confidence.

Similarly, we put "type 2" restrictions for a formal test. The X^2 statistic computed from the two log likelihood function values is 1.630. With 3 degrees of freedom, a X^2 statistic has a .05 probability of being larger than 7.815 by a pure change. We thus cannot reject the validity of the overidentifying restrictions at 99% confidence level, nor can we do so at 90 percent confidence level.

When the two types of restrictions are jointly imposed, the resulting X^2 statistic is 1.928, which does not lead us to reject the null hypothesis even at 90 percent confidence level: the associated X^2 value leading to the rejection is 10.645 at 6 degrees of freedom. Thus, all the restrictions that REH implies in terms of the evolution of exogenous variables and the structural details seem to be quite consistent with the available data.

3.9 Conclusions

Depending on the proxy measure one uses for the unobservable price expectations variable, the nature of the implied unanticipated inflation can be drastically different. In particular, the rational expectations hypothesis, as opposed to the conventional adaptive expectations formulation, rules out the existence of a persistent unanticipated inflation characterizing the economy. The main purpose of this chapter was to study certain derivable implications of different proxies for anticipated inflation in the context of two standard macro models of the U.S. economy, and to test the Rational expectations hypothesis. These tests would then throw light on the important question of the existence of short-run Phillips curves for pursuing stabilization policies. The empirical findings can be summarized as follows:

(1) In all the models that we estimated with REH, the natural rate hypothesis passed the statistical tests at a very high level of significance. The result was the same when we used the survey data, which is known to contain a substantial amount of persistent unanticipated inflation. In the context of McCallum's model with REH, complete structural details need to be utilized in estimation to accept NRH.

(2) The remarkable different between the models with survey data and models with REH was that the unemployment variable became statistically insignificant in all the wage-price models with REH. This was true even when we used disguised unemployment rate in addition to U_t^{-1} and treated U_t^{-1} as an endogenous variable. However, we found a significant relationship between the unemployment rate and the implied unanticipated rates of inflation. We also conducted some additional tests which indicated the innovations in the rates of unemployment are quite independent of innovations in monetary and fiscal policies. These results clearly support a rather naive version of the REH, where there is no way that the government can expect to conduct short-run stabilization policies in a meaningful manner. In the context of McCallum's model, however, short-run Phillips curve could still be identified even though it became steeper.

(3) To study the extent to which the statistical insignificance of the unemployment variable in the wage equation can be attributed to the instrumental variable estimation technique employed, we estimated all the models by explicitly trading-off the over-identifying restrictions with the under-identifiability introduced by the basic unobservable nature of the price expectations variable. At this stage, however, to avoid an obvious indeterminancy, we normalized the coefficient of price expectations in the wage equation to be unity and tested whether the REH is an adequate representation of the reality. On the average, our tests support the basic implication of the REH. In only one option with partly rational expectations, where the implied $\bar{R}^2$ in the auxiliary regression was as low as 0.35, did U_t^{-1} show up with a significant sign.

(4) To examine certain empirical implications of the assumption that unobservable expectations are formed rationally in Muth's sense, we have presented fully efficient estimates of the structural parameters of McCallum's macroeconomic model. As Wallis [1980] has recently point out, the full force of the econometric implications of REH has yet to be appreciated in applied econometric work. Since the wage equation is embedded in the system of structural equations, the limited-information instrumental variable estimator is inefficient. We have demonstrated that, once all the overidentifying restrictions together with the special factor-analytic structure of the disturbance-covariance matrix that REH implies is utilized in estimation, the Natural Rate Hypothesis is

accepted at a very high level of statistical confidence. These, however, are not all the restrictions implied by REH. Muthian rationality assumes that expectations depend specifically on the structure of the relevant system describing the economy and hence, it should depend on the expectations of future values of exogenous and policy variables. Thus, the data-based distributed lag structures of the exogenous processes in conjunction with the economic structure yield certain non-linear constraints across reduced form equations. In the context of both McCallum's model and Gordon's wage-price model, we find that these restrictions are quite consistent with the available data. These results can also be interpreted as direct evidence on the validity of rational expectations hypothesis.

Table 3.1 Maximum Likelihood Estimation of Wage-Price Models With Survey Data on Price Expectations* (1954:1 - 1973:1)

	Option I		Option II		Option III	
	OLS	MLE	OLS**	MLE	OLS**	MLE
P^e	.894 (11.175)	.810 (6.75)		.854 (10.948)		.982 (10.791)
U^{-1}	6.45 (2.780)	7.57 (3.22)		7.169 (3.288)		6.38 (2.995)
GD	-1.398 (6.269)	-1.31 (5.954)		-1.43 (6.777)		-1.27 (6.165)
SG	.393 (3.672)	.335 (3.284)		.368 (3.680)		.325 (3.421)
CONST	-.288 (-.620)	--		--		--
$\bar{R}^2$	.876	--		--		--
W	.803 (5.317)	.938 (6.131)	.573 (3.769)	.643 (4.202)	.379 (2.216)	.585 (3.078)
PR	-.190 (1.759)	-.140 (1.400)	-.191 (2.098)	-.173 (2.011)	-.101 (1.097)	-.100 (1.190)
UFK	--	--	--	--	.020 (1.428)	.010 (.666)
CMW	.323 (1.462)	.168 (.875)	.228 (1.145)	.178 (.994)	--	--
MG	.109 (1.253)	.063 (.732)	--	--	--	--
t	--	--	.067 (3.350)	.060 (3.000)	--	--
P_{t-1}	--	--	--	--	.610 (3.526)	.452 (2.469)
CONST	.159 (.406)	--	-.233 (.634)	--	.132 (.376)	--
$\bar{R}^2$	.595	--	.678	--	.675	--

* Absolute t-ratios are in brackets

** OLS estimates of wage equations are the same in all the options.

Table 3.2 Test of Existence of Observational Error in Survey Data*
(1954:1 - 1973:1)

$\hat{\bar{p}}^e$ is obtained by regressing $\bar{p}^e$ on	Regressors						
	CONST	U^{-1}	GD	SG	$\bar{p}^e$	$\hat{\bar{p}}^e$	$\bar{R}^2$
U^{-1}, GD, SG,	-.31	6.85	-1.42	.40	.93	-.07	.890
PR, CMW, MG	(.47)	(2.53)	(.23)	(.11)	(.11)	(.15)	
U^{-1}, GD, SG,	-.30	6.79	-1.41	.40	1.43	-.57**	.899
PR, CMW, t	(.48)	(2.25)	(.22)	(.10)	(.31)	(.32)	
U^{-1}, GD, SG,	-.25	5.63	-1.36	.38	.71	.26	.897
PR, UFK, P_{t-1}	(.45)	(2.32)	(.22)	(.10)	(.14)	(.17)	
U^{-1}, GD, SG,	-.29	6.44	-1.40	.39	.89	.004	.889
MG_{t-1}, MG_{t-2}, MG_{t-3}, MG_{t-4}	(.47)	(2.39)	(.22)	(.11)	(.15)	(.17)	
U^{-1}, GD, SG, P_{t-1}	-.26	5.90	-1.37	.38	.68	.26	.895
P_{t-2}, P_{t-3}, P_{t-4}	(.46)	(2.32)	(.22)	(.11)	(.17)	(.19)	

* Standard errors are in brackets.
**Significant at 5% level of significance.

Table 3.3 Instrumental Variable Estimation of Wage Equation*
(1954:1 - 1973:1)

	I.V. Estimates***			Partly Rational Expectation	
	Option 1	Option II	Option III	$P_{t-1}\ldots P_{t-6}$	$P_{t-1}\ldots P_{t-6}$ $MG_{t-1}\ldots MG_{t-6}$
P^{e}**	.965	.932	.979	1.04	.894
	(.173)	(.147)	(.128)	(.178)	(.139)
U^{-1}	-1.30	-.729	-1.54	-2.55	-.082
	(4.64)	(4.28)	(4.52)	(4.90)	(4.32)
GD	-.795	-.830	-.780	-.717	-.869
	(.409)	(.392)	(.406)	(.429)	(.381)
SG	.087	.104	.080	.050	.123
	(.196)	(.189)	(.195)	(.208)	(.183)
CONST	.089	.062	.100	.148	.032
$\bar{R}^2$	.656	.671	.649	.617	.686

* Standard errors are in brackets

** One period ahead percentage change in implicit deflators on personal consumption expenditures was used as a proxy for price expectations.

*** Option I, II and III are the same as in Table 3.1 all exogenous variables lagged two periods have been used to form the instruments.

Table 3.4 Estimation od Short-run Phillips Curve Under Rational Expectations Hypothesis*

	Option II	Option III	Partly Rational 6 Lags of Prices	Partly Rational 6 Lags of Prices and 6 Lags of Money Supply
U_t^N	4.98 (.149)	4.98 (.148)	4.98 (.125)	4.98 (.154)
$P_t-E_{t-1}P_t$	-.395 (.163)	-.417 (.161)	-.511 (.104)	-.307 (.171)

* Standard errors are in brackets.

Table 3.5 Tests of Rational Expectations Hypothesis*

Option I

$$1)\quad \hat{W}_t = p^e + \underset{(0.744)}{2.893}\, U_t^{-1} - \underset{(3.061)}{1.050}\, GD_t + \underset{(1.272)}{.210}\, SG_t \qquad \hat{Cov}(u) = \begin{bmatrix} \underset{(.167)}{.541} & \\ \underset{(.107)}{-.008} & \underset{(.106)}{.460} \end{bmatrix}$$

$$2)\quad \hat{P}_t = \underset{(6.912)}{.712}\, W_t - \underset{(2.285)}{.144}\, PR_t + \underset{(2.048)}{.252}\, CMW_t + \underset{(1.037)}{.055}MG_t$$

$$3)\quad \hat{P}_{t+1} = \underset{(.271)}{1.391}\, p^e \qquad \hat{\sigma}_{vv} = \underset{(.217)}{.166}$$

Option II

$$1)\quad \hat{W}_t = p^e - \underset{(4.076)}{.630}\, U_t^{-1} - \underset{(.369)}{.827}\, GD_t + \underset{(.177)}{.100}\, SG_t \qquad \hat{Cov}(u) = \begin{bmatrix} \underset{(.103)}{.311} & \\ \underset{(.075)}{-.070} & \underset{(.091)}{.390} \end{bmatrix}$$

$$2)\quad \hat{P}_t = \underset{(.103)}{.633}\, W_t - \underset{(.053)}{.143}\, PR_t + \underset{(.116)}{.203}\, CMW_t + \underset{(.013)}{.031}\, t$$

$$3)\quad \hat{P}_{t+1} = \underset{(.156)}{1.073}\, p^e \qquad \hat{\sigma}_{vv} = \underset{(.147)}{.524}$$

Option III

$$1)\quad \hat{W}_t = p^e - \underset{(4.365)}{1.536}\, U_t^{-1} - \underset{(.386)}{.707}\, GD_t + \underset{(.186)}{.080}\, SG_t \qquad \hat{Cov}(u) = \begin{bmatrix} \underset{(.118)}{.234} & \\ \underset{(.097)}{-.67} & \underset{(.113)}{.488} \end{bmatrix}$$

$$2)\quad \hat{P}_t = \underset{(.137)}{.625}\, W_t - \underset{(.061)}{.101}\, PR_t + \underset{(.009)}{.010}\, UFK_t + \underset{(.163)}{.195}P_{t-1}$$

$$3)\quad \hat{P}_{t+1} = \underset{(.159)}{1.005}\, p^e \qquad \hat{\sigma}_{vv} = \underset{(.170)}{.580}$$

---

* Standard errors are in brackets.

Table 3.6 Tests of Rational Expectation Hypothesis with Specific Information-Availability Assumptions*

With Six Lagged Inflation Rates

$$W = \underset{(2.48)}{8.853}\, U_t^{-1} - \underset{(.256)}{.713}\, GD_t + \underset{(.114)}{.349}\, SG_t + p^e + \hat{u}_1 \qquad \hat{\sigma}_{11} = \underset{(.137)}{.006}$$

$$p^e = \underset{(.138)}{.455}\, P_{t-1} + \underset{(.153)}{.139}\, P_{t-2} + \underset{(.153)}{.090}\, P_{t-3} + \underset{(.151)}{.119}\, P_{t-4} + \underset{(.146)}{.220}\, P_{t-5} - \underset{(.081)}{.042}\, P_{t-6} + \hat{u}_2$$

$$\hat{\sigma}_{22} = \underset{(.169)}{.427}$$

$$P_{t+1} = \underset{(.160)}{.960}\, p^e + \hat{u}_3 \qquad \hat{\sigma}_{33} = \underset{(.285)}{1.111}$$

With Six Lagged Inflation and Money Growth Rates

$$W = \underset{(2.75)}{3.398}\, U_t^{-1} - \underset{(.259)}{1.212}\, GD_t + \underset{(.130)}{.294}\, SG_t + p^e + \hat{u}_1 \qquad \hat{\sigma}_{11} = \underset{(.09)}{.190}$$

$$p^e = \underset{(.135)}{.342}\, P_{t-1} + \underset{(.149)}{.083}\, P_{t-2} - \underset{(.150)}{.130}\, P_{t-3} + \underset{(.146)}{.070}\, P_{t-4} + \underset{(.147)}{.136}\, P_{t-5}$$

$$- \underset{(.081)}{.183}\, P_{t-6} + \underset{(.050)}{.170}\, MG_{t-1} + \underset{(.061)}{.004}\, MG_{t-2} + \underset{(.060)}{.093}\, MG_{t-3} + \underset{(.53)}{.123}\, MG_{t-4}$$

$$+ \underset{(.050)}{.007}\, MG_{t-5} + \underset{(.49)}{.029}\, MG_{t-6} + \hat{u}_2 \qquad \hat{\sigma}_{22} = \underset{(.088)}{.147}$$

$$P_{t+1} = \underset{(.145)}{1.109}\, p^e + \hat{u}_3 \qquad \hat{\sigma}_{33} = \underset{(.226)}{.757}$$

* Standard errors are in brackets.

Table 3.7 A Joint Test on the Survey Data and Rational Expectations Hypothesis*

$$\hat{W}_t = p_t^e + \underset{(2.389)}{4.200}\, U_t^{-1} - \underset{(.220)}{1.298}\, GD_t + \underset{(.106)}{.322}\, SG_t \qquad \hat{\sigma}_{11} = \underset{(.088)}{.212}$$

$$\hat{P}_{t+1} = \underset{(.195)}{1.478}\, p^e \qquad \hat{\sigma}_{vv} = \underset{(.327)}{1.247}$$

$$\hat{\bar{p}}^e = \underset{(.105)}{1.003}\, p^e \qquad \hat{\sigma}_{\omega\omega} = \underset{(.077)}{.111}$$

* Standard errors are in the brackets.

Table 3.8 ML Estimation of Reduced Form Parameters With and Without Restrictions Implied by the REH*

	Wage Equation			Price Equation		
Variables	Unconstrained	Type 1 Restrictions	Type 1 & 2 Restrictions	Unconstrained	Type 1 Restrictions	Type 1 & 2 Restrictions
U_{-1}	- 5.86 (11.95)	- 6.38**	- 2.16**	34.00 (17.37)	33.59 (15.43)	15.22 (8.54)
U_{-2}	10.02 (11.34)	4.98 (6.77)	1.34 (3.42)	- 22.19 (16.48)	- 26.25 (14.22)	- 9.41 (10.79)
U_{-3}	- 9.77 (9.15)	- 4.45**	- 1.79**	19.12 (13.31)	23.41 (11.64)	12.58 (10.39)
U_{-4}	6.44 (4.91)	3.05**	1.54**	- 13.35 (7.14)	- 16.08 (6.54)	- 10.86 (6.34)
U	14.34 (6.42)	16.07 (5.03)	13.79 (4.08)	- 5.47 (9.34)	- 4.08 (8.47)	8.15 (3.41)
GD	- 1.72 (.34)	- 1.82 (.31)	- 1.91 (.31)	- 1.64 (.49)	- 1.72 (.46)	- 1.132**
SG	- .915 (.27)	- .885 (.27)	- .842**	- .114 (.40)	- .09 (.39)	- .498 (.22)
PR	.053 (.08)	.029 (.07)	.038 (.07)	.008 (.13)	- .012 (.12)	.010 (.04)
CMW	- .243 (.15)	- .261 (.14)	- .243 (.14)	.100 (.21)	.086 (.21)	- .063**
T	.085 (.01)	.084 (.01)	.085 (.01)	.113 (.02)	.112 (.02)	.020**
R^2	.862	.854	.852	.783	.779	.746
DW	2.12	2.09	2.10	1.95	1.89	1.88

*Standard errors are in the brackets. All variables are measured from their arithmetic means. The data are for the U.S. economy, covering the period 1954:1 - 1973:1 on half yearly basis. The maximized values of the log-likelihood functions for the two-equation model with no constraints, with type 1 restrictions and with type 1 & 2 restrictions were -82.357, -83.439, and -87.468 respectively.

**The coefficient estimates of the constrained parameters are computed by using the respective individual parameter values TSP provides under the constrained estimation.

Table 3.9* Explanatory Variables in First-Stage Regressions Used to Create Instruments For $\Delta \log P_{t+1}$

	I	II	III	Option IV	V[a]	VI	VIII
Constant[b]	X	X	X			X	X
$\log(y/n)_{t-1}$	X	X	X	X		X	X
$\log(y/n)_{t-2}$		X		X			
$\log w_{t-1}$	X	X	X	X		X	X
$\log w_{t-2}$				X			
$\Delta \log M_1$	X	X	X	X			
$\Delta \log M_{t-1}$				X		X	X
$\Delta \log G_t$	X	X	X	X			
$\Delta \log G_{t-1}$		X		X		X	X
$\Delta \log c_{t-1}$	X	X	X	X		X	X
$\Delta \log c_{t-2}$				X			
$\log q_1$	X	X	X	X			
$\log q_{t-1}$				X		X	X
t	X	X	X	X		X	X
$\log P_{t-1}$	X	X	X	X		X	X
$\log P_{t-2}$				X			
$\log y_{t-1}$	X	X	X	X		X	X
$\log y_{t-2}$				X			
$\Delta \log P_{t-1}$			X				X
$\Delta \log P_{t-2}$			X				X

[a] Ordinary least squares estimates computed.

[b] Seasonal dummies are also included in each option.

[c] Enters via the identity $\Delta \log y_t = \Delta \log y_{t-1}$.

* Taken from McCallum [1976, TABLE I, p. 48].

Table 3.10 Two-Stage Least Square Estimates of Wage Equation; U.S. Quarterly Data, 1952–70[a]

Explanatory Variables	Fully Rational Options[b]							Partly Rational Options[d]			
	I	II	III	IV	V[c]	VI	VII	1	2	3	4
$\log(y/n)_{-1}$	.0221 (.010)	.0221 (.010)	.0226 (.010)	.0293 (.010)	.0406 (.010)	.0175 (.010)	.0190 (.010)	.0139 (.006)	.0129 (.006)	.0131 (.006)	.0129 (.006)
$\log W_{-1}$	-.0350 (.011)	-.0351 (.011)	-.0355 (.012)	-.0369 (.012)	-.0510 (.012)	-.0312 (.012)	-.0325 (.012)	-.0275 (.008)	-.0275 (.008)	-.0275 (.008)	-.0275 (.007)
$\Delta\log P^*_{+1}$	.7616 (.125)	.7628 (.124)	.7535 (.126)	.7163 (.130)	.3862 (.160)	.8615 (.136)	.8346 (.138)	.8982 (.150)	.9528 (.138)	.9416 (.122)	.9524 (.120)
R^2	.6167	.6187	.6116	.5907	.5171	.6276	.6144	.4921	.5649	.5827	.5932
SE	.0023	.0023	.0023	.0024	.0026	.0023	.0026	.0024	.0024	.0024	.0023
DW	1.86	1.81	1.85	1.83	1.72	1.70	1.73	1.77	1.77	1.90	1.95

[a]Standard errors are in parentheses.

[b]Constant terms and seasonal dummies are included, though their coefficients are not reported here. 'Option' refers to various specifications of first-stage regressions of table 1.

[c]Option V corresponds to ordinary least squares estimate of the wage equation.

[d]Seasonal dummies are not added to the wage equation in order to conform to McCallum's orginal specification. Exogenous variables of the wage equation disappear in the first-stage regression. Seasonal dummies are also added. These options, in addition, include upto four lagged $\Delta\log P_{t-i}$ terms.

Table 3.11 3SLS Estimates for McCallum's Entire Model[1]

Wage Equation	Options I	II	III	IV
$\log(y/n)_{t-1}$	.0283	.0288	.0300	.0323
	(.010)	(.010)	(.010)	(.010)
$\log w_{t-1}$	-.0417	-0.422	-.0432	-0.450
	(.012)	(.012)	(.012)	(.012)
$\Delta \log P^*_{t+1}$	.7167	.7127	.6809	.6320
	(.132)	(.129)	(.130)	(.129)
R^2	.575	.584	.573	.561
DW	1.91	1.85	1.88	1.81
Output Equation[2]				
$\Delta \log M_t$	.1470	.1437	.1449	.1436
	(.197)	(.197)	(.198)	(.198)
$\Delta \log G_t$	.1860	.1863	.1845	.1826
	(.062)	(.062)	(.062)	(.063)
$\Delta \log P_t$	-.3330	-.3330	-.3294	-.3262
	(.093)	(.100)	(.095)	(.095)
$\Delta \log c_{t-1}$	.2048	.2074	.2078	.2104
	(.116)	(.116)	(.117)	(.117)
R^2	.953	.953	.953	.953
DW	1.76	1.76	1.76	1.76
Price Equation				
$\log(y/q)_t$	.0526	.0525	.0523	.0519
	(.010)	(.010)	(.010)	(.010)
$\log W_t$	.2200	.2170	.2148	.2090
	(.042)	(.042)	(.042)	(0.42)
t	-.0013	-.0013	-.0013	-.0013
	(.0002)	(.0002)	(.0002)	(.0002)
$\log P_{t-1}$	-.1363	-.1324	-.1309	-.1253
	(.041)	(.041)	(.041)	(.041)
R^2	.598	.599	.599	.600
DW	1.39	1.40	1.39	1.40

[1]See table 2 for details. Standard errors are in parentheses.

Table 3.12 Coefficient Estimates With and Without Restrictions Imposed by REH

Equation & Variables	Unrestricted	Type 1	Type 2	Type 1 & 2
Equation (13)				
DM1	-.062	-.059	-.019	-.022
	(.044)	(.045)	(.022)	(.023)
DG2	.012	.006	.011	.007
	(.011)			
DG3	.008	.010	.011	.012
	(.010)	(.010)	(.010)	(.009)
Q	.374	.368	.374	.370
	(.059)	(.058)	(.059)	(.058)
DC1	.003	.003	.001	.001
	(.019)	(.019)	(.019)	(.019)
YN1	.024	.025	.021	.022
	(.010)	(.010)	(.010)	(.010)
WP1	-.132	-.138	-.117	-.123
	(.046)	(.045)	(.044)	(.042)
T	-.003	-.003	-.003	-.003
	(.0006)	(.0006)	(.0006)	(.0006)
R^2	.670	.668	.664	.663
DW	1.653	1.640	1.717	1.706
Equation (14)				
DM	.888	.889	.880	.876
	(.257)	(.255)		
DG	.217	.217	.215	.215
	(.057)	(.057)	(.056)	(.056)
Q	-.698	-.717	-.698	-.710
	(.331)	(.325)	(.328)	(.322)
DM1	.137	.147	.271	.271
	(.253)	(.250)		
DG2	-.070	-.089	-.072	-.804
	(.058)		(.058)	
DG3	-.164	-.157	-.154	-.149
	(.056)	(.053)	(.055)	(.052)
DC1	.079	.078	.076	.076
	(.109)	(.108)	(.108)	(.107)
YN1	-.044	-.042	-.052	-.050
	(.057)	(.057)	(.056)	(.055)
WP1	-.169	-.188	-.124	-1.38
	(.257)	(.250)	(.252)	(.243)
T	.007	.007	.007	.007
	(.003)	(.003)	(.003)	(.003)
R^2	.969	.969	.969	.969
DW	2.012	2.020	2.044	2.049

Table 3.12 Continued

Equation & Variables	Unrestricted	Type 1	Type 2	Type 1 & 2
Equation (15)				
DM	.005 (.055)	.005 (.054)	-.008 (.036)	-.008 (.035)
DG	-.005 (.012)	-.005 (.012)	-.002 (.009)	-.002 (.009)
Q	.350 (.075)	.349 (.073)	.355 (.073)	.355 (.071)
DM1	-.049 (.057)	-.048 (.056)	-.026	-.028
DG2	.055 (.013)	.004	.005 (.013)	.004
DG3	.007 (.013)	.007 (.012)	.008 (.012)	.008 (.012)
DC1	-.027 (.025)	-.027 (.024)	-.025 (.023)	-.025 (.023)
YN1	0.25 (.013)	.025 (.013)	.023 (.013)	.023 (.013)
WP1	.030 (.058)	.029 (.057)	.037 (.057)	.035 (.056)
T	-.003 (.0007)	-.003 (.0007)	-.003 (.0007)	-.003 (.0007)
R^2	.603	.603	.602	.602
DW	1.294	1.290	1.344	1.341
Log-Likelihood	956.652	956.321	955.837	955.688

Note: Standard errors are in the parentheses. A constant term and three seasonal dummies are added, though their results are not reported here.

PART II

INFLATIONARY EXPECTATIONS IN FINANCIAL MARKETS

CHAPTER 4

INFLATIONARY EXPECTATIONS: THEIR FORMATION AND INTEREST RATE EFFECTS

In estimating the effects of inflationary expectations on nominal interest rates, distributed lags on past prices have traditionally been used as observable proxies for the supposedly unobservable price change expectations. Thus, Irving Fisher's famous explanation of the Gibson paradox is expressed in terms of two hypothesized relationships:

$$R_t = i_t + p_t^e \tag{4.1}$$

$$p_t^e = \sum_i w_i p_{t-i} \tag{4.2}$$

The first equation states that the nominal interest rate (R_t) for a particular asset with returns fixed in money terms is equal to the real rate of interest (i_t) plus the anticipated rate of inflation (p_t^e). He further assumed that ($i_t = \rho + u_t$ where ρ is the long-run real equilibrium rate of interest and where u_t is a random error term. Since equation (4.2) was used as a proxy for p_t^e in equation (4.1) the reduced form becomes

$$R_t = \rho + \sum_i w_i p_{t-i} + u_t \tag{4.3}$$

and the whole problem finally boils down to that of finding out a particular lag structure which best explains the interest rate variations. Gordon [1971] followed exactly the same approach to develop an independent measure of price expectations which was used for estimating wage-price equations.

It should be pointed out that the distributed lag coefficients of equation (4.2) can only be recovered from the reduced form estimates if the coefficient of price expectations in the interest rate equation is assumed to be unity; or some other assumption is made on w_i. As Gibson [1972] has pointed out, there are important theoretical and empirical studies which suggest that the nominal rate of interest may not fully adjust to changes in price expectations. Thus, equation (4.1) should be modified as

$$R_t = \alpha + \beta p_t^e + u_t \tag{4.4}$$

and ideally β should be subject to usual statistical tests. In the context of equation (4.3) another assumption which identifies the parameter β and which seems to be implicit in a number of studies is that w_i sums to one. This restriction means that eventually people will catch on and fully anticipate inflation. It is certainly reasonable to expect that a sustained constant inflation sooner or later would be fully anticipated; but this consideration is of very little use in producing a reasonable restriction to impose on w_i for the purpose of empirical estimation because during the periods used in estimation, inflation was never so sustained [see Sargent (1971)]. Another problem associated with the distributed lag proxy is that it is modeled in a deterministic form which may be quite restrictive in diverse periods. More properly, expectations should be modeled with an error:

$$p_t^e = \sum_i w_i p_{t-1} + \eta_t \tag{4.5}$$

Unfortunately modeling expectations stochastically results in a reduced form in which the explanatory variables are correlated with the composite error term. Hence ordinary least squares would give inconsistent estimates.

To overcome these difficulties Gibson [1972] and Pyle [1972] used Livingston's consensus forecasts on price expectations to test the Fisher effect. In some instances they found the value of β to be far below unity. Turnovsky and Wachter [1972] had noted in the context of their study of the Phillips curve that the coefficient might have been seriously underestimated due to the presence of some errors in the measurement of the variable. Gibson [1972] and Pyle [1972], too, pointed out the same.

Turnovsky [1970] used the same data to study the lag structure of past prices that best explains the data on price expectations. The purpose of the present chapter is to estimate the following structural model:

$$\bar{p}_t^e = p_t^e + u_{1t} \qquad (4.6)$$

$$R_t = \alpha + \beta p_t^e + u_{2t} \qquad (4.7)$$

$$p_t^e = \sum_{i=1}^{m} w_i P_{t-i} + u_{3t} \qquad (4.8)$$

where $\bar{p}_t^e$ = observed price expectations

p_t^e = unobservable price expectation variable

P_t = actual rate of change in prices

and u_1, u_2, u_3 are random error terms

Apart from testing Fisher's two hypotheses independently and in a unified framework, the model would take into account one of the simplest types of errors that might have blurred the observed price expectation variable. In the process we also get much more precise estimates of the lag structure than those obtained by Turnovsky [1970]. As we did in Chapter 1, we shall also incorporate a new model of formation of short-term expectations [Frenkel (1975)] into the structural model.

4.1 Interest rates and models on expectations

From Livingston's survey two series of expected prices can be obtained -- one from six months ahead (short term) and the other from twelve months ahead (long term) predictions of the price level. Since both Gibson and Pyle found the coefficients of the 6-month price expectations to be particularly low, this study has been restricted to the estimation of Fisher effect with short-term price expectations only. Data on market yields on 6-month bills were not available prior to 1959; hence yields on 3-month bills were used for the period 1952-70. The 6-month yield observations are monthly averages for June and December. All quantities are expressed as annual rates and past price changes are based on the Consumer Price Index.

Turnovsky's three expectation hypotheses were: unrestricted distributed lag, adaptive, and extrapolative. For the short-term expectations the equations are:

$$P_t^e = \sum_{i=0}^{\infty} w_i P_{t-i} \tag{4.9}$$

$$P_t^e = w_0 + w_1 P_{t-1}^e + w_2 P_t \tag{4.10}$$

$$P_t^e = w_0 + w_1 P_t + w_2 (P_t - P_{t-1}) \tag{4.11}$$

As we know, $w_1 + w_2 = 1$ and $w_0 = 0$ in equation (4.10) would give the original version of advaptive expectations. On the other hand, the original version of extrapolative hypothesis stipulated $w_0 = 0$ and $w_1 = 1$ in equation (4.11). The coefficient $w_2 < 1$ in (4.10) implies expectations to be regressive.

Frenkel's [1975] theory of the formation of expectations explains the impact of money supply on nominal interest rates in the short run as well as in the intermediate and the long run. Specfically he hypothesized that short-term expectations are influenced by two factors: (i) a regressive element, which is determined by the discrepancy between the actual rate of inflation P_t and an average long-term expected rate; and (ii) the usual adaptive element which is determined by the discrepancy between P_t and the expected short-term rate.

To test the above hypothesis we estimated equations of the following form:

$$\bar{P}_t^e = w_0 + w_1 P_{12}^e(t) + w_2 \bar{P}_{t-1}^e + w_3 \cdot P_t \tag{4.12}$$

The coefficient w_1 gives the coefficient corresponding to the regressive element and $(1 - w_2)$ would give the coefficient corresponding to the adaptive element. Thus Frenkel's hypothesis can be tested by introducing long-term expectations as an additional variable in the adaptive hypothesis given in equation (4.10).

4.2 The results

Ordinary least squares regression of r_t on $\bar{p}_t^e$ for the period 1952-70 produced the following results:

$$R_t = \underset{(.182)}{2.347} + \underset{(.063)}{0.586}\bar{p}_t^e$$

$$\text{D-W} = 1.449 \qquad \bar{R}^2 = 0.702$$

Regression results of four hypotheses to explain the formation of expectations are given in Table 4.1. The results are very similar to those obtained by Turnovsky though in this case the unrestricted distributed lag model is slightly better than the adaptive and the extrapolative models on the $\bar{R}^2$ criterion. In almost all the cases the constants were found to be insignificant and were accordingly dropped. Since the coefficient of P_t in the extrapolative case and the sum of the coefficients of P_t and P_{t-1} in the adaptive case were very close to unity, the original versions of these models were found to be successful in explaining the data. Apart from that, a negative coefficient value for $(P_t - P_{t-1})$ suggests strong regressivity. The introduction of $\bar{p}^e_{12}$ in equation (4.12) was found to be a very significant additional variable. The $\bar{R}^2$ was significantly higher and the value of D-W statistic was very close to 2. If $\bar{p}^e_{12}(t)$ can roughly be assumed to represent the (long-term) expected average rate of inflation, then the significance of the coefficient for $\bar{p}^e_{12}(t)$ implies regressivity corresponding to longer-term expectations. The coefficient of the lagged short-term expectation retained the same value as in the pure adaptive model. The low value for the coefficient of P_t is only expected since it really measures the difference between the coefficients corresponding to short-term and long-term adjustments.

The reduced form of the structural model (4.6) - (4.8) is

$$\bar{p}^e_t = \sum_{k=1}^{K} w_k P_{t-k} + u_{1t} + u_{3t} \tag{4.13}$$

$$R_t = \alpha + \beta \sum_{k=1}^{K} w_k P_{t-k} + u_{2t} + \beta u_{3t} \tag{4.14}$$

This can also be written in the following alternative structural form:

$$\bar{p}_t^e = \sum_{k=1}^{K} w_k P_{t-k} + u_{1t} + u_{3t} \tag{4.15}$$

$$R_t = \alpha + \beta \bar{p}_t^e + u_{2t} - \beta u_{1t} \tag{4.16}$$

Let $u_{1t} + u_3 = v_{1t}$ and $u_{2t} - \beta u_{1t} = v_{2t}$. Gibson and Pyle estimated the equation (4.16) by ordinary least squares (OLS) where $\bar{p}_t^e$ is really endogenous. Turnovsky estimated equations of the form (4.15). Though measurement error in the dependent variable does not lead to any bias in OLS estimates, the presence of the composite disturbance term v_{1t} may unnecessarily produce large standard errors of estimates. This would particularly be the case if P_{t-i} are correlated.

To obtain consistent estimates of α and β, the two-stage least squares (2SLS) procedure was used. The results are given in Table 4.2 where it is found that the estimated value of β has increased from .586 to as high as .906 in some cases. As expected, some loss in efficiency is noticeable since the standard errors have increased uniformly. Since a consistent estimate of the variance-covariance matrix of residuals showed rather high negative value for the covariance term, we computed the "full information" estimates. These are reported in Table 4.3.

The standard errors for all the coefficients have decreased considerably. The three-stage least squares (3SLS) estimates of β, though on the average little less than the corresponding 2SLS estimates, were appreciably higher than the OLS estimates. By comparing Tables 4.1 and 4.3, it can be seen that much more precise estimates of the lag structures in the formation of price expectations have been obtained.

It may be noted that Gordon's approach to develop an independent measure of the lag structure was to estimate equation (4.14) of the reduced form and to pick up the estimated coefficients of the lagged prices. By OLS we obtain the following estimate of equation (4.14):

$$R_t = \underset{(.202)}{1.562} + \underset{(.187)}{.467}P_t - \underset{(.198)}{.049}P_{t-1} + \underset{(.103)}{.406}P_{t-2}$$

Since the var(u_2 + bu_3) was 0.56, which is far less than var(u_1 + u_3), (which is 2.22), and since the true value of β is very close to unity, the lag structure developed in this way is much more precise than that obtained from equation (4.13). These estimates are strikingly similar to those obtained by 3SLS.

The estimates of error variances of the original structural model (4.6) - (4.8) are given in Table 4.4. Given the estimates of var(v_1), var(v_2), and cov(v_1, v_2), one can recover only three second-order moments of the structural disturbances (u_1, u_2, u_3). The three variances viz. var(u_1), var(u_2), and var(u_3) have been estimated under additional assumptions that cov(u_i, u_j) = 0 for i $\neq$ j, i, j, = 1, 2, 3. Though there is no way to test these assumptions, there is some indirect evidence which suggests that the assumptions may be roughly true. Note that the assumptions

$$\text{cov}\,(u_i, u_j) = 0 \quad i, j = 1, 2, 3, \quad i \neq j$$

would imply the following three independent restrictions;

$$\text{var}\ (v_1) = E[v_1^2(t)] = \sigma_1^2 + \sigma_3^2 \tag{4.17}$$

$$\text{var}\ (v_2) = E[v_2^2(t)] = \sigma_2^2 + \hat{\beta}^2\sigma_1^2 \tag{4.18}$$

$$\text{cov}\ (v_1,\ v_2) = E[v_1(t),\ v_2(t)] = -\ \hat{\beta}\sigma_1^2 \tag{4.19}$$

Thus, $\text{cov}(v_1, v_2)$ must have a sign opposite to that of β. Since in our case β is always positive, equation (4.19) implies that $\text{cov}(v_1, v_2)$ assumes negative values. This, then, would give a positive σ_1^2. Similarly, given that σ_2^2 and σ_3^2 are positive quantities we get two additional restrictions. In all the experiments these restrictions were always satisfied. In addition, the reduced form covariance β_1 $\text{var}(u_3)$ was always positive.

To the extent we can rely on these estimates, the calculations suggest that $\text{var}(u_1)$ is quite large, followed by the disturbance term in the expectation formation equation. In all the cases the error variance of the interest rate equation was found to be quite low.

4.3 Structural change around 1960

The structural model (4.6) - (4.8) is particularly suitable for an analysis of possible changes in one or more of the structural relations. Yohe and Karnosky [1969] when relating nominal interest rates to distributed lag of past prices found enough evidence to support a break in the sample around 1960. They attributed the break to a shift in the interest rate equation. But, as Gibson has pointed out, there is also the other possibility that the shift had occurred in the formation of price expectations equation. In fact, the latter possibility has been supported by the experiments reported by Turnovsky.

Gibson found a break in the context of the equation (4.16); Turnovsky found the same in the context of equation (4.15). But it is interesting to note that the observed break may be due to a break in relation (4.6). Also, if the reduced form relation (4.14) does not show any break in the sample, then this finding should suggest that the shifts in relation (4.15) and (4.16) are due to shift in the relation (4.6), and not due to shifts in relations (4.7) and (4.8). We tested the propositions with the help of all the four expectations-formation hypotheses (4.9) - (4.12). When "extrapolative" and "distributed-lag" hypotheses were used, the Chow tests for stability of the coefficients were resoundingly rejected against the alternative that there was a break by the end of 1959. However, with "adaptive expectations," the equality of regressions hypothesis was accepted at both the 1 and 5 percent level of significance, while with Frenkel's hypothesis it was accepted only at 1 percent level. Thus, it seems that the adaptive expectations hypothesis is quite successful in explaining the reduced form interest rate equation (4.14) for the whole period, 1952-70.

It may seem that with the help of the adaptive expectations hypothesis the observed breaks in equations (4.15) and (4.16) can be explained by a break in the equation (4.6). To test a simple proposition that there was a parallel shift in the relation (4.6) after 1960, I estimated the whole model (4.6) - (4.8) after introducing a (0-1) dummy variable in equation (4.6). The coefficients appeared with right signs and the value of β was 0.944. But the improvement in the fit on $\bar{R}^2$ criterion was only marginal; it was apparent that the introduction of the dummy variable was not adequate to explain the shift in equation (4.6).

With extrapolative and distributed-lag hypotheses, there is of course the real possibility that the break occurred in both the relations (4.7) and (4.8) around 1960. Accordingly, we estimated the model with all the four hypotheses on the formation of expectations for the periods 1952-59 and 1960-70 separately. While estimating the model for the subperiod 1960-70, I also used the 6-month Treasury Bill rates in place of 3-month rates. The results were not found to be significantly different. The estimates were very similar to those obtained by Gibson [1972] and Turnovsky [1970]; and support the hypothesis that after 1960 people have become more conscious in forming their price expectations and relating them to nominal interest rates.

4.4 Conclusions

To avoid certain problems associated with the use of a deterministic distributed lag function of past prices as an observable proxy for inflationary expectations, Gibson and Pyle used some survey data on price expectations. To substantiate the speculation that the data may contain errors, we proposed an Unobservable Variable Model which accommodates not only some errors in measurement but also the presence of stochastic error term in the distributed lag function determining the unobservable variable. Evidence was found again that the data on short-term expectations contain substantial error in measurement. This explains why both Gibson and Pyle obtained such low values for the cofficient corresponding to the price speculations variable in the Fisher equation.

Our calculations support earlier findings by Gibson and Turnovsky that both the interest rate equation and the expectations formation equation had a structural break around 1960. Yohe and Karnosky found the same in the context of their regressions of nominal interest rates on distributed lag of past prices. However, when we used the adaptive expectations hypothesis, the Chow test of equality of regressions did not support a break in the reduced form interest rate equation.

Table 4.1 Ordinary Least Squares to Explain The Formation of Expectations 1952-70

Expectations	$\bar{R}^2$	D-W
Weighted Expectations:		
$\bar{P}^e_t = \underset{(.361)}{.251}P_t + \underset{(.389)}{.102}P_{t-1} + \underset{(.195)}{.543}P_{t-2}$	.587	1.018
Adaptive Expectations:		
$\bar{P}^e_t = \underset{(.145)}{.426}P_t + \underset{(.164)}{.534}\bar{P}^e_{t-1}$	.580	1.989
Extrapolative Expectations:		
$\bar{P}^e_t = \underset{(419)}{.494} + \underset{(.148)}{1.011}P_t - \underset{(.183)}{.568}(P_t - P_{t-1})$	.555	1.354
Frankel's Hypothesis:		
$\bar{P}^e_t = \underset{(.251)}{.786}P^e_{12(t)} + \underset{(.177)}{.046}P_t + \underset{(.145)}{.535}\bar{P}^e_{t-1}$	.668	1.962

Note: Standard errors are in parentheses; $\bar{R}^2$ is adjusted R^2, and D-W is the Durbin-Watson statistic.

Table 4.2 Two-Stage Least Squares Estimates of the Interest Rate Equation

Expectations Hypotheses	Estimates	$\bar{R}^2$
Weighted:	$R_t = \underset{(.217)}{1.598} + \underset{(.075)}{.906}\ \hat{p}^e_t$	.778
Adaptive:	$R_t = \underset{(.205)}{2.044} + \underset{(.080)}{.765}\ \hat{p}^e_t$	.729
Extrapolative:	$R_t = \underset{(.238)}{1.976^a} + \underset{(.096)}{.796}\ \hat{p}^e_t$	.752
Frenkel's:	$R_t = \underset{(.262)}{2.077} + \underset{(.080)}{.723}\ \hat{p}^e_t$	.704

[a]This is an estimate of $\alpha + \beta W_0$.

Table 4.3 Three-Stage Least Squares Estimates of the Structural Parameters[a] 1952-70

Expectations Hypotheses	W_0[b]	W_1	W_2	W_3	α	β
Weighted	---	.482	-.038	.442	1.638	.892
		(.207)	(.221)	(.116)	(.149)	(.056)
Adaptive	---	.487	.469			.771
		(.112)	(.122)			(.058)
Extrapolative	-.510	1.018	-.558	---	1.984[c]	.791
	(.367)	(.119)	(.126)		(.193)	(.052)
Frenkel's	---	.510	-.558	.509		.723
		(.207)	(.126)	(.122)		(.062)

[a]Standard errors are in parentheses.

[b]The constant term W_0 was estimated only in the extrapolative case; in other cases constants were found to be insignificant and were accordingly dropped.

[c]This is an estimate of $\alpha + \beta W_0$.

Table 4.4 Estimates of the Error Variances of the Structural Model 1952-70[a]

Expectations	$V(u_1)$	$V(u_2)$	$V(u_3)$
Weighted	1.561	.032	.656
Adaptive	1.393	.166	.871
Extrapolative	1.435	.082	.897
Frenkel's	1.152	.304	.704

[a]Under additional assumption that $\text{cov}(u_i, u_j) = 0$, $i,j = 1, 2, 3$; $i \neq j$.

CHAPTER 5

RATIONAL EXPECTATIONS AND THE FISHER EFFECT

5.1 Search for a full Fisher effect

In a world with uncertainty where foresight is imperfect, the Fisher relation can be interpreted as an equality between nominal rate of interest and equilibrium expected real return plus the market's assessment of the expected rate of inflation. This relationship has been subjected to extensive econometric tests, including those by Fisher [1930] himself, utilizing distributed lag of past inflation rates as observable proxy for the price expectations variable. However, the success of these proxies, rather than the one-period-ahead rate of inflation (subsequently observed), is inconsistent with a well-functioning capital market. The efficient market literature, on the other hand, utilizes the rational expectations hypothesis which states that market's anticipations reflect all available information such that the anticipated value equals the model's expected value of the variable being predicted, cf. Muth [1961].

In a pioneering study, Fama [1975] claimed to have presented overwhelming evidence in favor of market efficiency in the context of U.S. Treasury Bill markets for widely different maturities with some reservations in respect to five- and six-month treasury bills.[19] Since Fama's tests are joint tests of the REH, a full Fisher effect, and the constancy of real rates, one can not readily identify the particular hypotheses being invalidated.

The main purpose of the present chapter is to test the rational expectations hypothesis and the Fisher effect as two disjoint propositions. A unitary price expectations coefficient in the Fisher equation should not be taken for granted because as Roll [1972] has pointed out, there is enough theoretical and empirical evidence against complete adjustment in some cases. Explicit test for market efficiency in terms of Muthian rationality has also been emphasized by Fama [1975], because market inefficiency may indicate a serious failure of a free market. An indirect proof of rationality in terms of efficient use of available information has earlier been presented by Hamburger and Platt [1975]. The idea here is that if markets are efficient, then price changes in these markets should follow approximately a random walk. If current price changes are somehow related to past prices, then all the information known at that point of time have certainly been not incorporated in forming that market price. Efficient prices are equilibrium prices conditional on all available information at the time the prices are formed

In recent years, the basic Fisherican proposition has been seriously questioned by a number of authors who argue that the Fisher equation should be viewed as a reduced form relationship derivable from a more general macroeconomic model.[20] The typical argument is that a change in the anticipated inflation affects employment and output in such a way that the assumption of independence of real interest rate is no longer tenable. The argument goes far beyond the imaginative analysis of Mundell [1963] who showed that real interest rate depends on expected inflation due to the real balance effect. Another type of complication in the context of the Fisher relation is the effect taxes on nominal interest, recently discussed by Darby [1975] and Feldstein [1976]. The temporal break in the Fisher relationship that we found in the last chapter can be justified in terms of these omitted factors.

Whether an expanded reduced-form Fisher equation or the simple Fisher hypothesis is entertained as a parsimonious descriptive device, the fundamental econometric problem of handling the price expectations variable remains. To highlight the implications of different expectational proxies on the estimated Fisher effect, we have also used the Livingston series in addition to the REH. Prompted by our findings in the previous chapters that reworking of Livingston's concensus forecasts by Carlson [1977] did improve upon the series as a measure of the underlying price expectations, we utilized Carlson-adjusted data in this chapter. The adjustments made by Carlson on Livingston's concensus forecasts can be justified only by comparing the relative performance of these two competing measures in the context of actual behavioral models. The original series, thus, can not be rejected as 'faulty' on *a priori* grounds.

The use of Livingston's adjusted data in interest rate equations of different maturities, however, typically produces the price expectations coefficient which are significantly more than one, cf. Carlson [1979]. Hendershott and van Horne [1973] have produced some evidence which shows that Livingston's data considerably underestimated the true price expectations implied by their interest rate equations. Thus, a systematic underestimation of true price expectations may very well explain the apparent overadjustment. We have tested the proposition by generalizing our econometric framework in which the survey measure and the REH were utilized as general *indicators*, rather than *proxies* for the unobservable price expectations variable.

The plan of this chapter is as follows: In Section 5.2 we report the full-information maximum likelihood (FIML) estimates of the Fisher effect by utilizing the REH and the survey measure as two different proxies. The methodology for FIML estimation in such unobservable-variable models was first analyzed by Zellner [1970] and Goldberger [1972]. The contrasting estimates of the Fisher effect depending on the nature of the proxy variable used will become apparent. In Section 5.3, we generalize our econometric framework by utilizing both the survey measure and the REH as indicators of the true price expectations. Apart from estimating the Fisher coefficient, this would then allow us to study the extent to which the two observable proxies deviate systematically from being unbiased measures of true price expectations. Finally, conclusions have been summarized in Section 5.4.

5.2 Maximum likelihood estimates

The Model:

Fisher's equation can be written as:

$$R_t = \alpha_0 + \alpha_1 p_t^e + U_t \tag{5.1}$$

where R_t = the nominal interest during period t; α_0 = the long-run equilibrium real rate; p_t^e = anticipated rate of inflation held during period t for the next period and $U_t \sim N(0, \sigma_{uu})$. From now onwards, let us define all variables as deviations from their respective means. Thus, (5.1) becomes:

$$R_t = \alpha_1 p_t^e + U_t. \tag{5.1'}$$

Since p_t^e denotes the anticipated value of the one-period-ahead actual price inflation (P_{t+1}), the rational expectations hypothesis, due to Muth [1960], specifies that:

$$p_t^e = E(P_{t+1}/I) = P_{t+1} + v_t \tag{5.2}$$

where $v_t \sim N(0, \sigma_{vv})$ and I is the available information utilized by market participants in forming expectations. The relevant information according to the partly rational expectations hypothesis (or the weak form of efficient market hypothesis) consists of present and past values of the variable being predicted. The conditional expectations in (5.2) can then be expressed as:[21]

$$E(P_{t+1}/I) = p_t^e = \beta_0 P_1 + \beta_1 P_{t-1} + \beta_2 P_{t-2} + \ldots + \eta_t . \tag{5.3}$$

Combining (5.1'), (5.2) and (5.3) we can write a three-equation structural model containing one unobservable variable:

$$\begin{aligned} R_t &= \alpha_1 p_t^e + U_t \\ P_{t+1} &= p_t^e - v_t \\ p_t^e &= \beta_0 P_t + \beta_1 P_{t-1} + \beta_2 P_{t-2} + \ldots + \eta_t . \end{aligned} \tag{5.4}$$

The structural system (5.4) can also be written as a two equation system after eliminating p_t^e:

$$\begin{aligned} R_t &= \alpha_1 P_{t+1} + \varepsilon_t \\ P_{t+1} &= \beta_0 P_t + \beta_1 P_{t-1} + \ldots + \psi_0 \psi_1 - v_t + \eta_t \quad \text{and} \end{aligned} \tag{5.5}$$

where $\varepsilon = U - \alpha_1 v$. Thus, one can use an instrument[22] for P_{t+1} generated from least squares regression of the last equation in (5.5) to obtain a consistent estimate of α_1.

As an alternative proxy for p_t^e, we also use the Livingston's measure $\bar{p}_t^e$. Under the assumption that true expectations can be expressed as a distributed lag function of past prices, $\bar{p}_t^e$ can then be used in an analogous fashion. We estimated the structural system (5.4) using the FIML algorithm developed by Goldberger [1972] and Zellner [1970].

The Estimation Technique

Consider the classical errors-in-the variables model:

$$y_1(t) = y^*(t) \cdot \nu + U_1(t) \tag{5.6}$$

$$y_2(t) = y^*(t) + U_2(t), \ t = 1, 2, \text{—}, T, \tag{5.7}$$

where we observe $y_1(t)$ and $y_2(t)$ but not the physically meaningful variable y^*. Zellner [1970] considered efficient estimation of the above model where y^* is related to a number of explanatory exogenous variables:

$$y^*(t) = x'(t) \cdot \beta , \tag{5.8}$$

where x is a k x 1 vector of observable independent variables, ν is a scalar parameter and β is a k x 1 parameter vector. Assuming that the disturbances U_1 and U_2 have zero expectations, non-zero variances and zero covariance, the contemporaneous variance-covariance matrix of the structural disturbances can be written as

$$\Sigma = E \begin{bmatrix} U_1(t) \\ U_2(t) \end{bmatrix} [U_1(t) \quad U_2(t)]$$

$$= \begin{bmatrix} \sigma_{11} & \sigma_{12} \\ \sigma_{12} & \sigma_{22} \end{bmatrix} = \begin{bmatrix} \sigma_{11} & 0 \\ 0 & \sigma_{22} \end{bmatrix} \tag{5.9}$$

The structural model (5.6), (5.7) and (5.8) has the reduced form:

$$y_1 = x'\beta\nu + \nu_1 = X\cdot\Pi_1 + \nu_1 \tag{5.10}$$

$$y_2 = x'\beta + \nu_2 = X\cdot\Pi_2 + \nu_2 \tag{5.11}$$

or, in obvious notations,

$$Y = X\cdot\Pi + V. \tag{5.12}$$

The contemporaneous variance-covariance matrix of the reduced form disturbances is denoted by:

$$\Omega = E \begin{bmatrix} \nu_1(t) \\ \nu_2(t) \end{bmatrix} [\nu_1(t) \quad \nu_2(t)]$$

$$= \begin{bmatrix} \omega_{11} & \omega_{12} \\ \omega_{12} & \omega_{22} \end{bmatrix} = \begin{bmatrix} \omega_{11} & 0 \\ 0 & \omega_{22} \end{bmatrix} \tag{5.13}$$

$$\begin{bmatrix} \sigma_{11} & 0 \\ 0 & \sigma_{22} \end{bmatrix}$$

Thus, the force of the structural specification is that (i) there are cross-equation restrictions on parameters Π, and (ii) Ω is diagonal. Zellner [1970] sketched a generalized least squares (ZEF) procedure for estimating (β,ν) under these restrictions.

Under a more realistic assumption that the multiple-cause function is stochastic, we get

$$y^*(t) = x'(t) \cdot \beta + \varepsilon \tag{5.14}$$

where $\varepsilon \sim IID(0, \sigma_\varepsilon^2)$. Since the resulting estimation equations have not been reported in the literature, we shall now present a brief description of the procedure. With $\sigma_{\varepsilon\varepsilon} \neq 0$ (and $\sigma_{12} = 0$),

$$\Omega = \begin{bmatrix} \omega_{11} & \omega_{12} \\ \omega_{12} & \omega_{22} \end{bmatrix} = \begin{bmatrix} \sigma_{11} + \nu^2\sigma_{\varepsilon\varepsilon} & \nu\sigma_{\varepsilon\varepsilon} \\ \nu\sigma_{\varepsilon\varepsilon} & \sigma_{22} + \sigma_{\varepsilon\varepsilon} \end{bmatrix} \tag{5.15}$$

With Ω non-diagonal, the ZEF estimator can be obtained as follows: First, by minimizing the ZEF criterion function $\text{tr} \cdot S^{-1}(Y-X\Pi)'(Y-X\Pi)$ with respect to β we obtain

$$\beta(\nu) = (1/h)[h_1\hat{\pi}_1 + h_2\hat{\pi}_2]. \tag{5.16}$$

where $h_1 = \nu S_{22} - S_{12}$; $h_2 = S_{11} - \nu S_{12}$

$$h = S_{11} - 2\nu S_{12} + \nu^2 S_{22} = \nu h_1 + h_2 \; .$$

$S_{ij}(i,j = 1, 2)$ are the estimated reduced form variances and covariance. Substituting the value of $\beta(\nu)$ for β in the ZEF criterion function, we get

$$G = \text{Const.} - \{h/\det.(S)\} \cdot \beta'(\nu)X'X\beta(\nu) \; , \tag{5.17}$$

which is to be minimized with respect to ν. Setting $(\partial G/\partial \nu) = 0$, we find that ν satisfies the quadratic

$$\nu^2 \cdot a + \nu \cdot b - c = 0 \tag{5.18}$$

where $a = l_{12}S_{22} - l_{22}S_{12}$; $b = l_{22}S_{11} - l_{11}S_{22}$;

$c = l_{12}S_{11} - l_{11}S_{12}$ and $l_{ij} = \hat{y}_i' \hat{y}_j/T$,

$\hat{y}_i = X\hat{\Pi}_i (i,j = 1,2)$.

We take

$$\hat{\nu} = \{- b + \sqrt{b^2 + 4ac}\}/2a \tag{5.19}$$

as the ZEF estimate of ν since one can show that only the root (5.19) of the quadratic is consistent for ν.

On the assumption that $\beta'X'X\beta = Q$ exists, plim. $\hat{y}_1'\hat{y}_1/T = \nu^2 \cdot Q$; plim. $\hat{y}_1\hat{y}_2/T = \nu Q$ and plim. $\hat{y}_2'\hat{y}_2/T = Q$. Noting that $l_{ij} = \hat{y}_i'\hat{y}_j/T$ and plim. $S_{ij} = \omega_{ij}$, we verify plim. $a = \nu \cdot Q\omega_{22} - Q\omega_{12}$, plim. $b = Q\omega_{11} - \nu^2 Q\omega_{22}$, and plim. $c = \nu \cdot Q\omega_{11} - \nu^2 \cdot Q\omega_{12}$. Then writing $\mu = \omega_{11}/\omega_{22}$ and $\omega_{12} = \rho\sqrt{\omega_{11}\omega_{22}}$, where ρ = Corr. $(\omega_{11}, \omega_{12})$, it is seen that

$$\text{plim. } \hat{\nu} = \nu^2 + \mu + \sqrt{(\mu - \nu^2) + 4\nu(\nu - 2\sqrt{\mu})\ (\mu - \nu \cdot \rho\sqrt{\mu})}/2(\nu - \rho\sqrt{\mu}) = \nu. \tag{5.20}$$

With variances and covariance unknown, Goldberger [1972a] has proved that the FIML estimates are identical with the first round estimates obtained by using (5.16) and (5.19). Thus, we need not iterate on Ω to attain the maximum likelihood estimates.

Data and the Estimates

We used six-month treasury bill rates over the period 1959-1973. Annualized percentage change in the Consumer's Price Index was used to construct the inflation variable. The time period chosen was partially motivated by Cargill's [1976] finding that around 1960 there has been a serious structural break in the Fisher equation. The R_t series is six-monthly averages[23] (June and December); i.e., if R_{tj} denotes the bill rate for the jth month in the half year "t", then

$$R_t = \sum_{j=1}^{6} R_{tj}/6$$

Similarly, P_t has been defined as $P_t = (CPI_t - CPI_{t-1})^2 - 1) \times 100$ where

$$CPI_t = \sum_{j=1}^{6} CPI_{tj}/6$$

and CPI_{tj} = price index for the jth month. Since Livingston's data represents expectations held at specific points of time (viz. April and October), we approximated the expectation held during the half year t by taking the mean of the expectation held right before t and the expectation held at the latter part of t. (See Appendix C).

Using equation (5.19), we estimated the Fisher coefficient for the two structural models with $\bar{P}_t^e$ (i.e., survey data) and P_{t+1} (rational expectations). The estimates of α_1 using 3-9 lags of past price changes have been reported in Table 5.1.

The estimates of α_1 with survey data is around 1.15; whereas in simple ordinary least squares regression α_1 was calculated to be only .97. Thus, use of the survey data in an errors-in-the variables framework suggests that the sampling errors are indeed significant. It is worth noting that the Livingston's data when regressed against interest rates of different maturities typically produces Fisher coefficients which are significantly more than one.[24]

In a recent paper, Feldstein [1976] has developed a monetary growth model where the presence of corporate and personal income taxes can justify such overadjustments of nominal interest rates to inflationary expectations. Darby [1975] has also argued independently that the nature of our tax laws are such that interest rates should rise by $1/(1-\tau)100\%$ more than an increase in expected inflation where τ is the marginal tax rate. However, there are additional complications which tend to offset the initial effect of taxes: (i) a typical investment project depreciates and the problem is that tax deductions are based on historic cost of an asset rather than its current replacement cost. As a result, the real value of tax-deductible depreciation is reduced by inflation; (ii) firms typically maintain a balance between equity and debt, rather than engaging solely in debt financing. To the extent that firms must expand their base of equity capital, they cannot capture the full potential benefit of the tax deductibility of interest. In fact, Feldstein and Summers [1978] have illustrated in their calculations that an increase in the maximum potential interest rate associated with an extra point of inflation can range anywhere between 0.8 and 1.3, depending on the assumptions made about the yield differentials and the risk premium between equity capital and bonds. Carlson [1979] also found very little evidence in favor of the Darby-Feldstein hypothesis.[25] [See also Tanzi [1980] for a similar conclusion].

The observable-variable model with the survey data estimated α_1 to be around 1.15. On the other hand, with rational expectations hypothesis it was only around 0.62. To see how robust this estimate is with respect to different specifications of the conditional expectations equation (5.3), we estimated the REH model using a number of current and lagged values of relevant exogenous variables that appear in our wage-price models. The exogenous variables were: inverse of official unemployment rate, Guide-post dummy, percentage change in the ratio of actual to trend productivity, percentage change in the ratio of total compensation to wage, and percentage change in the ratio of unfilled orders to capacity. The rationale behind the variables and their definitions were presented earlier. Current and two lagged values of these variables were utilized to generate the instrumental variable estimates of α_1 in (5.5). We conducted ten experiments with different combinations of the above variables. In all the experiments, the estimated Fisher effect was around .54 with very high t-ratios. Thus, under the maintained hypothesis that expectations are formed rationally, we are led to accept a value of the Fisher effect which is consistently less than one, even in an extended reduced form framework of the interest rate equation.

The overadjustment of nominal interest rates to expected inflation when $\bar{p}^e_t$ is used as a proxy, and the apparent underadjustment when REH is used as a proxy for p^e is possibly complicated by the assumed constancy of the real interest rate in the present framework. In fact, in the experiments reported by Pyle [1972] using Livingston's original series based on 'consensus' forecasts, introduction of some liquidity preference variables substantially reduced the magnitude of the Fisher effect. We have used Sargent's [1969] reformulation of the Leonable Funds theory to introduce three additional variables which can take care of possible variations in the real rate. Specifically, we utilized the following regression framework to test the constancy of real rates:

$$R_t = \alpha_0 + \alpha_1 p_t^e + \beta_1 \cdot \underline{RGNP}_t + \beta_2 \cdot \Delta\underline{RGNP}_t + \beta_3 \cdot \underline{RMG}_t + W_t \tag{5.21}$$

where $\underline{RGNP}_t$ = aggregate output in period t in constant dollars; $\Delta\underline{RGNP}_t$ = first different in $\underline{RGNP}$; and $\underline{RMG}_t$ = percentage change in real money stock.[26] The instruments for p_t^e in (5.21) were generated by regressing $\bar{p}_t^e$ and P_{t+1} on P, P_{-1}, P_{-2}, $\underline{RGNP}$, $\Delta\underline{RGNP}$ and $\underline{RMG}$. The null hypothesis (H_0) that real rates were roughly constant over the sample period is equivalent to test H_0; $\beta = 0$ against the alternative hypothesis $\beta \neq 0$ where $\beta = (\beta_1, \beta_2, \beta_3)$. The appropriate F-statistics associated with the survey-data approach and the REH came out to be only 1.73 and 1.95 respectively, which are not statistically significant at the 5% level (cf. $F_{3.25}^{.05} = 3.01$). Hence, the assumption that real rates were constant seems to be a serviceable approximation, at least in the context of our model.[27]

Actually, it is the independence between p_t^e and the real rate which is critical for the robustness of the estimates of the Fisher coefficient we have obtained so far. Carlson [1979] used two variables - the percentage of capacity utilization and a liquidity variable to account for possible variation in the real rate, and found a significantly negative liquidity effect. However, the introduction of these two variables in the Fisher equation did not change the estimated Fisher coefficient by any significant amount. His ordinary least squares estimate of the Fisher coefficient decreased from 1.298 to 1.250 when the two additional variables were included. This indicates that the independence assumption is not too restrictive in the persent context. It should be pointed out that Carlson's [1979] liquidity variable was defined as the excess of the growth rate of last period's money supply over the rate for the last three years. His experience with RMG was same as ours -- it was not significant.

Levi and Makin [1978, 1979] have argued, as did Turnovsky [1974], that the impact of price expectations upon nominal interest should be studied in the context of a reduced-form interest rate equation based on a general-equilibrium macro-economic model. To them the break in the interest rate equation that we found in Chapter 4 can be explained in terms of assumed zero correlation between anticipated inflation and the real rate. In testing the Fisher hypothesis, they apparently controlled for changes in employment and output (i.e., the Phillips effect) and in the level of uncertainty about inflation that is likely to result from changes in the level of anticipated inflation (the so-called Friedman effect). More specifically, Levi and Makin [1979] included the growth in real national income ($\dot{y}_t$) and a variable that measures the degree of uncertainty about the anticipated inflation (σ_t) as two additional variables in the Fisher equation. They used Livingston's data on price expectations for p^e and Carlson's [1979] computation of the standard deviation of implied inflation forecasts as a measure of the degree of uncertainty. Over 1950-70, $\dot{y}_t$ and σ_t were significantly negative, and the Fisher coefficient became very close to unity. However, the notable result for our purposes is that the inclusion of $\dot{y}_t$ and σ_t had insignificant effect on the Fisher coefficient. Over 1950-70, it was statistically not different from unity in all the three cases reported by them.

Tanzi [1980] has recently introduced yet another variable representing the difference between potential and actual GNP to take into account the effect of fluctuations in real output on expected real interest rates. In addition to the price expectations variable, this variable turned out to be statistically significant in explaining 6-month and 12-month treasury bill rates. However, the relevant question in our context is whether the addition of this variable affects the Fisher coefficient by any significant magnitudes. One potentially serious problem with Tanzi's [1980] estimates is that price expectations formed in April and October each year are related to the 6- and

12-months yeilds beginning in June and December respectively. To overcome this problem we reestimated these equations with the 6-month yeilds quoted at the end of April and October. Our results with and without the GNP gap measure (G_t) have been reported in table 5.2 over three different sample periods, viz. 1959-71, 1959-75, and 1959-80. These estimates have been corrected for auto-correlation in the residuals and for possible errors-in-measurement in $\bar{p}^e_t$. In generating the instrument for $\bar{p}^e_t$, we have used a distributed lag spanning three years. Our G_t was defined as percentage change in GNP gap over the same six months. A remarkably consistent result is that G_t did not affect the Fisher coefficient by any appreciable amount. Except for the Tamzi's sample period, 1959-75, the Fisher coefficient was not statistically different from unity whether G_t was included or not. However, contrary to Tanzi's finding, the Fisher coefficient was significantly less than one for the period 1959-75 even when G_t was included in the regression. What all these results imply is that possible variability in the real rate will not serve as an explanation for the apparent underestimation of the Fisher coefficient when REH is used and the apparent over/complete adjustment when Livingston's new series is used as a proxy for anticipated inflation. Thus, the question arises whether a systematic underestimation of p^e by $\bar{p}^e_t$ and a systematic overestimation by P_{t+1} can possibly explain the apparant anomalous results on the Fisher effect. We study these aspects of the proxy measures in the next section.

5.3 Three indicator Models

Hendershott and van Horne [1973] have produced evidence indicating that over a comparable sample period, the Livingston's measure has substantially underestimated the true price expectations implied by their interest rate equation. We shall now generalize our econometric framework to that of a three-indicator model to look into this possibility. The model would also be able to test whether the subsequently observed actual price inflation has in fact over-estimated the true inflationary expectations. We consider the structural model:

$$R_t = \alpha_1 p_t^e + U_t \tag{5.25}$$

$$\bar{p}_t^e = \beta p_t^e - \varepsilon_t \qquad \beta > 0, \text{ and} \tag{5.26}$$

$$P_{t+1} = \nu p_t^e - v_t \quad \nu > 0, \tag{5.27}$$

where $U_t \sim N(0, \sigma_{\mu\mu})$; $\varepsilon_t \sim N(0, \sigma_{\varepsilon\varepsilon})$ and $v_t \sim N(0, \sigma_{\nu\nu})$. In addition, we assume

$$\begin{aligned} &\text{Cov}(U, v) = \text{Cov}(\varepsilon, v) = \text{Cov}(U, \varepsilon) = 0 \\ &\text{Cov}(p^e, U) = \text{Cov}(p^e, v) = \text{Cov}(p^e, \varepsilon) = 0 \end{aligned} \tag{5.28}$$

A value of $\nu = 1$ would indicate the validity of the basic implication of the REH, whereas $\beta = 1$ would indicate that the survey measure can be used as an unbiased proxy. The variance of unanticipated inflation in the rational expectations framework is given by $(1 - \nu)^2 \sigma_{pp} + \sigma_{\nu\nu}$, where σ_{pp} is the variance of p^e. Similarly, the sampling variance associated with the survey measure is given by $(\beta - 1)^2 \sigma_{pp} + \sigma_{\varepsilon\varepsilon}$. Since there are seven (viz. α_1, β, ν, σ_{pp}, σ_{uu}, $\sigma_{\varepsilon\varepsilon}$ and $\sigma_{\nu\nu}$) parameters to be estimated and there are only six equations in terms of observable moments:

$$S = \begin{bmatrix} S_{11} & & \\ S_{21} & S_{22} & \\ S_{31} & S_{32} & S_{33} \end{bmatrix} = \begin{bmatrix} \alpha_1^2 \cdot \sigma_{pp} + \sigma_{uu} & & \\ \alpha_1 \cdot \beta \cdot \sigma_{pp} & \beta^2 \cdot \sigma_{pp} + \sigma_{\varepsilon\varepsilon} & \\ \alpha_1 \cdot \nu \cdot \sigma_{pp} & \beta \cdot \nu \cdot \sigma_{pp} & \nu^2 \cdot \sigma_{pp} + \sigma_{\nu\nu} \end{bmatrix} \tag{5.29}$$

we need one identifying restriction to avoid the obvious indeterminacy. Normalizing either $\nu = 1$ or $\beta = 1$ would give an exactly identified system. The estimators for the model with $\nu = 1$ are;

$$\hat{\alpha}_1 = S_{21}/S_{32};\ \hat{\beta} = S_{21}/S_{31};\ \hat{\sigma}_{pp} = S_{32}/\hat{\beta}$$
$$\hat{\sigma}_{uu} = S_{11} - \hat{\alpha}_1^2\,\hat{\sigma}_{pp};\ \sigma_{\varepsilon\varepsilon} = S_{22} - \hat{\beta}^2\hat{\sigma}_{\nu\nu}S_{33} - \hat{\sigma}_{pp}. \tag{5.30}$$

Estimates for the model with $\beta = 1$ are obtained as

$$\hat{\alpha}_1 = S_{31}/S_{32};\ \hat{\nu} = S_{31}/S_{21};\ \hat{\sigma}_{pp} = S_{32}/\hat{\nu}$$
$$\hat{\sigma}_{uu} = S_{11} - \hat{\alpha}_1^2\,\hat{\sigma}_{pp};\ \hat{\sigma}_{\varepsilon\varepsilon} = S_{22} - \hat{\sigma}_{pp};\ \hat{\sigma}_{\nu\nu} = S_{33} - \hat{\nu}^2\cdot\hat{\sigma}_{pp}. \tag{5.31}$$

In addition, one can normalize both $\nu = \beta = 1$ and obtain an overidentified system. The latter model was solved by using LISREL-III, a general computer algorithm developed by Joreskog and Sorbom [1976]. For the exactly identified models, LISREL-III can not compute the associated standard errors of estimates.

As reported in Table 5.3, the estimates with $\beta = 1$ and $\nu = 1$ are very similar to the estimates obtained in the previous section using the survey measure and the REH respectively. However, now we obtain estimates of ν and β which are seen to be significantly different from unity. The estimated Fisher effect in the overidentified case is 1.02, which is a weighted average of the estimates implied by the two exactly identified models.

It may be noted that $\hat{\beta} = S_{21}/S_{31}$ in the model with $\nu = 1$ is just the reciprocal of $\hat{\nu} = S_{31}/S_{21}$ in the model with $\beta = 1$. Thus, a more reasonable identifying restriction seems to be $\nu\beta = 1$. This model will then allow both the survey measure and the REH to deviate simultaneously from being unbiased measures of true price expectations. Under this normalizing constraint, the estimates are obtained as:

$$\begin{aligned}
&\hat{\nu} = (S_{31}/S_{21})^{1/2};\ \hat{\sigma}_{pp} = S_{32};\ \hat{\beta} = 1/\hat{\nu} \\
&\hat{\alpha}_1 = S_{21}/\hat{\beta}\cdot\hat{\sigma}_{pp} = S_{31}/\hat{\nu}\cdot\hat{\sigma}_{pp};\ \hat{\sigma}_{uu} = S_{11} - \hat{\alpha}_1{}^2\hat{\sigma}_{pp} \qquad (5.32) \\
&\hat{\sigma}_{\nu\nu} = S_{32} - \hat{\nu}^2\hat{\sigma}_{pp};\ \sigma_{\varepsilon\varepsilon} = S_{22} - \hat{\beta}^2\hat{\sigma}_{pp} .
\end{aligned}$$

The estimates of all the seven parameters for different time periods have been reported in Table 5.4. For the relatively "clean" time period 1959:1-1971:1, the Fisher coefficient was always very close to unity with both ν and β significantly different from their hypothesized values. One-period-ahead prices seem to overestimate the true price expectations by nearly 30%; the survey data, on the other hand, underestimated the price expectations by nearly 23%.[29] This finding is strikingly similar to the evidence produced by Hendershott and van Horne [1973]. It also explains why a straightforward use of the survey data produces the Fisher coefficients which are significantly greater than one; and the use of REH yields a Fisher coefficient which are substantially less than unity. Also, Fama's somewhat discouraging finding with respect to five- and six-month treasury bill rates can be explained by the fact that subsequently-observed one-period-ahead price inflation tends to overestimate the true price expectations. However, given the conventional Fisherian framework where a number of simplifying assumptions are made, we feel that Fisher's hypothesis is borne out quite well, particularly when one considers the constraints imposed by the cost of obtaining and using additional information.

All the estimated variances came up with proper signs and reasonable magnitudes. The variance of the error term in the interest rate equation, σ_{uu}, is quite stable over different sample periods. However, $\sigma_{\nu\nu}$ and $\sigma_{\varepsilon\varepsilon}$ seem to have increased substantially during the 1970's. This can partially be explained by the increased uncertainty brought about by the distortions associated with the wage-price controls during the first half of 1970's. During these latter time periods, together with increasing uncertainty in future price movements, the Fisher coefficient also seems to be drifting away from its hypothesized value.

Rather than using $\nu\beta = 1$, we also used $\nu + \beta = 2$ as an alternative normalization. The parameter estimates were very similar. Since our study suggests that Livingston's survey data substantially underestimated the true price expectations, instead of using the above identifying restrictions, (viz. $\nu\beta = 1$ or $\nu + \beta = 2$) we also experimented with various values of β which are smaller than one, and obtained the corresponding estimates of ν and α_1. The results are consistent with those obtained with normalization $\nu\beta = 1$ (see Table 5.5). It is interesting to note that the efficient market hypothesis (i.e., $\nu = 1$) is consistent only with a value of β which is substantially less than unity. This estimate is independent of possible covariance between anticipated inflation and real rate. Secondly, a value of the Fisher coefficient close to one is also consistent only with values of β which is less than unity. This estimate is <u>not</u> independent of possible non-zero covariance between p_t^e and i_t. However, a negative covariance between p_t^e and i_t will imply that a full Fisher effect is consistent with even a lower value for β.

5.4 Conclusions

In this chapter, we presented some additional econometric evidence on the "efficiency" of the treasury bill market. To highlight the contrasting estimates that one obtains by utilizing different proxy measures for the unobservable price expectations, we have used the rational expectations framework and the Livingston's series to estimate the Fisher coefficient. The models fall neatly into Goldberger's unobservable-variable framework which implies certain non-linear constaints on the parameters across the reduced form equations. The main conclusions can be summarized as follows:

(i) The rational expectations hypothesis implied a Fisher coefficient which was only around .54. This estimate was roughly the same when a number of lagged actual inflation rates and a number of current and lagged values of relevant exogenous variables were used to generate the instruments.

(ii) Cargill [1976] has used the Livingston's data to estimate the Fisher coefficient. Our estimates, utilizing an errors-in=the variables framework indicated that there are substantial sampling errors in the survey data. Thus, simple ordinary least squares estimates will tend to underestimate the true coefficient. The FIML estimates of the Fisher coefficient in our 'errors-in-variables' framework, however, tended to be greater than one.

(iii) Using three loanable funds variables (cf. Sargent) to track possible variations in the real rates, we failed to reject the null hypothesis that the real rates were constant over the sample period. This result is quite different from the one obtained by Pyle, who used the Livingston's data based on "consensus" forecasts.

(iv) In the context of a simple, yet very general three-indicator model, we directly tested whether the survey measure and the one-period-ahead price inflation can be used as unbiased proxies for the price expectations variable. The results indicate that P_{t+1} overestimated the true price expectations by nearly 30% over the sample period, whereas the Livingston's measure underestimated it by roughly 23%. The estimated Fisher coefficient in this generalized framework was found out to be very close to unity. The evidence on the inadequacy of the Livingston's measure in predicting the increase in the rate of inflation in the sixties is very similar to those obtained by Hendershott and van Horne. Since we have worked only with the six-month treasury bill rates, where Fama's [1975] results were particularly discouraging, it is certainly possible that more positive evidence may turn out if one conducted the same experiments with bill rates of other maturities. In fact, when we experimented with three-month treasury bill rates, the parameter estimates seem to be more consistent with rational expectations with a Fisher effect very close to unity. For example, for $\beta = .8$, ν is now 1.07 with $\alpha_1 = 1.04$. The results are given in Table 5.5. For the same values of β the 3-month bills yield values of ν which are much closer to unity than one finds using the 6-month bills; the values of α_1, on the other hand, are very close to each other in both the cases. In this chapter, we studied the validity of a particular version of the rational expectations hypothesis which posits that the expected rate of inflation in each period is an unbiased prediction of the actual inflation rate subsequently observed. The apparent overestimation of true anticipated inflation in terms of actual inflation while using the 6-month treasury bill rates seems to be due to the assumed independence between anticipated inflation and real rate. In Chapter 6, we shall show how models which allow the real rates to vary and be correlated with price expectations become more consistent with the efficient market hypothesis.

Table 5.1 FIML Estimates of the Fisher Coefficient*: 1959:1-1973:2

Variables in the price expectations Equation	With $\bar{p}_t^e$	With P_{t+1}
P, P_{-1}, P_{-2}	1.17	.62
$P, P_{-1}, P_{-2}, P_{-3}$	1.15	.61
$P, P_{-1}, P_{-2}, P_{-3}, P_{-4}$	1.14	.62
$P, P_{-1}, P_{-2}, P_{-3}, P_{-4}, P_{-5}$	1.14	.61
$P, P_{-1}, P_{-2}, P_{-3}, P_{-4}, P_{-5}, P_{-6}$	1.14	.62
$P, P_{-1}, P_{-2}, P_{-3}, P_{-4}, P_{-5}, P_{-6}, P_{-7}$	1.14	.62
$P, P_{-1}, P_{-2}, P_{-3}, P_{-4}, P_{-5}, P_{-6}, P_{-7}, P_{-8}$	1.16	.62

*Estimates are based on the model (5.4).

Table 5.2. 2SLS Estimates of the Fisher Equation with GNP Gap*

Explanatory Variables	1959 - 71		1959 - 75		1959 - 80	
Const.	2.46 (.523)	2.68 (.427)	2.77 (.456)	2.789 (.301)	2.28 (.616)	2.33 (.483)
$\bar{P}^e$	.994 (.235)	.892 (.196)	.759 (.131)	.774 (.137)	.881 (.118)	.890 (.098)
G	-	.113 (.052)	-	.138 (.043)	-	.126 (.057)
ρ**	.36	.25	.48	.29	.66	.60
DW***	1.91	1.88	1.98	1.98	2.15	2.16

* Estimates are corrected for serial correlation. Dependent variable is six-month T.B. bills quoted at the end of April and October. Standard errors in paranthesis.

** ρ is the autocorrelation coefficient before correction for serial correlation.

*** DW is Durbin-Watson statistic after correction.

Table 5.3 Alternative Estimates of the Three-Indicator Models: 1959:1-1973:2

		α_1	ν	β	σ_{pp}	σ_{uu}	$\sigma_{\varepsilon\varepsilon}$	σ_{vv}
Overidentified Case*		1.02 (.174)	-	-	1.53 (.47)	.48 (.25)	.13 (.20)	2.4 (.65)
Just-identified Cases	(β=1)	1.18	2.09	-	1.29	.62	.29	.76
	(ν=1)	.57	-	.48	5.64	.34	.29	.76

*Standard errors in brackets

Table 5.4 Parameter Estimates for the Three-Indicator Model*
Structural Parameters

Sample Period	α_1	ν	β	σ_{pp}	σ_{uu}	σ_{vv}	$\sigma_{\varepsilon\varepsilon}$
1959:2 ∿ 67:2	.99	1.29	.77	.46	.26	.37	.03
∿ 68:1	.91	1.30	.77	.71	.26	.35	.02
∿ 68:2	.86	1.32	.76	.94	.25	.35	.02
∿ 69:1	.89	1.38	.72	1.19	.23	.33	.03
∿ 69:2	.98	1.38	.72	1.46	.26	.32	.03
∿ 70:1	1.01	1.34	.75	1.63	.25	.35	.03
∿ 70:2	1.02	1.29	.77	1.67	.22	.42	.06
∿ 71:1	.97	1.30	.77	1.68	.31	.29	.19
∿ 71:2	.98	1.28	.78	1.63	.27	.32	.26
∿ 72:1	.94	1.29	.77	1.60	.32	.23	.32
∿ 72:2	.87	1.29	.77	1.71	.39	.28	.29
∿ 73:1	.83	1.36	.73	2.04	.37	.62	.28
∿ 73:2	.81	1.44	.69	2.70	.34	.76	.29
∿ 74:1	.73	1.45	.69	3.82	.39	.76	.27
∿ 74:2	.73	1.35	.74	4.44	.32	1.05	.43
∿ 75:1	.68	1.33	.75	4.97	.39	.79	.63
∿ 75:2	.70	1.30	.76	4.73	.34	1.06	.72

*The model is given by (5.25)-(5.27) with $\nu\beta = 1$ as the normalization.

Table 5.5 Estimates of ν and α_1 for different values of β: 1959:1-1973:2

Assumed Values of β	ν		α_1	
	Six-month T.B. Rates	Three-month T.B. Rates	Six-month T.B. Rates	Three-month T.B. Rates
.6	1.253	.81	.710	.69
.7	1.461	.94	.828	.81
.8	1.670	1.07	.946	.92
.9	1.775	1.21	1.005	1.04
1.0	2.088	1.34	1.183	1.182

CHAPTER 6

VARIABILITY OF REAL INTEREST RATES AND THE EFFICIENT MARKET HYPOTHESIS

As we have noted in the last chapter, in a pioneering article, Fama [1975] presented some evidence in favor of the joint hypotheiss that the real rate of interest is constant and that the U.S. Treasury Bills market is _efficient_. Under this joint hypothesis, the _ex post_ real interest rate (EPRR) is simply the _ex ante_ real rate (EARR) plus a random forecasting error associated with a _rational expectations_ scheme. Thus, one of Fama's tests was to examine the simple autocorrelations in the _ex post_ real rate which by definition is the difference between the market interest rate and the _subsequently observed_ rate of inflation. However, Nelson and Schwert [1977] have demonstrated that Fama's tests were not powerful enough to reject the joint hypothesis; low autocorrelation observed in the EPRR could indicate rather strong autocorrelation and significant variation in the EARR, since the latter might have been substantially overlaid with forecast errors. Under the assumption that EARR follows an autoregressive scheme, they considered different combinations of autocorrelation in the EPRR under hypothetical value for the forecast-error variance.

The main purpose of the present chapter is to show that all the structural parameters of the Nelson-Schwert model are identifiable and can be consistently estimated; as such, the random forecasting errors do not confound the problem of identifying variations in the _ex ante_ real rate. In Section 6.1, we present the structural estimates utilizing the six-month treasury bill rates. The choice of the six-month bill rate was partly motivated by the fact that Fama obtained some discouraging results with respect to bills of five- and six-month maturities (see Fama [1975, p. 279]).

However, models with a variable EARR bring in an additional parameter to be identified -- the correlation between EARR and the anticipated inflation. Mundell [1963] has argued that an increase in the anticipated rate of inflation will be accompanied by a fall in the *ex ante* real rate. Although the evidence on the *Mundell effect* obtained by Nelson and Schwert is rather mixed, their analysis suggests that a significant Mundell *effect* would substantially increase the estimate of the variance in the EARR. In order to identify the *Mundell effect* in the context of the Nelson-Schwert *two-indicator* model,[30] we have used the Livingston data on price expectations (six-months ahead), as reported in Carlson [1977a], as an additional *indicator*. We have utilized the survey data in such a way that the structural model be able to ascertain the extent to which the series deviates from being an unbiased measure of the true price expectations.[31]

Since empirical measures of temporal movements in real rates of interest have very important implications for the understanding of macroeconomic adjustment mechanisms, we have generated an experimental series for the real interest rates which explicitly incorporates the rational expectations scheme in a Fisherian framework. Previous empirical formulations of the real rate have typically defined the real rate as the difference between the nominal rate and an estimated distributed lag on past inflation rates with nominal rate as the regressand (eg. Yohe-Karnosky [1969]). However, Elliott [1977] has recently demonstrated that this formulation makes very little use of current available information and is a poor representation of Muthian rationality. In Section 6.3, we have analyzed a number of alternative procedures to generate rationally expected EARR in a Fisherian Framework and compared their predictive efficiencies. Finally, the conclusions have been summarized in Section 6.4.

6.1 A structural model of ex-ante real rate

The model considered by Nelson and Schwert can be written as[32]

$$r_t = i_t - \varepsilon_t \tag{6.1}$$

$$i_t = \phi i_{t-1} + w_t \tag{6.2}$$

where r_t = the ex post real interest rate, i_t = the ex ante real rate, and ε_t is the market's forecasting error for the rate of inflation. Also, ε and w are assumed to be independently and identically distributed random variables with zero means and variances σ^2_ε and σ^2_w respectively.

Equations (6.1) - (6.2) can be written in terms of the observable r_t as:

$$r_t = \phi r_{t-1} + u_t \, , \tag{6.3}$$

where $u_t = -\varepsilon_t + \phi\varepsilon_{t-1} + w_t$. Since u_t is correlated with r_{t-1}, an ordinary least squares regression (LS) of r_t on r_{t-1} will yield inconsistent estimate of the parameter ϕ. The probability limit for the OLS estimate of ϕ, which is also the correlation coefficient between r_t and r_{t-1}, is given by:

$$\text{plim. } \hat{\phi}_{OLS} = \text{Corr }(r_t, r_{t-1}) = \frac{\phi\sigma^2_i}{\sigma^2_i + \sigma^2_\varepsilon} \tag{6.4}$$

where σ^2_i is the variance of the EARR. Thus, the first-order autocorrelation in the EPRR may be considerably less than ϕ if the variance of forecast errors is large relative to the variance of the EARR. However, since r_{t-2} is uncorrelated with u_t, it can, in general, be used as an instrumental variable. By taking

$$\hat{\phi}_{INS} = \frac{\text{Cov}(r_t\ r_{t-2})}{\text{Cov}(r_{t-1}\ r_{t-2})}, \tag{6.5}$$

we shall have plim. $\hat{\phi}_{INS} = \phi$. We next use the estimated residuals $\hat{u}_t = r_t - \hat{\phi}_{INS} \cdot r_{t-1}$ to get estimates of the residual variances. Since

$$\text{Var}\ (u_t) = \text{Var}\ (-\varepsilon_t + \phi\varepsilon_{t-1} + w_t)$$

$$= \sigma^2_\varepsilon\ (1 + \phi^2) + \sigma^2_w,\ \text{and} \tag{6.6}$$

$$\text{Cov}\ (u_t,\ u_{t-1}) = -\phi\sigma^2_\varepsilon\ , \tag{6.7}$$

we can estimate the other structural parameters as:

$$\sigma^2_\varepsilon = -\text{Cov}\ (\hat{u}_t,\ \hat{u}_{t-1})/\hat{\phi} \tag{6.8}$$

$$\sigma^2_w = \hat{\sigma}^2_u - (1 + \hat{\phi}^2)\hat{\sigma}^2_\varepsilon,\ \text{and} \tag{6.9}$$

$$\sigma^2_i = \hat{\sigma}^2_w/(1-\hat{\phi}^2). \tag{6.10}$$

Thus, all the four structural parameters of the model (6.1) - (6.2) are identifiable and can be consistently estimated, given some suitable instrument for r_{t-1} in (6.3). In the context of our model, however, r_{t-2} is not a powerful instrument because, over the period 1/1959 - 1/1971, the estimated first-order autocorrelation in r_t is very low. We followed Durbin's [1954] suggestion of using the ranks of r_{t-1} as the instrumental variable (IV). Fortunately, in all the experiments, the covariance between the ranks and r_{t-1} was found to be very close to unity (0.95 on the average), which indicates that the loss in efficiency will be quite minimal.[33]

The estimated parameters over different overlapping sample periods have been reported in Table 6.1.[34] Over the period 2/1959 - 1/1971, which is approximately the sample period chosen by Fama, we find that the variance of the <u>ex ante</u> real rate constitutes nearly 49% of the variance in the <u>ex post</u> real rate. This can partially explain why some of Fama's experiments with five- and six-month treasury bill rates did not yield encouraging results. However, over the different sample periods from 2/1959 - 2/1971, the percentage of total annual variance in the EPRR attributable to variations in the EARR fluctuated remarkably from nearly 14% to 56%. Thus, a constant <u>ex ante</u> real rate does not seem to be a robust approximation in efficient market models.[35] Over this relatively "clean" time period, the autoregressive parameter is only around 0.3. Since the IV procedure takes care of the contemporaneous correlation between r_{t-1} and u_t, $\hat{\phi}_{INS}$ is always significantly greater than the simple autocorrelation in the EPRR. These results illustrates the Nelson-Schwert point that low autocorrelation observed in the EPRR could in fact be indicative of rather sizable variation in the EARR. However, the autocorrelations in the EARR are not very high.

The estimates covering the time periods 2/1959 to 2/1973 give quite a different picture. The first-order autocorrelation in the EPRR increased substantially together with the implied variance of the EARR. As Fama has pointed out, this can be explained by the distortions introduced by the wage-price controls, beginning August 1971.[36]

6.2 Estimation of covariance between ex-ante real rate and anticipated inflation

Robert Mundell has argued that an increase in the anticipated rate of inflation will be accompanied by a fall in the <u>ex ante</u> real rate, because inflation reduces real money balances which stimulates savings due to the resulting wealth effect. Since the EARR shows substantial variation over the sample period, Nelson and Schwert tried to identify the Mundell effect in the context of their two-indicator model. Under an additional assumption[37] employed to identify all the four parameters, they estimated the effect to be positive and very small. However they found a significant negative Mundell effect in seasonal variation.

To estimate the Mundell effect together with the variance in the EARR, we consider the following three-indicator model:

$$R_t = p_t^e + i_t \tag{6.11}$$

$$P_{t+1} = p_t^e + \varepsilon_t \tag{6.12}$$

$$\bar{p}_t^e = \beta p_t^e + \eta_t \qquad \beta > 0 \tag{6.13}$$

wehre r_t is the observed nominal interest rate, p_t^e is the unobservable market forecast of the inflation rate P_{t+1}, i_t is the unobservable EARR, and $\bar{p}_t^e$ is the survey data on price expectations. Thus, a value of β different from unity would indicate that the survey measure cannot serve as an unbiased proxy. The error term η_t, of course should take care of possible sampling variability that may be associated with the surveys.[38] The covariance terms between i and ε and between p^e and ε can be eliminated due to the rationality hypothesis; we shall further assume that η_t is uncorrelated with p^e, ε_t and i_t. The latter assumption can be justified by noting that η_t, in our analysis, represents random sampling error associated with Livingston's surveys; since the scope, procedure and the number of experts surveyed in these surveys have been almost the same over the relevant sample period, the assumption seems, *a priori*, to be reasonable.

The six observable second order moments in (6.11) - (6.13) can then be written as:

$$S = \begin{bmatrix} S_{11} & & \\ S_{21} & S_{22} & \\ S_{31} & S_{32} & S_{33} \end{bmatrix} = \begin{bmatrix} \sigma_i^2 + \sigma_\rho^2 + 2\sigma_{i\rho} & & \\ \sigma_\rho^2 + \sigma_{i\rho} & \sigma_\rho^2 + \sigma_\varepsilon^2 & \\ \beta(\sigma_\rho^2 + \sigma_{i\rho}) & \beta\sigma_\rho & \beta^2\sigma_\rho^2 + \sigma_\eta^2 \end{bmatrix}, \quad (6.14)$$

where σ_ρ^2 = variance of the anticipated inflation and $\sigma_{i\rho}$ is the Mundell effect. The six parameters (viz. β, σ_ρ^2, $\sigma_{i\rho}$, σ_ε^2, σ_η^2 and σ_i^2) can be solved as follows:

$$\hat{\beta} = S_{31}/S_{21};\ \hat{\sigma}_\rho^2 = S_{32}/\hat{\beta};\ \sigma_{i\rho} = S_{21} - \hat{\sigma}_\rho^2$$

$$\hat{\sigma}_i^2 = S_{11} - \hat{\sigma}_\rho^2 - 2\hat{\sigma}_{i\rho};\ \hat{\sigma}_\eta^2 = S_{33} - \hat{\beta}^2\sigma_\rho^2, \text{ and} \quad (6.15)$$

$$\hat{\sigma}_\varepsilon^2 = S_{22} - \hat{\sigma}_\rho^{\ 2}$$

The estimates of all the parameters for the sample period 1/1959 - 2/1971 have been reported in Table 6.2. The Mundell effect ($\sigma_{i\rho}$) turns out to be quite significant and is around -.69. The estimates of σ_i^2 and σ_ε^2 are very close to the corresponding estimates reported in Table 6.1 and σ_i^2 constitutes nearly 25% of the total variation in the nominal interest rate.

It is interesting to note that β came out to be around .60, which implies that Livingston's data systematically underestimated the true price expectations implied by an interest rate equation.[39] The parameter estimates using the three-month Treasury Bill rates are also given in Table 6.2. The survey data performs a little better now; β is estimated to be .80 with the Mundell effect around -.42. This evidence is consistent with what we found in the last chapter; the survey data seems to perform somewhat better in the context of three-month bill rates. The failure of the survey data to track the price inflation during the 1960's was first demonstrated by Hendershott and van Horne [1973]. A value of β less than unity is consistent with the fact that over the sample period, the variance of $\bar{p}^e_t$ was only 1.28 (with mean 1.85) whereas the variance of P_{t+1} was 3.42 (with mean 2.72). Also $\beta = 1$ in our framework means that $\mathrm{var}(\bar{p}^e_t) \geq \mathrm{var}(p^e_t)$, which would imply that the Livingston data contains all of the information available to form the market's expectations of future inflation.

6.3 Rationality of Livingston's survey data

Using the so-called consistency and efficiency properties of rational expectations, Pesando [1975] first showed that the original Livingston's data based on consensus forecasts did not satisfy rationality in Muth's sense. Carlson [1977] reached the same conclusion even using the new adjusted series. Mullineaux [1978] has, however, argued that due to possible heteroskedasticity in errors, their test results can not be unambigiously interpreted. His tests, in fact, could not reject the hypothesis of Muthian rationality.

The consistency and efficiency tests of rationality for the Livingston data are based on the following equations (see Modigliani and Shiller [1973]):

$$P_{t+1} = w_0 + w_1 P_t + w_2 P_{t-1} + \ldots + w_n P_{t-n} + U_{1,t} \quad (6.16)$$

$$\bar{P}^e_t = w'_0 + w'_1 P_t + w'_2 P_{t-1} + \ldots + w_n P_{t-n} + U_{2,t} \quad (6.17)$$

$${}_2\bar{P}^e_t = w''_0 + w''_1 (\bar{P}^e_{t-1}) + w''_2 P_{t-2} + \ldots + w_n P_{t-n} + U_{3,t} \quad (6.18)$$

where ${}_2\bar{P}^e_t$ is the forecast for current inflation made two periods ago. This two-period ahead forecast is derived as the forward rate implicit in the 12-month forecast of CPI that are available through the Livingston's surveys (see Pesando [1975, p. 852]). The composite hypothesis of rationality incorporating both consistency and the efficiency is tested as: $w_i' = w_i'' = w_i'''$ (i = 0, 1, 2, ...). The first equality states that realizations and one-period forecasts are generated by the same autoregressive model ("efficiency"), while the second equality requires that multispan forecasts be generated recursively via Wold's [1963] chain principle ("consistency"). By using the Chow test of equality of regressions, Carlson [1977] strongly rejected rationality. Mullineaux's point, however, is that the error terms in (6.16), (6.17) and (6.18) are not identically distributed; thus the Chow tests really rejected the homoskedasticity assumption rather than the hypothesis of equality of the regressions. His solution was thus, to subtract (6.17) from (6.16) and (6.17) from (6.18), to estimate the resulting models, and then test the hypothesis that all the coefficients in both the regressions are zero. Mullineaux fails to reject rationality.

In a recent paper, Pearce [1979] compares the characteristics of forecast errors of the Livingston data to those from a constructed expectations series that explicitly satisfies the rationality criterion and reaches a conclusion similar to Carlson [1977] and Pesando [1975]. The fact that the forecasting errors associated with the Livingston data is not random is also evident in Mullineaux's calculations.

A more fundamental problem with Mullineaux's procedure becomes evident if we restate the "efficiency" aspect the REH. The underlying structural model is

$$P_{t+1} = p_t^e + \varepsilon_t \tag{6.19}$$

$$\bar{p}_t^e = \beta_0 + \beta_1 p_t^e - \eta_t \tag{6.20}$$

$$p_t^e = E(P_{t+1} | I_t) = w_o + w_1 P_t + w_2 P_{t-1} + \ldots + \eta_1 MG_t + \eta_2 MG_{t-1} + \ldots \tag{6.21}$$

Equations (6.19) and (6.21) are obtained from the rational expectations hypothesis where the relevant conditioning information comes from past prices, etc. In this framework, (β_0=0, β_1=1) together with ε_t being a white noise would imply rationality on part of the Livingston data. Thus, the rationality can be tested by testing the equality of the coefficients of the reduced form equations (6.16) and (6.17) that one obtains by substituting (6.21) into (6.19) and (6.20) with the assumption (β_0=0, β_1=1). However, asymptotically the most efficient way of inferring about β_0 and β_1 will be to estimate β_0, β_1 and w_i and η_i (i=0,1,2,...) in

$$P_{t+1} = w_0 + w_1 P_t + w_2 P_{t-1} + \eta_1 MG_t + \eta_2 MG_{t-1} + \dots + \varepsilon_t \tag{6.22}$$

$$\bar{P}_t^e = (\beta_0 + \beta_1 w_0) + \beta_1 w_1 P_t + \beta_1 w_2 P_{t-1} + \dots + \beta_1 \eta_1 MG_t + \beta_1 \eta_2 MG_{t-1} + \dots \eta_t \tag{6.23}$$

After considerable experimentation, we found four lagged inflation and money growth rates as the optimal specification in terms of $\bar{R}^2$ criterion. This is consistent with our findings in chapter 3. With this specification, we estimated (6.22) - (6.23) over 1960/1 - 1979/2 by Zellner's seemingly unrelated regression procedure with cross-equation constraints across equations. The maximum likelihood estimates of β_0 and β_1 turned out to be .348 and .765 with standard errors .431 and .078, respectively. Durbin's h-statistic indicated no evidence for serial correlation in residuals for the actual inflation equation; however, it was significantly negative for (6.23). R^2 for (6.22) and (6.23) were .73 and .80 respectively. Since the other structural parameters are not of direct relevance here, we are not reporting them. Since β is less than one even at the 1% level of significance, our empirical evidence overwhelming support the view that Livingston's data systematically underestimated the true price expectations. Thus, apart from the possibility that Mullineaux's test might not have been sufficiently powerful to reject the rationality hypothesis, his maintained assumption that a fifth-order autoregressive process adequately represents the stochastic process in (6.21) might have contributed to his contradictory result. One advantage of restating the efficiency criterion of REH in terms of (6.19) - (6.21) is that it clearly specifies the alternative should the rationality be rejected.

The responses to the Livingston's surveys are, however, representative of informed opinion of experts about the state and direction of the price level in the near future, and the data has been treated here with sufficient generality.

6.4 An estimated real rate series

It is well-known that according to the rational expectations hypothesis,

$$P_t^e = E\,(P_{t+1}|I) = P_{t+1} - \varepsilon_t \tag{6.24}$$

where I is the available information utilized by market participants in forming expectations. The relevant available information, according to the weak form of the rationality hypothesis consists of past values of the variable actually involved in the process in question. Thus, the conditional expectation in (6.24) can be written as:

$$E\,(P_{t+1}|I_t) = \delta_0 + \delta_1 P_t + \delta_2 P_{t-1} + \ldots. \tag{6.25}$$

To generate the experimental real rate series we thus consider the structural model:

$$R_t = i_t + P_t^e \tag{6.26}$$

$$P_{t+1} = P_t^e + \varepsilon_t, \text{ and} \tag{6.27}$$

$$P_t^e = \delta_0 + \delta_1 P + \delta_2 P_{t-1} + \ldots \tag{6.28}$$

which has the following reduced form:

$$R_t = i_t + \delta_0 + \delta_1 P_t + \delta_2 P_{t-1} + \ldots. \tag{6.29}$$

$$P_{t+1} = \delta_0 + \delta_1 P_t + \delta_2 P_{t-1} + \ldots. + \varepsilon_t \tag{6.30}$$

Under the Fisherian assumption that $i_t = \alpha + v_t$, where α and v_t are the long-run equilibrium real rate and a small random disturbance term determined by short-run changes in financial markets (term uncorrelated with p_t^e), earlier formulations (e.g., Gibson [1970], Yohe-Karnosky [1969], etc.) yielded a form of the equation (6.29) which is typically estimated:

$$R_t = (\alpha+\delta_0) + \delta_1 P_t + \delta_2 P_{t-1} + \ldots + v_t \tag{6.29a}$$

The real rate series is then obtained as $R_t - \hat{\delta}_1 P_t - \hat{\delta}_2 P_{t-1} - \ldots.$, where $\hat{\delta}_i$ (i=1,2,...) is the estimated least squares coefficient (see, for example, Yohe-Karnosky [1969, p. 38]). Looking at the reduced form equations (6.29a) and (6.30), we find at least three potentially troublesome problems with the procedure. First, if δ_0, which can be interpreted as the long-run expected inflation rate, is non-zero the above procedure is expected to yield a real rate series which is apt to be unduely inflated.[40] Secondly, the real rate generated in this way may not satisfy a basic prediction of the rational expectations hypothesis, viz. equation (6.27). In other words, the real rate is generated solely on the basis of equation (6.29) without imposing the cross-equation constraints implied by equations system (6.29) - (6.30). These constraints are, however, testable in principle. The third problem results from our evidence that the variance of i_t is indeed substantial and that i_t is significantly correlated with p^e_t. Thus, v_t will be contemporaneously correlated with the explanatory variables in (6.29a), and as a result, ordinary least squares estimates in (6.29a) will be biased. It is, thus, not surprising that in Elliott's [1977] study, the so-called Fisherian autoregressive model, when compared with four other macroeconomic alternatives, did so poorly in terms of predictive efficiency.

Under the strict Fisherian hypothesis, a regression of R_t-P_{t+1} on $(P_t, P_{t-1}, \ldots)$ should be statistically insignificant. After experimenting with lags of different lengths in the context of (6.29a) and (6.30), nine lagged inflation variables were chosen on $\bar{R}^2$ criterion. The results have been reported in Table 6.3. The sign pattern of the estimated coefficients were remarkably similar and the serial correlation in the residuals were statistically insignificant in both the equations. However, the F-test statistic for the third regression was calculated to be 4.01 which was more than the critical F-value at the one percent level of significance ($F^{.01}_{9,16} = 3.78$). The serial correlation coefficient of the residuals was however insignificant. Thus, we are led to reject the hypothesis of zero correlation between EARR and the expected inflation.

In view of these results, a logical way to obtain the EARR will be to generate the in-sample predictions from a regression of r_t $(= R_t-P_{t+1})$ on $(P_t, P_{t-1}, \ldots)$.[41] Though simple, this procedure (call it Method I) circumvents the problems associated with the so-called Fisherian autoregressive method discussed earlier. Another closely similar procedure noted briefly by Elliott [1977, p. 438, Fn. 16] to estimate the *ex ante* real rates is by first generating the rationally forecasted inflation rates on the basis of equation (6.30), (Elliott regressed P_t on past money growth rates) and then subtracting the series from R_t in (6.29). Elliott rejected this procedure (Method II in this paper) in favour of his best fitting Neo-keynesian Monetary model on the argument that the average absolute error of one-period ahead prediction of r_t obtained on a in-sample basis was 1.06 as compared to only 0.88 associated with his best fitting model. It should be obvious, however, that this particular version of the Fisherian rationally expected real rate model will not possess the least squares optimality property in terms of in-sample predictive efficiency that is achievable by simply regressing r_t on past values of P_t.

The root mean square errors (RMSE) and the average absolute errors (AAE) related to these three Fisherian real rate models have been given in Table 6.4. The inefficiency of the Fisherian Autoregressive model in relation to the other two rationally expected Fisherian real rate models are well illustrated by the RMSE and AAE figures. The notable result, however, is the revealed relative efficiency of the rationally expected real rate Method I when compared with the Fisherian indirect method introduced by Elliott [1977]; we find almost a 35% gain in predictive efficiency on the average.

The problem with the latter method is that R_t is known at the beginning of the period, and hence should also be used in the prediction of P_{t+1}. The resultant forecasted inflation rate can then be subtracted from the corresponding nominal rate to obtain a more efficient rationally expected EARR series. (Call it Method III) The results of the regressions of P_{t+1} on R_t, and P_{t+1} on (R_t, P_t, P_{t-1}, ...) were similar to those obtained by Fama [1975, 1977] and Nelson and Schwert [1977]; the introduction of R_t in the regression of P_{t+1} on (P_t, P_{t-1}, ...) was highly significant and the additional explanatory power of $(P_t, P_{t-1}, \ldots)$ in a regression of P_{t+1} on $(R_t, P_t, P_{t-1}, \ldots)$ turned out to be significant at a 5% level of significance (but not at the 1% level). The RMSE and AAE of this EARR series in relation EPRR over the sample period were .39 and .33 respectively (see Table 6.4) and are very close to those obtained by Method I. As a result, the estimated EARR series associated with these two methods were almost identical. The reason for the similar predictive efficiency is that the estimated coefficient of R_t in the regression of P_{t+1} on $(R_t, P_t, P_{t-1}, \ldots)$ was statistically not different from unity. The means of all the three EARR series were, however, the same (=1.58) as that of the ex-post real rates series.

The estimated real rate series generated by Method III together with the 6-month treasury bill rates have been presented in Table 6.5 and Figure 1. It is interesting to note that the economic recessions of 1960-61 and 1969-70 are clearly captured by the series. Also, the estimated EARR series serves to show why the sole use of changes in nominal rates are indicators of monetary ease or tightness may give misleading information about the direction of movements in ex ante real rates. On thirteen occasions out of a total of twenty-five, the rationally forecasted real rate changed in a direction opposite to that of the nominal rate due to the underlying movements in, and the effects of unobserved price expectations.

The real rate series reported by Carlson [1977b] has also been plotted in Figure 1 for the sake of comparison. Carlson's data tracks the nominal rate very closely primarily due to the sluggish behavior of his series on inflationary expectations. The average value of his real rate series over the comparable time period is considerably more than the average value of the rationally forecasted real rates. This is due to the fact that Carlson's [1977a] data on inflationary expectations contain substantial amount of systematic unanticipated inflation, and is consistent with our evidence presented so far. In addition, a rather steady but slow downward drift in our real rate series together with a steady increase in the nominal rate during 1959-71 explains our dual evidence on the Mundell effect and the real rate autoregressive parameter.

6.5 Conclusions

In reply to Fama's tests on market efficiency and the constancy of the *ex ante* real rate, Nelson and Schwert have pointed out that his tests might not be sufficiently powerful to reject the joint hypothesis. In particular, they have shown that a substantial variation in the EARR is compatible with a very low autocorrelation observed in the EPRR. By using the Nelson-Schwert framework as a convenient starting point, we have attempted further to decompose the variation in the EPRR into underlying variations in the EARR and price expectations. The main conclusions can be summarized as follows: (i) Over the sample period considered by Fama, the variation in the EARR constitutes nearly 49% of the variation in the EPRR on a semi-annual basis. However, the estimate fluctuated from nearly 14% to 56% depending on the particular sub-sample period chosen over 2/1959 - 2/1971. The autocorrelation in the *ex ante* real rate was calculated to be only around 0.3. (ii) The Mundell effect was found to be around 0.50. The percentage of the total variance in the nominal rate attributable to variations in the EARR stabilized around 25%, once the Mundell effect was taken into account. Thus, models which allow the EARR to vary and be correlated with price expectations appear to be more consistent with the efficient market hypothesis. (iii) We have reported a rationally forecasted real interest rate series which possesses the optimality property in terms in-sample predictive efficiency. The advantages of this method over the conventional Fisherian autoregressive procedure (e.g., Yohe and Karnosky) have been studied. Elliott has recently considered a real rate series obtained first by generating the rationally forecasted inflation variable and then subtracting the series from the nominal rates. Following Nelson and Schwert, we have shown that the in-sample predictive efficiency of this procedure can be substantially increased by including the nominal rate as another explanatory variable in the first stage regression. A downward drift in the estimated real rate series together with a steady increase in the nominal rate during 1959-71 is consistent with our evidence on the Mundell effect.

Table 6.1 IV Estimates of the Structural Parameters and Other Statistics*

Sample Period	σ_r^2	σ_i^2	σ_ε^2	ϕ	Corr.$(r\ r_{-1})$	σ_w^2
2/1959-1/1968	.743	.209	.528	.230	-.128	.198
2/1959-2/1968	.825	.330	.435	.324	.019	.296
2/1959-1/1969	.888	.317	.410	.294	.147	.289
2/1959-2/1969	.847	.355	.343	.277	.159	.328
2/1959-1/1970	.807	.453	.230	.240	.159	.427
2/1959-2/1970	.778	.182	.497	.381	.159	.155
2/1959-1/1971	.795	.386	.292	.192	.128	.372
2/1959-2/1971	.764	.104	.560	.299	.109	.094
2/1959-1/1972	.775	.567	.336	.364	.093	.492
2/1959-2/1972	.994	1.533	.076	.535	.191	1.094
2/1959-1/1973	1.620	2.097	.010	.647	.446	1.219
2/1959-2/1973	2.240	2.760	.107	.760	.638	1.168

* The structural model is given by (6.1) - (6.2). The variance estimates are annualized.

Table 6.2 Estimates of Structural Parameters in the Three-Indicator Model*

	$\sigma_{i\rho}$	β	σ^2_ρ	σ^2_i	σ^2_ε	σ^2_η
Six-Month Treasury Bills. 1/59 - 2/71	-.633	.611	2.66	.432	.317	.258
Three-month Treasury Bills. 1/1953-2/1973	-.420	.801	3.00	.612	1.60	.102

* The structural model is given by (6.11) - (6.13). The variance estimates are annalized.

Table 6.3* Test for 'No Mundel Effect' Where Expectations are Rational: 1959/1–1971/2

Dependent Variable	const.	Independent Variables P_t	P_{t-1}	P_{t-2}	P_{t-3}	P_{t-4}	P_{t-5}	P_{t-6}	P_{t-7}	P_{t-8}	R^2**	DW
R_t	3.70 (.266)	.830 (.112)	-.193 (.145)	.164 (.141)	.145 (.132)	-.362 (.130)	.065 (.115)	-.058 (.118)	.098 (.119)	-.481 (.111)	.833	2.18
P_{t+1}	1.02 (.412)	.959 (.173)	-.012 (.224)	.051 (.218)	.186 (.204)	-.407 (.201)	.201 (.178)	-.326 (.183)	.252 (1.83)	-.404 (.172)	.789	2.12***
$R_t - P_{t+1}$	2.68 (.255)	-.129 (.107)	-.181 (.139)	.113 (.135)	-.041 (.126)	.045 (.124)	-.136 (.110)	.068 (.113)	-.154 (.114)	-.773 (.106)	.488	2.06***

* Observations are biannual. R_t is the arithmetic average of six-month Treasury Bill rates, annualized and P_t is the annualized rate of inflation (percent). Sources: Federal Reserve and Bureau of Labor Statistics, respectively.

** F-tests were significant at the 1% level of significance in all the regressions. at the

*** Durbin's h-test for serial correlation (in the presence of lagged dependent variables) is insignificant at the 1% level.

Table 6.4 In-Sample Predictive Efficiency of Different Fisherian Real Rate Models; 1951/1-1971/2*

Model	Root Mean Square Errors (RMSE)	Average Absolute Error (AAE)
Fisherian Rationally Expected Real Rate Models:		
Method I	.41	.35
Method II	.66	.52
Method III	.39	.33
Fisherian Auto-regressive Model	2.26	2.18

* RMSE and AAE figures are in percentage. Method I generates EARR by regressing EPRR on lagged inflation variables. In Method II rationally forecasted inflation rate is first generated by regressing P_t on lagged inflation variables and then subtracting the results from nominal rate. Method III is similar to Method II except that R_t is also used as a regressor while generating the price forecasts.

Table 6.5 Estimated EARR and the Price Expectations: 1/1959-2/1971

Time Periods	Six-month Treasury Bill Rate	Ex-ante Real Rates*	Price Expectations*
1/59	3.24	2.65	.60
2/59	4.38	2.19	2.18
1/60	3.75	2.17	1.58
2/60	2.67	1.42	1.25
1/61	2.51	1.50	1.00
2/61	2.67	1.86	1.00
1/62	2.85	1.84	1.00
2/62	2.94	1.71	1.23
1/63	2.99	2.49	.49
2/63	3.52	2.01	1.50
1/64	3.64	2.23	1.40
2/64	3.72	1.76	1.96
1/65	3.95	2.19	1.76
2/65	4.14	2.03	2.10
1/66	4.75	1.93	2.81
2/66	5.35	1.57	3.78
1/67	4.18	1.84	2.34
2/67	5.04	1.54	3.49
1/68	5.44	1.89	3.56
2/68	5.49	1.19	4.29
1/69	6.29	1.10	5.19
2/69	7.42	.60	6.82
1/70	6.93	.75	6.18
2/70	6.01	.05	5.95
1/71	4.18	.88	3.20
2/71	4.83	.73	4.09

* Estimates are based on Method III (cf. table 6.4).

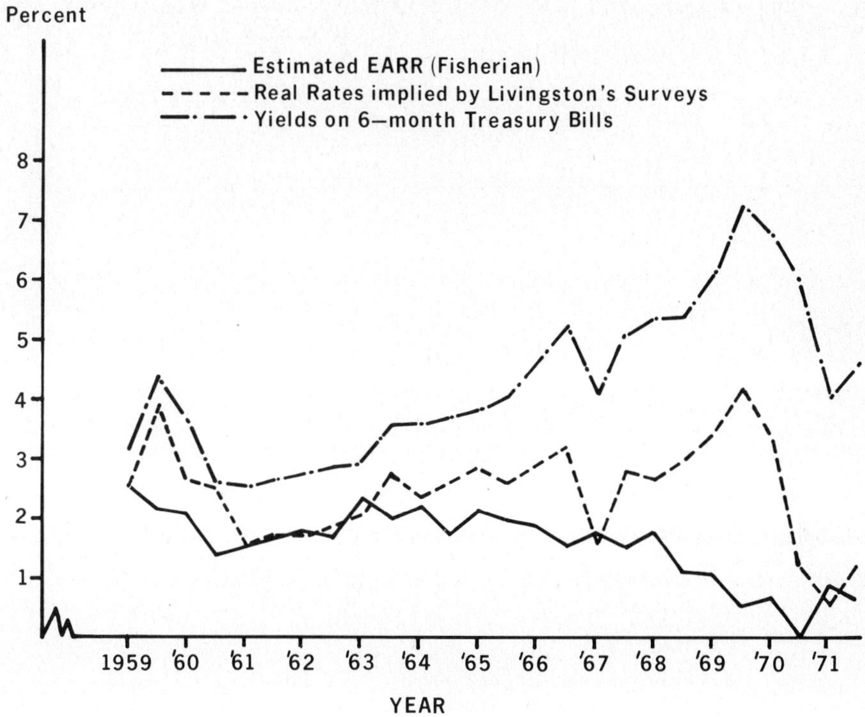

Figure 1. Rationally Expected EARR (Fisherian) and EARR Implied by Livingston's Surveys.

CHAPTER 7

CONCLUDING REMARKS

The main purpose of this study is to analyze inflationary expectations in such a way that econometric implications of different hypothesis on the formation of expectations can be delineated from the more fundamental behavioral implications in the context of certain standard monetary models. More specifically, we studied the role of price expectations in the wage-price dynamics of the U.S. economy and in the determination of short-term interest rates. Since expectations *per se* are unobservable, the relevance of any hypothesis on how they form has to be studied in relation to actual behavioral models. However, the problem with this approach is that the structure of behavioral models themselves are subject to controversy and consequently to usual econometric tests. Thus, the appropriate methodology for analyzing a variable like inflationary expectations has to evolve through a scientific interplay between the available data, conflicting hypotheses, and one's own degree of belief about beliefs regarding competing structures. Starting with the presumption that different markets may have different views about the future rate of inflation because they are exposed to different sets of information, we analyze the wage-price models and the models of interest rate determination in two separate parts. This proligative approach of treating expectations heterogenous across markets turned out to be fruitful.

Without being unduly repetitive, I shall now summarize the analysis of the preceding chapters, discuss some of the more important hypotheses we tested, and indicate the major conclusions that can be drawn from the material presented in parts I and II.

Three different models of expectations have been widely used in empirical works: adaptive, extrapolative and unrestricted distributed lag. Using a time series for the expected rate of inflation constructed from the 'consensus' forecasts of Livingston's surveys, Turnovsky [1970] tested these hypotheses directly. The same series was used by Turnovsky and Watcher [1972] to test the Accelerationist hypothesis. They found that though the observed data on price expectations are important in explaining wage changes, the coefficient is only around 0.20. Carlson [1977] has argued that the price expectations data is fundamentally flawed, because the series has been judgmentally adjusted by Livingston in an inconsistent fashion. To substantiate this speculation, we proposed in Chapter I an 'unobservable-variable' model which accommodates not only some random errors in measurement, but also the presence of a stochastic error term in the distributed lag model determining the true unobservable variable. Our calculations suggest that the survey data do, indeed, contain substantial errors in measurement. This partially explains why Turnovsky and Watcher [1972] found such low values for the coefficient corresponding to the price expectations variable in their wage equation. We also find that the size of the response of actual wage change to expectations is not invariant with respect to different measures of the tightness in the labor market. In particular, it is very sensitive to the presence of Perry's [1970] unemployment dispersion index.

Gibson [1972] and Pyle [1972] utilized this survey data on price expectations to test the celebrated Fisher relation, independent of any assumption on the formation of expectations. By using our general econometric framework in the context of interest rate equations, we again reach the conclusion that the series contains substantial errors in measurement. This also explains why both Gibson and Pyle obtained very low values for the price expectations coefficient. Our calculations also support earlier findings by Gibson and Turnovsky that both the interest rate equation and the expectations formation equation had a structural break around 1960. These results have been presented in Chapter 4.

We have also tested a new model of formation of expectations, recently formulated by Frenkel [1975] and Auernheimer [1979], which is a mixture of both adaptive and regressive elements. Specifically, the idea is that short-term expectations are influenced by two factors: (i) a regressive element, which is determined by the discrepancy between the actual inflation rate and an average long-term expected rate; and (ii) the usual adaptive element which is determined by the discrepancy between actual price and the expected short-term rate. In the context of both the wage and the interest rate equations, we found that the adaptive-regressive scheme outperformed all the three hypothesis considered by Turnovsky [1970].

In Chapter 2, we generalized the model presented in Chapter 1 by estimating a set of simultaneous wage-price models without any explicit modeling of the unobservable inflationary expectations. In addition to Livingston's survey measure, McGuire [1976] utilized an interest rate equation as an additional 'indicator' to estimate the wage-price equations. Gordon [1976] has pointed out certain methodological problems of using the Fisher relation in the context of wage-price models. Instead of using the interest rate equation, we exploited the overidentifying restrictions obtained by explicitly bringing in the simultaneity between wages and prices. The parameter estimates of the wage-price equations were found to be quite stable over the sample period 1951-73 when the Chow tests were applied to the reduced form equations. Thus, we show that the widely found parameter instability in the wage-price equations can partly be explained on the basis of a failure to take care of simultaneity together with the deterministic modeling of the price expectations variable (cf. Oi 1976).

We also point out that a dynamic implication of the Natural Rate hypothesis would predict the price expectations coefficient in the reduced form wage and price equations to be unity. For a wide range of models, our estimates support the Natural Rate hypothesis. This also highlights Cukierman's [1974] view that tests based on ordinary least squares estimates of structural wage-price equations may produce misleading conclusions. We also evaluated the Wage-Price Controls Program of the Nixon administration in terms of counterfactual predictions of the model. Since we do not use any fixed distributed lag proxy for price expectations, the current procedure is not vulnerable to Lucas [1976] type criticism that standard econometric policy evaluation permits policy rules to change but does not allow expectations mechanism to respond as economic theory predicts they will. Our results failed to indicate any restraining effect on wages; however, it showed large effects on price increases during the early phase of the Freeze, with a partial rebound in 1973.

In Chapter 3, we studied certain derivable implications of the rational expectations hypothesis and tested its validity in the context of our wage-price models. To examine the implications of a persistent unanticipated inflation on the existence of short-run Phillips curves, we have also used the Livingston's series on expected inflation which has been adjusted by Carlson [1977a]. A remarkable difference, that we found, between the models with survey data and the models with REH was that a number of labor market variables became statistically insignificant in all the models with REH. We, however, found a significant relationship between unemployment rate and the implied unanticipated rates of inflation. We experimented with a number of assumptions on the available information used in forming the expectations. The models with survey data, on the other hand, reveal a rather strong relationship between wage inflation and unemployment. Friedman [1979] has argued that the policy-ineffectiveness results in the Sargent-Wallace [1975] model are due to the extreme information-availability assumption used in their estimation. The prediction error implied by the REH is orthogonal to all the conditioning variables including the money supply. Thus, it is not surprising that the deviation of output from its 'natural' level in Sargent-Wallace's model is also independnet of monetary policy. Our evidence that the implementation of REH in the context of these models do wipe out the conventional short-run Phillips curves - are obtained without explicitly introducing the orthogonality assumption between the expectational errors and the policy variables.

Given the drastic policy implications associated with the REH, it is thus very important to test the REH itself. Here, we have utilized two approaches. In the first approach, we directly tested whether the actual price inflation can be taken as an unbiased proxy for the true underlying price expectations implicit in the wage-price models. In the second approach we tested the econometric implications of the REH after bringing in certain 'data-based' distributed lag functions for the exogenous variables. Wallis [1980] has shown that the restrictions generally take the form of cross-equation non-linear constrains across reduced form equations. All these tests overwhelmingly supported the Muthian rationality. It is interesting to note that the Carlson-adjusted Livingston's data on price expectations also appeared to be consistent with the wage equation.

In order to study the nature of price expectations in the determination of short-term interest rates, we tested three distinct hypotheses in Part II: (i) complete adjustment of nominal rates to changes in anticipated inflation; (ii) the rationality in the formation of expectations, i.e., the efficient market hypothesis; and (iii) the constancy of real interest rates. The problem in testing the above three hypotheses is that the validity of one of them can not be studied in isolation of the other two. The famous Fisher relation has been subjected to extensive econometric tests, including those by Fisher [1930] himself, utilizing distributed lag of past inflation rates as the observable proxy for inflationary expectations. However, the success of these proxies rather than the actual rate of inflation is inconsistent with a well-functioning capital market. In Chapter 5, we used the survey data and the one-period-ahead rate of inflation as two different indicators for the latent price expectations variable and found evidence in favor of a full Fisher effect. Our estimates associated with the six-month Treasury Bill rates indicated that the one-period-ahead prices tend to overestimate the true price expectations to a certain extent. While obtaining these estimates, we, however, did not allow for any correlation between real rates and the price expectations. It thus became apparent that a small negative correlation between anticipated inflation and real rate should be accommodated in the simple Fisherian framework in order to maintain the efficient market hypothesis. We also concluded that the use of certain income tax variables, loanable funds variables, capacity utilization rate, variables representing employment-output effects, and the level of uncertainty about inflation to explain possible variations in the real rate have no significant effect on these estimates, including that of the Fisher coefficient.

In Chapter 6, we analyzed interest rate models where the real rate could drift due to possible transitory real balance effects. Nelson and Schwert [1977] have demonstrated that low anticorrelation observed in the *ex-post* real rate could indicate rather strong autocorrelation and significant variation in *ex ante* real rate. By using the Nelson-Schwert framework as a convenient starting point, we have further decomposed the variation in the *ex post* real rate into underlying variations in the *ex ante* real rate and price expectations. It is demonstrated that all the structural parameters of the Nelson-Schwert model are identifiable and can be consistently estimated; as such, the random forecasting errors associated with the REH need not confound the problem of identifying variations in the *ex ante* real rate. We also found a significantly negative correlation between real rate and price expectations. The percentage of total variance in the nominal rate attributable to variations in the EARR stabilized around 25%, once the *Mundell effect* was taken into account. Thus, models which allow the *ex ante* real rates to vary and be correlated with price expectations appear to be more consistent with the efficient market hypothesis. We have also calculated a rationally forecasted real interest rate series, which possesses the optimality property in terms of in-sample predictive efficiency. The advantages of this method over the conventional autoregressive procedure (e.g, Yohe and Karnosky) have been studied in greater detail. It is also demonstrated that our real rate series based on the sample Fisherian framework is as good as the best performing Keynesian model in Elliott [1977] in terms of predictive efficiency. The performance of the so-called Fisherian autoregressive model (cf. Elliott) is generally very poor because the rationality criterion is not imposed while estimating the model.

It is interesting to note that the interest rate equations tend to imply that Livingston's data on price expectations systematically underestimated true price expectations implicit in the financial-assets market. On the other hand, the wage-price models considered in Part I do not seem to imply any such systematic errors in measurement. Thus, it appears that the underlying price expectations in the financial assets market and in the markets for labor and output, may not fundamentally be homogeneous. Financial markets are much well organized, the items traded are highly standardized, and there are substantial incentives to gather new information. The speculators in these markets are able to force prices to adjust to the levels consistent with most complete information. Thus, agents in different markets may be exposed to different bits of information. (See Cukierman and Watchel 1979). Labor markets, however, do not behave in this way. There is no such arbitrage mechanism to force rapid adjustment because adjustment and mobility costs very often prohibit instantaneous changes in labor contracts. Thus, the variation in the underlying price expectations implied by the wage-price dynamics can, indeed, be less than the variation in the actual inflation rate. Also, the institution of overlapping long-term labor contracts (implicit and explicit), which has been rationalized as a risk shifting device, inject an element of short-run wage stickiness in the wage-price process (see, for instance Barro [1977], Fischer [1977], and McCallum [1977]). There are losses incurred, in terms of real resources, by too-frequent or too-precipitate revisions of price lists and wage scales (see Phelps and Taylor [1977]). In addition, Turnovsky [1979] has argued that oligopolistic elements in both the labor market and the output market may deter instantaneous adjustment to new information. Thus, the apparently sluggish behavior of the price expectations series may as well be consistent with rationality, given the environment in which wages and prices are set.

APPENDIX A

FULL-INFORMATION MAXIMUM-LIKELIHOOD ESTIMATION IN TRIANGULAR MODELS

The structural specification of some of the econometric models we estimated in Chapters 1, 3 and 4 were <u>triangular</u>. Here we shall discuss certain very unusual properties of such models. These models are triangular in the sense that there exists an ordering of endogenous variables and equations such that the ith equation contains the ith endogenous variable, and may also contain endogenous variables whose position in the ordering is less than i, but does not contain endogenous variables whose position in the ordering is greater than i. To be more explicit, let us write the model as

$$YB + XC + U = 0 ,$$

where Y is the TxG matrix containing T observations on teh G endogenous variables; X is the TxK matrix containing observations on the K predetermined variables; U is a TxG matrix of distrubances; and B and C are GxG and KxG matrices of unknown parameters. The model is triangular if the matrix B is upper triangular; thatis, if $B_{ij} = 0$ for $i > j$.

A recursive model is a special type of triangular model, which is characterized by the additional requirement that the disturbance covariance matrix, Σ, be diagonal. Recursive models have been widely studied and are of considerable theoretical interest because of their unusual statistical properties. Most notably, it is well known that in a recursive model, the ordinary least squares (OLS) estimates are consistent and in fact are identical to the full information maximum likelihood (FIML) estimates.

On the other hand, triangular systems with non-diagonal disturbance covariance matrix have received very little attention, despite the fact that they have appeared repeatedly in economics and other Social Sciences. For example, the method of "path analysis," which is widely used in sociology, involves structural models which are triangular but which need not be recursive; see, for example, Land [1973].

Triangular systems have been treated briefly in Hausman [1975] and Zellner [1971]. Hausman observes that in a triangular system, the Jacobian term in the likelihood function vanishes, so that the likelihood function is the same so for the usual seemingly unrelated regressions problem. He then observes that this implies that "the generalized least squares estimator is appropriate to use," [1975, p. 730] but he does not go on to investigate the precise sense in which this is true. On the other hand, Zellner [1971, pp. 252-253] treats triangular systems from a Bayesian point of view, and finds that the posterior p.d.f. is the seme as for a seemingly unrelated regressions problem. However, Zellner does not investigate the implications of this observation for the usual two-step generalized least squares estimation procedure.

In an interesting paper, Chow [1974] systematically catalogs a family of estimators for systems of simultaneous stochastic equations obtained by modifying the statistical assumptions concerning the model and/or simplifying the computations based on the solution of the likelihood equations by Newton's method. The simplifying statistical assumptions are that (i) the variance-covariance matrix of structural disturbances (Σ) may be diagonal or block diagonal with B triangular or block-triangular; (ii) Σ is diagonal or block diagonal with B full. But he does not discuss the case where B is triangular but Σ is non-diagonal.

First, we shall demonstrate that generalized least squares (GLS), based on any consistent estimator of Σ, gives consistent estimates of the parameters in triangular models. This is analogous to the result that OLS gives consistent estimates in recursive models, but it is somewhat counter-intuitive since the right-hand-side endogenous variables are correlated with the disturbances. We shall then compare the asymptotic efficiency of the GLS estimates to that of the FIML and 3SLS estimates. It will be proved that an iterative GLS based on consistent estimate of Σ is in fact the full-information maximum likelihood estimator in such models.

Consistency of Generalized Least Squares

The model is

$$YB + XC + U = 0 \ ,$$

with B upper triangular. We can write the ith equation as

$$\begin{aligned} y_i &= Y_i\beta_i + X_i\gamma_i + u_i \\ &= Z_i\alpha_i + u_i \ , \qquad Z_i = (Y_iX_i) \ , \ \alpha_i = \begin{bmatrix} \beta_i \\ \gamma_i \end{bmatrix} . \end{aligned}$$

Here y_i is the vector of observations on the ith endogenous variable; Y_i and X_i are matrices of observations on the endogenous and predetermined variables that actually appear in the ith equation; and β_i and γ_i are appropriate vectors of parameters. Note that because the model is triangular,

$$Y_i = (y_1, y_2, \ldots, y_{i-1}) \ .$$

We can write all G equations as

$$\begin{bmatrix} y_1 \\ y_2 \\ \cdot \\ \cdot \\ \cdot \\ y_G \end{bmatrix} = \begin{bmatrix} Z_1 & 0 & 0 \ldots & 0 \\ 0 & Z_2 & 0 \ldots & 0 \\ \cdot & & \ddots & \cdot \\ \cdot & & & \cdot \\ 0 & 0 & 0 \ldots & Z_G \end{bmatrix} \begin{bmatrix} \alpha_1 \\ \alpha_2 \\ \cdot \\ \cdot \\ \cdot \\ \alpha_G \end{bmatrix} + \begin{bmatrix} u_1 \\ u_2 \\ \cdot \\ \cdot \\ \cdot \\ u_G \end{bmatrix}$$

or, in compact notation,

$$y_* = Z_* \alpha_* + U_* ,$$

The covariance matrix of U_* is $\Sigma \otimes I_T$, so the GLS estimate of α_* -- based on the assumption that Σ is known -- is

$$\hat{\alpha}_* = \{Z_*'[\Sigma^{-1} \otimes I]Z_*\}^{-1} Z_*' (\Sigma^{-1} \otimes I)y_*$$

$$= \alpha + \{Z_*'[\Sigma^{-1} \otimes I]Z_*\}^{-1} Z_*' (\Sigma^{-1} \otimes I)U_* .$$

Clearly then

$$\text{plim}\ \hat{\alpha}_* = \alpha + \text{plim}\ \{\frac{1}{T} Z_*'(\Sigma^{-1} \otimes I)Z_*\}^{-1} .\ \ \text{plim}\ \frac{1}{T} Z_*'(\Sigma^{-1} \otimes I)U_* ,$$

and the consistency of $\hat{\alpha}_*$ hinges on whether or not it is true that

$$\text{plim}\ \frac{1}{T} Z_*'(\Sigma^{-1} \otimes I)U_* = 0 .$$

At first glance the above condition would seem very unlikely, since Z_* and U_* are correlated. However, let us look more carefully. It is true that

$$\text{plim}\ \frac{1}{T} Z_*'(\Sigma^{-1} \otimes I) U_* = \text{plim}\ \frac{1}{T} \begin{bmatrix} \sum_j \sigma^{1j} Z_1' u_j \\ \sum_j \sigma^{2j} Z_2' u_j \\ \vdots \\ \sum_j \sigma^{Gj} Z_G' u_j \end{bmatrix} \tag{A1}$$

Clearly the first term in this vector is zero, since Z_1 contains only predetermined variables. However, to calculate the other terms we need an expression for $\text{plim}\ (1/T) Z_i' u_j$.

It is easy to verify that

$$\text{plim}\ \frac{1}{T} Y'U = -(B^{-1})'\Sigma \ .$$

This is true whether or not B is triangular. But if B is upper triangular, so is B^{-1}. Therefore

$$\text{plim}\ \frac{1}{T} Y'U = - \begin{bmatrix} B_{11} & 0 & 0 \cdot\cdot & 0 \\ B^{12} & B^{22} & 0 \cdot\cdot & 0 \\ \cdot & & & \\ \cdot & & & \\ B^{1G} & B^{2G} & \cdot\cdot\cdot\cdot\cdot & B^{GG} \end{bmatrix} \begin{bmatrix} \sigma_{11} & \sigma_{12} & \cdot\cdot & \sigma_{1G} \\ \sigma_{21} & \sigma_{22} & \cdot\cdot & \sigma_{2G} \\ \cdot & & & \\ \cdot & & & \\ \cdot & & & \\ \sigma_{G1} & \sigma_{G2} & \cdot\cdot & \sigma_{GG} \end{bmatrix}$$

of which the i, j th element is

$$\text{plim}\ \frac{1}{T}y_i'u_j = -\sum_{k=1}^{i} B^{ki}\sigma_{kj}\ . \tag{A2}$$

We return now to the second element in the vector in equation (A1)

$$\text{plim}\ \left(\frac{1}{T}\sum_j \sigma^{2j} Z_2'u_j\right) = \text{plim}\ \frac{1}{T}\sum_j \sigma^{2j}\begin{bmatrix} y_1'u_j \\ X_2'u_j \end{bmatrix}$$

$$= \begin{bmatrix} \sum_j \sigma^{2j}\ \text{plim}\ \frac{1}{T}y_1'u_j \\ 0 \end{bmatrix},$$

X_2 contains predetermined variables. But

$$\sum_j \sigma^{2j}\ \text{plim}\ \frac{1}{T}y_1'u_j = \sum_j \sigma^{2j}B^{11}\sigma_{1j} \qquad \text{(using (A2) above)}$$

$$= B^{11}\sum_j \sigma^{2j}\sigma_{1j} = 0\ .$$

A similar result holds for all elements in the vector in (A1) above. For example, the mth element is

$$\text{plim}\ \frac{1}{T}\sum_j \sigma^{mj} Z_m'u_j\ ,$$

of which the only possible non-zero elements are of the form

$$\text{plim}\ \frac{1}{T}\sum_j \sigma^{mj} y_i'u_j \qquad (i<m)$$

$$= \sum_j \sigma^{mj}\sum_{k=1}^{i} B^{ki}\sigma_{kj}$$

$$= \sum_{k=1}^{i} B^{ki}\sum_{j=1}^{G}\sigma^{mj}\sigma_{kj} = 0 \quad (\text{since } k\leq i<m)\ .$$

This implies that the probability limit in (A1) is equal to zero. As a result, it has been established that, in a triangular system, the GLS estimator is consistent. This is somewhat remarkable since the GLS estimator does not "correct for" the simultaneity of the model.

The same demonstration would be valid if the GLS estimator were based on any consistent estimator of Σ. But note that we can not get a consistent estimator of Σ from OLS residuals, as OLS is inconsistent here. As a result the usual two-step procedure of estimating seemingly unrelated regressions (Zellner [1972]) would have to be modified slightly. For example, we could first estimate the model by 2SLS, to get a consistent estimate of Σ, and then apply GLS. This estimator would differ from the usual 3SLS estimator in that it does not substitute instruments for the right-hand-side endogenous variables in the final step.

From a theoretical point of view, it is somewhat interesting that in 3SLS the consistency of $\hat{\Sigma}$ is not necessary for the consistency of the resulting coefficients; it is necessary for their asymptotic efficiency. (See Hendry [1976, p. 56]). However, in GLS the consistency of $\hat{\Sigma}$ is necessary for the consistency of the resulting coefficient estimates.

Relative Efficiency of Generalized Least Squares

In this section we compare the (asymptotic) efficiency of GLS to that of 3SLS and FIML. This comparison turns out to be different when Σ is known than when it it not known.

Consider first the case in which Σ is known. In this case it is well known that FIML is efficient relative to 3SLS. Furthermore, GLS (based on known Σ) is numerically identical to FIML in a triangular system. This can be seen more clearly by writing the logarithmic likelihood function as

$$L = -\frac{GT}{2}\log(2\pi) - \frac{T}{2}\log|\Sigma| + T\log|B| \tag{A3}$$

$$-\frac{1}{2}(y_* - Z_*\alpha_*)'(\Sigma^{-1}\otimes I)(y_* - Z_*\alpha_*) .$$

When B is upper triangular (and normalized in the usual way, i.e., $B_{ii} = -1$ for all i), $\log|B| = 0$. Furthermore, when Σ is known, $\log|\Sigma|$ is constant, and the maximum likelihood estimator will simply minimize the sum of squares

$$(y_* - Z_*\alpha_*)'(\Sigma^{-1}\otimes I)(y_* - Z_*\alpha_*). \tag{A4}$$

But this is precisely the sum of squares minimized by the GLS estimator of α_* (based on known Σ).

The result is that when Σ is known, GLS is identical to FIML. It is more efficient than 3SLS in this case. However, cases in which Σ is known are apt to be zero.

We now consider the case in which Σ is unknown, so that GLS is based on some consistent estimator $\hat{\Sigma}$. It is well known that when Σ is unknown, FIML and 3SLS are equally efficient. However, GLS turns out to be inefficient, unless it is based on an efficient estimate of Σ.

To show this, consider the GLS estimator

$$\tilde{\alpha}_* = [Z_*'(\hat{\Sigma}^{-1}\otimes I)Z_*]^{-1}Z_*'(\hat{\Sigma}^{-1}\otimes I)y_* .$$

We note that the FIML estimator of α_* is of this form, with $\hat{\Sigma}$ equal to the FIML estimator of Σ. The relevant question is therefore whether the asymptotic distribution of $\tilde{\alpha}_*$ depends on the asymptotic distribution of $\hat{\Sigma}$.

We therefore consider the asymptotic distribution of

$$\sqrt{T}\,(\tilde{\alpha}_* - \alpha_*) = [\,\tfrac{1}{T}Z_*'(\hat{\Sigma}^{-1}\otimes I)Z_*]^{-1}\,\tfrac{1}{\sqrt{T}}Z_*'(\hat{\Sigma}^{-1}\otimes I)U_* \,. \tag{A5}$$

It is clear that

$$\text{plim}\,[\,\tfrac{1}{T}Z_*'(\hat{\Sigma}^{-1}\otimes I)Z_*]^{-1} = \text{plim}\,[\,\tfrac{1}{T}Z_*'(\Sigma^{-1}\otimes I)Z_*]^{-1}$$

as long as $\hat{\Sigma}$ is consistent. The problem is therefore reduced to considering the asymptotic distribution of

$$\frac{1}{\sqrt{T}}\,Z_*'(\hat{\Sigma}^{-1}\otimes I)U_* = \frac{1}{\sqrt{T}}\begin{bmatrix}\sum_j \hat{\sigma}^{1j}Z_1'u_j \\ \sum_j \hat{\sigma}^{2j}Z_2'u_j \\ \vdots \\ \sum_j \hat{\sigma}^{Gj}Z_G'u_j\end{bmatrix} \tag{A6}$$

The second (block) element of this vector is typical (but simple), so we consider

$$\frac{1}{\sqrt{T}}\sum_j \hat{\sigma}^{2j}Z_2'u_j = \frac{1}{\sqrt{T}}\sum_j \sigma^{2j}Z_2'u_j + \frac{1}{\sqrt{T}}\sum_j(\hat{\sigma}^{2j} - \sigma^{2j})Z_2'u_j \,. \tag{A7}$$

We first need to establish that the first term on the right hand side of (A7) has a well defined asymptotic distribution. To do so note that

$$Z_2 = (y_1, X_2) = (\bar{y}_1, X_2) + (v_1, 0) \equiv \bar{Z}_2 + v_1^*$$

where $\bar{y}_1 = E(y_1)$, as given by its reduced form, and v_1 is the first reduced form disturbance. As a result we can write

$$\frac{1}{\sqrt{T}} \sum_j \sigma^{2j} Z_2' u_j = \frac{1}{\sqrt{T}} \sum_j \sigma^{2j} \bar{Z}_2' u_j + \frac{1}{\sqrt{T}} \sum_j \sigma^{2j} \begin{bmatrix} v_1' u_j \\ 0 \end{bmatrix} \qquad \text{(A8)}$$

Now, the first term on the right hand side of (A8) is exactly the quantity encountered in the aysmptotic distribution of 3SLS, and has a well defined asymptotic distribution. On the other hand, the non-zero part of the second term can be written as

$$\frac{1}{\sqrt{T}} \sum_j \sigma^{2j} v_1' u_j = -B^{11} \sum_j \frac{1}{\sqrt{T}} \sigma^{2j} u_1' u_j \quad ,$$

using the fact that $v_1 = -B^{11} u_1$ (due to triangularity of B^{-1}). The central limit theorem implies that this is asymptotically normal with mean

$$-B^{11} \sum_j \sigma^{2j} \sigma_{1j} = 0$$

and finite variance. Thus we are justified in concluding that the first term on the right hand side of (A8) has a well-defined asymptotic distribution.

As a result, we turn to the second term on the right hand side of (A7),

$$\frac{1}{\sqrt{T}} \Sigma(\hat{\sigma}^{2j} - \sigma^{2j}) Z_2' u_j = \sum_j \sqrt{T}\, (\hat{\sigma}^{2j} - \sigma^{2j}) \, \frac{1}{T} Z_2' u_j \ . \qquad \text{(A9)}$$

Unfortunately, this term does not vanish asymptotically, since $\sqrt{T}\,(\hat{\sigma}^{2j} - \sigma^{2j})$ has a well-defined asymptotic distribution, while $\frac{1}{T} Z_2' u_j$ has a non-zero probability limit. This is the essential difference between GLS and 3SLS; in 3SLS we would be dealing with $\frac{1}{T} \hat{Z}_2' u_j$, which has a probability limit of zero.

The implication is that the asymptotic distribution of

$$\frac{1}{\sqrt{T}} Z_*'(\hat{\Sigma}^{-1} \otimes I)U_*$$

depends on the asymptotic distribution of $\hat{\Sigma}$. Therefore, so does the asymptotic distribution of $\sqrt{T}\,(\tilde{\alpha}_* - \alpha_*)$. GLS, based on any $\hat{\Sigma}$ which does not have the same asymptotic distribution as the FIML estimate of Σ, will be inefficient relative to FIML (and 3SLS). This considerably limits the desirability of using GLS (rather than 3SLS) in triangular systems.

One way out of this difficulty is to <u>iterate</u> GLS. This estimator, sometimes referred to as "IZEF" (see, e.g., Kmenta and Gilbert [1968]) minimizes the sum of squares in (A4), and is therefore just a computational algorithm for FIML in this case.

APPENDIX B

THE MAXIMUM-LIKELIHOOD FRAMEWORK FOR GENERATING PRICE FORECASTS FROM SRC DATA

The purpose of this section is to develop an appropriate econometric methodology for analyzing data on price expectations collected by the Survey Research Center (SRC) of the University of Michigan. These responses have been collected approximately every quarter since 1948 and represent a random sample of approximately 2,000 U.S. households on the average. This is in contrast to the Livingston data which is composed of forecasts by professional economists (see Appendix C). The SRC data is, for the most part, qualitative in nature and design. In the early years of the questionnaire only a respondent's feeling about the direction of future prices is investigated. In the later years, price forecasts are only received from respondents who think prices will increase. As a result, the analysis of these data is not as straight-forward as with the Livingston data, where actual price forecasts were received from each respondent. We shall generate a series on one-year ahead price change expectation together with a measure of variability of forecasts. Our price expectations series will then be compared with the Livingston series and the series generated by deMenil and Bhalla [1975]. The latter study also use the SRC data.

Since the SRC Surveys cover a much wider cross-section of the population, this series may perform pretty well in the estimation of Phillips curves. In addition, we can also study the role of uncertainty of price forecasts in explaining the observed patterns of inflation and unemployment in recent years.

The SRC Price Expectation Questions

The SRC has asked respondents several different questions concerning inflationary expectations over the years. The specific questions asked and the frequency of these questions is documented in Juster [1973] and deMenil and Bhalla [1975]. The most consistently asked question concerns the behavior of price levels in the coming year. Specifically, the question is

> Q1: "Thinking about prices of things you buy in general, do you think they will go up in the next year or so, or go down, or stay where they are now?"

A careful reading of Q1 will reveal that the question is addressing changes in price levels and not changes in the rate of inflation. So it would seem reasonable to take price level forecasts *per se* as the point of departure in modeling Q1 and then to infer the expected rate of inflation from these forecasts. This is in essence what is done when the Livingston data is analyzed. Livingston's survey asked specifically for price level forecasts which are converted to expected inflation rates before examination.

Starting in 1966:2 the SRC has asked a follow-up question to those who replied "prices would go up" to Q1. This question is

> Q2: "How large a price increase do you expect? of course, nobody can know for sure, but would you say that a year from now prices will be about 1 or 2% higher, 5%, or closer to 10% higher than now or what?"

The responses to Q2 tended to be grouped about the prompted values, even though they could be chosen from five categories: 1-2%, 3-4%, 5%, 6-9% or 10+%. Ordinarily this prompting might bias these responses in such a way that they are not true measures of price forecasts. However, in this instance there is reason to believe that the prompting has no effect on the true responses. The evidence to support this comes from supplementary surveys conducted by the SRC during the 1970's. In these surveys an open-ended version of Q2 was asked -- "About how much do you expect prices to go up?" -- where the responses are not grouped in any specific price range. Here again, most of the responses tended to fall in the groupings 1-2%, 5%, 10%, and also 15% and 20%. So it seems unlikely that the prompting will bias the responses to Q2.

Modeling the Survey Responses

To model these questions one needs an assumption about the process generating price expectations and a method of utilizing the "prices will stay the same" responses. Using a price level interpretation of these questions, we will posit

$$P^*_{it} = \mu_t + u_{it} \tag{B.1}$$

to describe price level forecasts made by $i = 1, \ldots, N_t$ individuals in quarter $t = 1, \ldots, T$, where μ_t is the mean forecast at each period t and u_{it} is a random forecast error with zero mean and variance σ_t^2. The forecast horizon for both questions is one year. Thus P^*_{it} will represent the forecast distribution of P_{t+4} with mean μ_t and variance σ^2, where P_{t+4} is the actual price level four quarters from now.

A more general representation of (B.1) would have μ_t a function of exogenous variables that these individuals utilize in making their forecasts. At the present this is an unnecessary complication, since we are mainly interested in describing how to use the SRC data and not what variables determine expectations.

To incorporate (B.1) and the "stay the same" responses into a model of the directional question we will use the notion of a difference limen, denoted as δ_t. This will effectively avoid the possibility of mass points in our probability distribution. The <u>difference limen</u> represents a range $(-\delta_t, \delta_t)$ where a change in prices is not perceivable. We will assume this range to be a constant fraction of the current price level, i.e., $\delta_t = \delta P_t$. Hence, using the <u>difference limen</u> notion and the above model, we can separate the responses to the directional question into three mutually exclusive categories. These may be grouped using the following index:

$$I_{it} = \begin{cases} 1 & \text{iff } u_{it} > P_t - \mu_t + \delta P_t \\ 0 & \text{iff } P_t - \mu_t - \delta P_t \le u_{it} \le P_t - \mu_t + \delta P_t \\ -1 & \text{iff } P_t - \mu_t - \delta P_t > u_{it} \end{cases} \tag{B.2}$$

where, by implication, $I_{it} = 1$ if the reply was "prices will go up," $I_{it} = 0$ if the reply was "prices will remain the same," and $I_{it} = -1$ if the reply was "prices will go down."

This formulation of the directional question assumes that all individuals are informed about the value of P_t. If this was not the case it would be more appropriate to analyze these responses in terms of the rate of inflation. This could be done by dividing the conditioning terms in (B.2) by P_t. Thus, our model is transformed into one of positive ($>\delta$) or negative ($<\delta$) rates of inflation.

Now, turning our attention to the follow-up question, we must be mindful of the fact these responses are only obtained from individuals who said "prices will go up." Hence, simple averages of these numbers will not be unbiased estimates of the mean μ_t in (B.1). These responses must be weighted to prevent an upward bias in this average. A complete solution to this problem will also include the information in the directional question. Specifically, we will now observe P^*_{it} when an individual replies "prices will go up." As such, instead of (B.2), we will observe

$$P^0_{it} = \begin{cases} P^*_{it} & \text{iff } P^*_{it} - P_t > \delta P_t \\ \phi & \text{if } -\delta P_t \leq P^*_{it} - P_t \geq \delta P_t \\ \phi & \text{if } -\delta P_t > P^*_{it} - P_t \end{cases} \tag{B.3}$$

Here ϕ is the empty set and P^*_{it} is the forecasted price level of the ith individual.

Thus, our problem becomes one of estimating the parameters of (B.1) using the directional question alone or both questions together. We are only interested in utilizing all of the information in the sample so we will use the responses to both questions jointly to estimate the parameters of our model.

The idea of examining Q1 in terms of the rate of inflation is used by Shuford [1970], deMenil [1973], Carlson and Parkin [1975] and Wachtel [1977]. These papers assume that the rate of inflation may be described by

$$p^e_{it} = \mu_t + \varepsilon_{it} , \tag{B.4}$$

where p^e_{it} is the rate of inflation forecast at period t by individual i, μ_t is the mean rate of inflation, and ε_{it} is a random error with mean zero and variance $\sigma^2_{\varepsilon t}$. If the ε_{it} are independent random variables we may use the sample proportions in any time period to estimate μ . That is to say, with the mean only a function of time if we have a large sample then the sample proportion can be considered a good estimate of the true population proportion. Thus, if we define A_t = Pr {"prices will go up"} and B_t = Pr {"prices will go down"}, then

$$A_t = \Pr\left\{\frac{p^e_{it} - \mu_t}{\sigma_{\varepsilon t}} > \frac{\delta - \mu_t}{\sigma_{\varepsilon t}}\right\}$$

$$B_t = P\left\{\frac{p^e_{it} - \mu_t}{\sigma_{\varepsilon t}} < \frac{-\delta - \mu_t}{\sigma_{\varepsilon t}}\right\} \quad . \qquad \text{(B.5)}$$

Given a distributional assumption for ε_{it}, (B.5) may be solved to give estimates of δ and μ_t, δ and $\sigma_{\varepsilon t}$, or μ_t and $\sigma_{\varepsilon t}$, but not all three parameters simultaneously. Thus the estimates of μ_t will be scaled by either $\sigma_{\varepsilon t}$ or δ. The usual approach is to scale the estimates by δ, where δ is often arbitrarily chosen. This approach is somewhat suspect because the estimates will be very sensitive to the scale parameter. For the normal distribution these estimates will be linearly related to δ, and thus a systematic and constant underestimate or overestimate of the rate of inflation may be eliminated by the proper choice of δ. In Fishe and Lahiri [1981] a logistic formulation was used to avoid this identification problem.

Now, turning our attention to Q2, we shall first examine how others have utilized these grouped estimates in generating a series of inflationary expectations. deMenil and Bhalla [1975] calculate a price expectation series by computing a weighted average of the responses to Q2. The midpoint of each category is used for the price forecast with a zero substituted for those who expected prices to remain the same or go down. The same procedure is followed in Juster [1973] except that -3% is used as the point estimate for the "go down" category and also, in Juster and Comment [1978] except that here the responses are not grouped into categories thus enabling them to estimate exact sample means. Once these weighted averages are calculated the techniques used in each paper differ greatly. Juster [1973] stops here in the sense that these estimates are not used to back-calculate pre-1966:2 forecasts. However, Juster and Comment [1978] and deMenil and Bhalla [1975] work backwards from these estimates and the responses to Q1 to generate forecasts back to 1948. The linking mechanism is somewhat arbitrary, but essentially involves a scheme whereby the difference between the percentage expecting prices to increase and the percentage expecting prices to decrease is related to these weighted averages. The main problem with this procedure is that it ignores the fact that the weighted averages from Q2 are derived only from respondents who felt prices would increase. In this respect their estimates for both pre-1966 and post-1966 price expectations are biased upwards.

Joint Estimation of Price Expectations

There are several techniques that may be used to estimate the parameters of (B.1) from the responses to these questions. The most direct approach, and the one used here, is to specify a distribution for u_{it} and apply the method of maximum likelihood to the specification in (B.3). We will assume that the errors in the price forecasts are normally distributed. The index I_{it} defined in (B.2) may be used to separate the sample here: define $\psi_1 = \{i|I_{it} = 1\}$, $\psi_2 = \{i|I_{it} = 0\}$, and $\psi_3 = \{i|I_{it} = -1\}$. The likelihood function for (B.3) is

$$L = \prod_{\psi_1} f(P^0_{it} - \mu_t) \prod_{\psi_2} (\Phi(D_t) - \Phi(C_t)) \prod_{\psi_3} \Phi(C_t), \tag{B.6}$$

where $C_t = \sigma_t^{-1}(P_t - \mu_t - \delta P_t)$, $D_t = \sigma_t^{-1}(P_t - \mu_t + \delta P_t)$, $\Phi(\cdot)$ is the standard normal distribution function, and $f(\lambda)$ is the normal density function evaluated at λ. The log likelihood function becomes

$$\log L = -\sum_t^{\psi_1} \frac{N_{1t}}{2} \log 2\pi - \sum_t^{\psi_1} \frac{N_{1t}}{2} \log \sigma_t^2 - \sum_t^{\psi_1} \sum_i \left(\frac{P_{it}^0 - \mu_t}{\sigma_t}\right)$$

$$+ \sum_t^{\psi_2} N_{2t} \log[\Phi(D_t) - \Phi(C_t)] + \sum_t^{\psi_3} N_{3t} \log[\Phi(C_t)] \tag{B.7}$$

where N_{1t} = the number of responses in the "go up" category at time t,

N_{2t} = the number of responses in the "stay the same" category, and

N_{3t} = the number of responses in the "go down" category.

Maximizing (B.6) will give consistent and efficient estimates for μ_t, σ_t, and δ. To solve for these estimates, we treat (B.6) as conditional on δ and iterate over μ_t and σ_t^2. The equations for μ_t and σ_t^2 are obtained as follows:

$$\frac{\partial \log L}{\partial \mu_t} = \frac{1}{\sigma_t^2} [\sum_i^{\psi_1} P_{it}^0 - N_{1t}\mu_t] - \frac{N_{2t}}{\sigma^t} [\frac{\phi(D_t) - \phi(C_t)}{\Phi(D_t) - \Phi(C_t)}]$$

$$- \frac{N_{3t}}{\sigma_t} \frac{\phi(C_t)}{\Phi(C_t)} = 0 \tag{B.8}$$

$$\frac{\partial \log L}{\partial \sigma_t^2} = -\frac{N_{1t}}{2\sigma_t^2} + \frac{1}{2\sigma_t^4} \sum_i^{\psi_1} (P_{it}^0 - \mu_t)^2$$

$$- \frac{N_{2t}}{2\sigma_t^2} [\frac{D_t\, \phi(D_t) - C_t\, \phi(C_t)}{\Phi(D_t) - \Phi(C_t)}] = 0 \tag{B.9}$$

where $\phi(\cdot)$ is N (0,1).

Equations (B.8) - (B.9) can be solved to yield solutions for μ_t and σ_t as:

$$\mu_t = N_{1t}^{-1} [\sum_i^{\psi_1} P_{it}^0 - \sigma_t N_{2t} [\frac{\phi(D_t) - \phi(C_t)}{\Phi(D_t) - \Phi(C_t)}] - \sigma_t N_{3t} \frac{\phi(C_t)}{\Phi(C_t)}] \tag{B.10}$$

$$\sigma_t^2 = \sum_i^{\psi_1} (P_{it}^0 - \mu_t)^2 [N_{1t} + N_{2t}(\frac{D_t\phi(D_t) - C_t\phi(C_t)}{\Phi(D_t) - \Phi(C_t)}) + N_{3t} \frac{C_t\phi(C_t)}{\Phi(C_t)}]^{-1} \tag{B.11}$$

The final maximum likelihood estimates are obtained by solving (B.10) - (B.11) successively over different values of δ until the log-likelihood value reaches a maximum. The ML estimate of δ was found out to be .02 which implies that during this sample period, the respondents' average rate of imperceptability for a price change was -2.0% to +2.0%. Carlson and Parkin [1975] did not directly estimate δ from the British data; instead they used δ to scale p_t^e such that the mean of their price forecasts is equal to the average rate of inflation over the sample period. The value of δ obtained by this method was 1.76%. On the other hand, Juster and Comment [1978] assumed a value of δ equal to 1.25%. Even though these estimates are arbitrary, they compare favorably with our estimates of δ, although they appear to be somewhat low. The final estimates for μ_t and σ_t are given in table B.1. Given actual price levels, the expected rate of inflation and its standard deviation can, then, be calculated from the estimated μ_t and σ_t series. These are also presented in table B.1. It is interesting to note that the standard deviations implied for the rate of inflation forecast are of an order two or three times that found in the Livingston data set--reflecting, perhaps, that professional economists tend to 'stick together' on their forecasts of the economy. It is thus important to use economy-wide estimates such as these when analyzing the relationship between the variance of the expected rate of inflation and the variance of the actual rate of inflation as is done in Cukierman and Wachtel [1979]. Otherwise, by using the Livingston series one is likely to understate the true level of uncertainty about inflation in the economy.

Concerning the accuracy of this series vis-a-vis those of Livingston and deMenil and Bhalla, it appears to do no worse than the former and much better than the latter on the basis of mean square errors. The Livingston series over this period has a root mean square error of 2.79; whereas this series give a figure of 2.84, a difference of .05. The deMenil and Bhalla series was only computed up to 72:3. Over this period the root mean square error was 2.19, and for the same period our error was 1.53, a difference of .66, or rather one-half a percentage point in forecast accuracy.

A final observation that can be drawn from Table B.1 is that the periods 1968:2 - 69:4 and 1973:2 - 74:2 seem to signify spells of unanticipated inflation. These periods are characterized by rapidly increasing rates of inflation. More importantly though, these periods are also the ones that Carlson [1975] in his analysis of the Livingston data labels as spells of substantial unanticipated inflation. Given that these series are generated by two independent surveys we feel that this period represents a spell of genuine unanticipated inflation. Brown and Maital [1981] has recnetly argued for a more thorough analysis of the Livingston data because, in their opinion, "properties of experts' expectations likely to form an upper bound for those of laymen." The analysis here suggests that laymen do no worse than so-called experts.

Table B.1 -- Estimates of Price Expectations and Their Uncertainty From SRC Data

Period (t)	Price Level Expectation (μ_t)	Uncertainty in Price Level Expectation (σ_t)	Actual Rate of Inflation (P_t)	Uncertainty in Expected Rate of Inflation (s_t)	Expected Rate of Inflation (P_t^e)
66:2	99.94	3.974	2.58	3.17	4.10
66:3	101.50	4.182	2.76	3.89	4.28
67:1	102.13	3.733	3.64	3.34	3.78
67:3	104.26	4.116	4.38	3.85	4.10
67:4	106.05	4.272	4.21	4.13	4.19
68:2	107.50	3.847	5.48	3.94	3.72
3	109.11	4.613	5.53	4.12	4.40
4	109.73	4.300	5.75	3.40	4.05
69:1	111.38	4.750	6.24	3.73	4.42
2	113.98	4.959	6.02	4.48	4.55
3	115.45	5.259	5.73	4.39	4.76
4	115.72	5.403	5.65	3.11	4.81
70:1	119.19	5.855	4.79	4.49	5.13
2	121.14	6.297	4.44	4.73	5.44
3	121.06	5.777	4.30	3.53	4.94
4	123.83	5.937	3.48	4.44	5.01
71:1	124.21	6.547	3.55	3.92	5.48
2	125.35	5.677	3.23	3.77	4.70
3	125.50	6.144	3.12	2.89	5.04
4	126.84	5.916	3.42	3.38	4.82
72:1	128.59	5.150	4.06	3.90	4.16
2	127.42	6.345	5.56	2.19	5.09
3	129.93	5.962	6.76	3.32	4.53
4	131.05	5.598	8.33	3.27	4.41
73:1	135.14	7.575	9.91	4.92	5.88
2	137.65	8.316	10.54	4.58	6.32
3	141.32	10.407	11.47	5.25	7.75
4	143.52	9.734	12.19	4.40	7.08
74:1	152.48	9.277	11.06	7.71	6.55
2	155.24	10.676	9.69	6.69	7.34
3	160.25	10.341	8.71	7.07	6.91
4	166.53	11.167	7.33	7.98	7.24
75:1	163.08	12.485	6.42	3.72	7.94
2	161.88	12.035	6.03	1.43	7.54
3	172.53	10.037	5.45	6.04	6.17
4	174.29	10.669	4.98	5.30	6.45

Table B.2 - Estimates of the Uncertainty-Augmented Phillip Curve*

Variables	Without s		With s	
	SRC data**	Livingston data***	SRC data**	Livingston data***
Const	-.713 (.329)	1.05 (.368)	3.45 (.967)	3.48 (.508)
$P_t - P_t^e$	.115 (.115)	.13 (.140)	.320 (.103)	.26 (.097)
s_t	-	-	-.844 (.188)	-2.25 (.414)
R^2	.02	.04	.40	.61

*Standard errors in parantheses. Dependent variable is percentage change in the seasonally adjusted number of employees on payrolls of nonagricultural establishments.

**Sample period is 1966:2 - 1975:4 (quarterly) without 66:4, 67:2, and 1968:1 due to lack of data. That is why DW statistics are not reported. Data on p^e and s are taken from Table B.1.

***cf. Levi and Maken [1980]. The sample period is 1965-1975.

Uses of SRC Data

To explain the apparent positive or non-association between unemployment and inflation during the late 60's, Friedman [1977] has argued that higher uncertainty associated with higher rates of inflation should be taken into consideration while estimating a Phillips Curve. Because of institution rigidities in a society without appropriate indexing of nominal contracts, higher variability produces a reduction in the efficiency of the price system and a consequent reduction in output. In a recent paper, Levi and Makin [1980] have tested this proposition by using the Livingston data on price expectation and the standard deviation of individual forecasts computed by Carlson [1977]. They estimated the following equation:

$$dN_t = b_0 + b_1 (P_t - \overline{P}^e_t) + b_2 s_t + \mu_t \tag{B.12}$$

where dN_t is the percentage change in employment, $(P_t - \overline{P}^e_t)$ in forecast error implied by the Livingston data, and s_t is the standard deviation of forecasts in individual surveys. Thus, the coefficients of $(P_t - \overline{P}^e_t)$ and s_t should have positive and negative signs respectively. If a sustained unanticipated inflation is matched by high uncertainty of inflation, the expansionary effect of the former will be offset by the latter. As a result, omission of the uncertainty term in (b.12) should result in a systematic underestimation of b_1. Even though the use of the standard deviation of individual forecasts may be criticized on the ground that it really measures the degree of disagreemant amongst individual respondents, their empirical results unequivocally supported the Friedman conjecture. Our s_t series, however, has the straight forward interpretation of being an uncertainty measure of the underlying subjective probability distribution of price forecast of a respondent. Also, the forecast error reported in Table B.1 should be more appropriate in the context of a short-run

Phillips curve because these are generated from the responses of a wide variety of agents. The impirical results together with those obtained by Levi and Makin [1980] have been reported in Table B.2. The remarkable result is that both the Livingston data and the SRC data yield almost identical estimates of b's in (B.12). Over the sample period 1966:2 - 1975:4, we obtain the same result that the separate effect of forecast errors on employment growth can be properly estimated only when $(\dot{P}_t - \dot{P}_t^e)$ is used in conjunction with the uncertainty measure in the regression. Also, the uncertainty effect is relatively more important than forecast errors in the context of this particular version of Phillips Curve. It is worth pointing out, however, that in section 3.3 we did find negative relationships between unemployment and forecast errors associated with rational expectations even without any uncertainty variable. Also, b_0, which can be interpreted as the normal growth rate of employment, is estimated to be around 3.4 in both the cases. Since these empirical results using data from two independent surveys conform to each other so well, they can taken as very strong evidence supporting Friedman's [1977] description of the so-called Phillips Curve in it's third stage.

APPENDIX C

SOURCES AND THE DESCRIPTION OF VARIABLES

Being determined by the availability of observed price expectations data, we constructed six-monthly indices from the monthly and/or quarterly data and then, calculated the compounded annual percentage changes. For notational convenience let us denote a six-month period as "t", quarter as "i" and a month as "j". Thus,

x(t) = the value of the variable x during the half year "t",

x(i) = the value for the latter quarter of the half year "t", and

x(j) = the value of x for the last month of half year "t".

In this appendix, <u>BCD</u> denotes <u>Business Conditions Digest</u> and <u>SCB</u> denotes <u>Survey of Current Business</u>.

1) W_t = Annual percentage change in standard unit labor cost occurring during the half year "t".

Basic data and sources:

(a) WI(i) = Quarterly wage index (1967=100)

1964-1975: Average hourly earnings, production workers in private non-farm economy, adjusted for overtime (in manufacturing only) and interindustry employment shifts.

1947-1963: Fixed weight wage index net of fringes. Source: Professor R. J. Gordon.

(b) WS (i) = Wages and salaries in national income accounts, quarterly data.

Source: 1975 statistical supplement to the SCB and various issues of SCB.

(c) COMP (i) = Compensation of employees in national income accounts, quarter data. Source: 1975 Statistical Supplement to the SCB and various issues of SCB.

(d) Q (i) = Quarterly index of output per hour, all persons, total private nonfarm (1967 = 100). Source: BCD June 1976.

Method of Construction:

WI (t) = 1/2 (WI (i-1) + WI (i)).

WS (t) = 1/2 (WS (i-1) + WS (i)).

COMP (t) = 1/2(COMP (i-1) + COMP (i)).

WF (t) = WI (t) (COMP (t)/WS (t)).

QT (i): A trend line was extended between values of actual productivity (Q) in 1950:4, 1955:2 and 1966:1 to construct trend productivity (QT). For details, refer to the construction of PR_t.

QT (t) = 1/2(QT (i-1) + QT (i))

WFP (t) = WF(t)/QT (t)

$W_t = ((WFP\ (t)/WFP\ (t-1))^2 - 1) \times 100.$

2) P_t = Annual percentage change in Consumer Price Index.

Basic Data: CPI(i) = Quarterly Consumer Price Index.

Source: BCD, March 1976 and August 1976.

Method of Construction: CPI(t) = 1/2(CPI(i-1) + CPI(i)).

$P_t = ((CPI(t)/CPI(t-1))^2 - 1) \times 100.$

3) $\overline{p}_t^e$ = Expected percentage change in consumer prices held during half year "t" for the next 6 months.

Basic Data:

Livingston's survey responses. Mr. Joseph Livingston, a financial columnist now with the Philadelphia Inquirer, has been surveying nearly fifty financial analysts since 1946 on a bi-annual basis. Over various time periods, twenty-two variables have appeared consistently on the questionnaire. Among these are measures of consumer and wholesale prices, national output, and activity in various sectors of the economy including unemployment and housing construction.

Listings of Livingston survey respondents, 1947 and 1970.

June 1947. (Source: Washington Post).

Charles O. Hardy, adviser to the Joint Committee on the Economic Report; C.A. Sienkiewicz, president, Central-Penn National Bank, Philadelphia; Rufus Tucker, General Motors; Frank L. Valenta, vice president, Distributors Group, Inc.; Robert R. Nathan of Robert R. Nathan Associates; J. Frederic Dewhurst, Twentieth Century Fund and author of the recent monumental work, "America's Needs and Resources"; Boris Shisken, American Federal of Labor. Also, E.G. Bennion, Standard Oil Co., (N.J.); Alan H. Temple, vice president, National City Bank of New York; Woodlief Thomas, director of research and statistics, Federal Reserve Board; James F. Hughes, Auchincloss, Parker & Redpath, members of the New York Stock Exchange; Herbert Stein, economist for the Committee for Economic Development, and winner of the $25,000 Pabst award; Donald R. Smith, partner, Scudder, Stevens & Clark, investment counsel; Joseph K. Heyman, Joseph K. Heyman Co., Atlanta; Morris A. Copeland, Federal

Reserve Board; Dexter M. Keezer, McGraw-Hill Publishing Co.; Charles D. Stewart, U.S. Bureau of Labor Statistics; Robert C. Shook, vice president, International Statistical Bureau; Donald F. Bishop, investment counsel, Philadelphia; Solomon Barkin, director of research, Textile Workers Union of America; O.C. Stine, U.S. Department of Agricultural; Arthur R. Upgren, University of Minnesota; Robert Coltman, vice president, Provident Trust Co., Philadelphia; Nathaniel R. Whitney, Procter & Gamble Co.; John Patterson, National Shoe Manufactueres, Ass.; Lazare Teper, International Ladies' Garment Workers Union; F.E. Richier, General Foods Corp.; Wilson Wright, Armstrong Cork Co.; Glen G. Munn, Paine, Webber, Jackson & Curtis, members of the New York Stock Exchange; Adolf G. Abramson, SKF Industries.

December 1970. (Source: The Sunday Bulletin).

Gardner Ackley, Henry Carter Adams Professor, University of Michigan; Daniel S. Ahearn, vice president, Wellington Management Co.; Louis H. Bean, Arlington, Va.; Edward G. Boehne, Federal Reserve Bank of Philadelphia; Karl Brandt, emeritus professor, Stanford University; Ewan Clague, Washington, D.C.; Carrol L. Coburn, director of research, United Auto Workers; Philip E. Coldwell, president, Federal Reserve Bank of Dallas; George W. Coleman, American Bankers Association; Andrew T. Court, Detroit, Mich.; James M. Dawson, vice president, National City Bank of Cleveland; John V. Deaver, manager, economics department, Ford Motor Co.; Robert J. Eggert, Staff vice president, RCA Corp.; Richard W. Everett, vice president, Chase Manhattan Bank; Phillip John Fitzgerald, Dean Witter & Co.; William C. Freund, vice president, New York Stock Exchange; Douglas Greenwald, McGraw-Hill, Inc.; David L. Grave, International Business Machines Corp.; A. Gilbert Heebner, Senior vice president,

Philadelphia National Bank; Peter Henle, Bureau of Labor Statistics; Homer Jones, vice president, Federal Reserve Bank of St. Louis; Vernon E. Jirikowic, research director, International Association of Machinists and Aerospace Workers; J.W. Kendrick, American Airlines, Inc.; L.R. Klein, Wharton School, University of Pennsylvania; Richard W. Lambourne, vice president, Crocker-Citizens National Bank; Robert J. Landry, Dun & Bradstreet, Inc.; Werner Lehnberg, Goodbody & Co.; Wesley Lindow, senior vice president and secretary, Irving Turst Co.; Carl H. Madden, U.S. Chamber of Commerce; Edmund A. Mennis, senior vice president, Republic National Bank of Dallas; H. LeBrec Micoleau, General Motors Corp.; Robert R. Nathan, Robert R. Nathan Associates, Washington, D.C.; Robert J. Oster, Bank of America; Louis J. Paradiso, senior associate, Tyson, Belzer, and Associates, Inc.; Sanford F. Parker, Fortune Magazine, Robert W. Paterson, School of Business and Public Administration, University of Missouri; W.H. Peterson, United States Steel Corp.; Francis H. Schott, vice president, Equitable Life Assurance Society; Irving Schweiger, Graduate School of Business, University of Chicago; Beryl W. Sprinkel, vice president, Harris Trust & Savings Bank, Chicago; Lazare Teper, director of research, International Ladies Garment Workers Union; W.W. Tongue, University of Illinois; M.I. Upchurch, U.S. Department of Agriculture; Henry C. Wallich, Yale University; Robert L. Weidenhammer, Rockville, Md.; Rudolph L. Weissman, W.E. Hutton & Co.; Gary M. Wenglowski, Goldman, Sachs & Co.; J.P. Wernette, University of Michigan; Simon N. Whitney, New York University; Hans A. Widenmann, Loeb, Rhoades & Co.; Seymour Wolbein, Dean, School of Business Administration, Temple University.

Description of Carlson's adjustments (Carlson 1977a):

In order to describe the adjustments done by Professor Carlson on Livingston's survey data on Consensus forecasts, let us suppose that we want to obtain price expectations for the first half of a certain year. First point to note is that the panel of economists and businessmen, in fact, had to forecast over the coming eight months rather than six months (in six-month ahead predictions). This is because, by the time the respondents face the questionnaire, they only know the CPI of October, but they are asked to predict the CPI of next June.

Another problem regarding Livingston's published data is related to the following situation: Suppose October index was 121.1 and the panels predicted the CPI of next June to be 121.2. Also, suppose the index of November turned out to be 121.6 by the time the questionnaires are collected. If we compare the predicted index with the November index, we may think that the panels predicted a deflation. However, Mr. Livingston reasoned that this was contrary to the economists real expectations. In this case Livingston would add .5 to the predicted CPI for June (121.2), and show a June forecast of 121.7. Thus the survey data as published by Livingston incorporated his own arbitrary judgement.

In order to overcome these problems, Carlson adjusted the price expectations variable based on original data as follows:

$$\pi^*_{6,j} = (CPI^*_{6,j}/CPI_{j-2})^{12/8} - 1,$$

where $\pi^*_{6,j}$ = expected inflation at annual rates held in month "j" for the coming "6" months, $CPI^*_{6,j}$ = the forecast in month "j" of what the index will be "6" months later. CPI_{j-2} = the actual price index for month "j-2". However, since Carlson's data represents expectations held at specific points of time (viz. April and October), we approximated the expectation during the half year "t" by taking the mean of the expectations held right before "t" and the expectations held at the latter part of "t". Alternatively, we have also related Carlson's data directly to nominal yields quoted at the end of April and October.

Up-to-date data on Livingston's surveys incorporating Carlson's adjustments can now be obtained from the Federal Reserve Bank of Philadelphia.

4) CD_t : Annual percentage change in implicit price deflators on personal consumption expenditures.

Basic Data: CDI(i) = quarterly index of implicit deflators on personal consumption expenditures.

Source: Business Statistics, 1975 Edition.

$$CDI(t) = 1/2((CDI\ (i-1) + CDI(i)).$$

$$CD_t = ((CDI(t)/CDI(t-1))^2 - 1) \times 100.$$

5) U_t^{-1} : Unemployment inverse during "t".

UL (i) : Number of persons unemployed, quarterly average.

Source : BCD. April 1976 and August 1976.

L (i) : Total civilian labor force, quarterly average.

Source: BCD Apr. 76 & Aug. 76.

U (i) = (UL (i-1)/ L (i-1)) x 100.

$U_t = 1/2(U\ (i-1) + U\ (i))$.

$U_t^{-1} = 1/U_t$

6) TE_t : Total Employment rate in percentage terms.

$$TE_t = (1 - (U_t + U_t^D)) \times 100$$

where U_t: Official unemployment rate during t

U_t^D: Disguised unemployment rate during t (cf. Gordon 1971)

Source: Professor R. J. Gordon.

7) TUI_t: The inverse of Total Unemployment rate

$$TUI_t = 1/((U_t + U_t^D) \times 100)$$

Source: Professor R. J. Gordon.

8) SG_t: Percentage change in Social Security tax paid by employers (cf. Gordon 1971)

Source: Professor R.J. Gordon.

9) GD_t: Guidepost dummy was set equal to .575 in 1962: 1, .875 in 1962: 2, 1.0 in 1963: 1 to 1966: 2, .625 in 1967: 1, .125 in 1967: 1 and 0.0 in other periods.

10) PR_t: Annual percentage change in the ratio of actual to trend productivity during t.

Basic Data: Q (i): Quarterly index of output per hour, all persons total private nonfarm (1967 = 100). Source: <u>BCD</u> June 1976.

<u>Method of Construction</u>

a) QT (i): A trend line was extended between values of actual productivity (Q) in 1950:4, 1955:2 and 1966:1 to construct trend productivity.

An example is given below:

50:4 index - 68.6, 55:2 index - 74.2

$68.6 \times (1 + r_1)^{n_1} = 74.2,$

where n_1 = number of quarters between 50:4 - 55:2 (=18),

r_1 = compound rate of change per quarter during 50:4 - 55:2.

Hence r_1 = .004369 and it follows that

QT (51:1) - $68.6 \times (1 + .004369) = 68.6997$:

QT (51:2) = $68.6 \times (1 + .004369)^2 = 69.2007$, etc.

b) Q(t) = 1/2 (QT (i-1) + QT (i))

PROD (t) = Q (t)/QT (t).

$PR_t = ((PROD\ (t)/PROD\ (t-1))^2 - 1) \times 100.$

11) CMW_t: Annual percentage change in the ratio of total compensation per man hour to wage rate during t.

Basic Data: CMH (i) = Average hourly compensation, all employees in private nonfarm economy (index: 1967 = 100). Source: <u>BCD</u> June 1976.

<u>Method of Construction</u>

CMH (t) = 1/2 (CMH (i-1) + CMH (i))

CMWI (t) = CMH (t) /WF (t).

(For the description of WF(t), refer to the construction of W_t.

$CMW_t = ((CMWI\ (t)/CMWI\ (t-1))^2 - 1) \times 100.$

12) UFK_t = Annual percentage change in the ratio of unfilled orders to capacity during t.

Basic Data: UO (j) = unfilled orders, durable goods industries, (adjusted for seasonal variation), monthly data.

Source: 1975 Statistical Supplement to the Survey of Current Business and various issues of SCB.

OC (i): Ratio of output to capacity in manufacturing (5), quarterly data.

Source: BCD, July 1976.

Method of Construction: From the above basic data, UFK_t for the six-month period t was calculated as follows:

UO (i) = 1/3 (UO (j-2) + UO (j-1) + UO (j)).

UFKI (i) = UO (i) x OC (i).

UFKDT (i); UFKI (i) was detrended by dividing by values along a trend line extended between peaks.

UFKDT (t) = 1/2(UFKDT (i-1) + UFKDT (i))

$UFK_t = ((UFKDT\ (t)/UFKDT\ (t-1))^2 - 1) \times 100.$

13) MP_t = Annual percentage rate in material prices during t.

Basic Data: MPI (i): Quarterly index of industrial material prices (1967 = 100).

Source: BCD Oct. 1974 and various issues.

Method of Construction:

MPI (t) = 1/2(MPI (i-1) + MPI (i))

$MP_t = ((MPI\ (t)/MPI\ (t-1))^2 - 1) \times 100.$

14) MG_t = Annual percentage change in money supply (MI) during t.

Basic Data: MS (j) = Money supply (defined as currency outside bank and demand deposits), monthly data.

Source: 1975 Statistical Supplement to <u>SCB</u>.

$$MS(t) = 1/6 \left(\sum_{n=0}^{5} MS(j-n)\right)$$

$$MG_t = ((MS(t)/MS(t-1))^2 - 1) \times 100.$$

15) $RGNP_t$ = The level of real GNP during t.

Basic Data: RGNP (i) (1972 constant prices)

Source: <u>BCD</u> 1976 Issues

$$RGNP(t) = 1/2(RGNP(i-1) + RGNP(i))$$

$$\Delta RGNP(t) = RGNP(t) - RGNP(t-1).$$

16) RMG_t: Annual percentage change in real money supply (M1) during t

Basic Data: MS(i) (cf. MG(t))

DEF(i): quarterly index of GNP Deflator

Source: <u>BCD</u> 1976 Issues

$$RM(i) = MS(i)/DEF(i) \times 100$$

$$RM(t) = 1/2(RM(i-1) + RM(i)$$

$$RMG_t = ((RM(t)/RM(t-1))^2 - 1) \times 100.$$

17) R_t: Six Month Treasury Bill Rate during t.

Basic Data: r(j): Monthly Data on Six Month Treasury Bill Rate.

Source: Federal Reserve Bulletin, Various Issues.

$$r_t = 1/6 \left(\sum_{n=0}^{5} r(j-n)\right)$$

Finally, the trend variable was set at 1 in the first sample period and increased by 1 for the successive periods.

FOOTNOTES

1. See, for example, Friedman [1968], Phelps [1967], Lucas and Rapping [1969] and Mortenson [1972]. The literature has been surveyed in Laidler and Parkin [1975] and Santomero and Seater [1978].

2. Auernheimer [1979] has recently proposed a reformulation of the adaptive-regressive expectations hypothesis. See also Mussa [1975].

3. It may be pointed out that the $\bar{p}^e_{12}(t)$ series behaves quite differently from the $\bar{p}^e_t$ series. Whereas the mean and the variance for the $\bar{p}^e_{12}(t)$ series are 1.157 and 1.472 respectively, the same for the $\bar{p}^e_t$ series are 1.774 and 5.110. The correlation coefficient between them is 0.683.

4. Using the Livingston data, we have also tested a hypothesis on variable inflation coefficients originally proposed by Gordon [1972, pp. 404-405). The variant of the hypothesis which we tested implies that $\bar{p}^e_t$ be replaced by $(\bar{p}^e_t)^2$ in the wage equation. The coefficient value thus obtained was, however, insignificant.

5. We constructed a number of variables representing the 'catch-up' term. None of them succeeded. It may be noted that though the catch-up term was significant, our model does, however, allow error adjustment in price expectations (viz. eq. (1.7)) which, in turn, affects the behavior of actual wage changes.

6. It may be noted that eq. (I) is the same as the one estimated by Eckstein and Brinner [1972], except that their composite inflation variable has been replaced by our Livingston's measure and the personal income tax variable has been dropped. Since the tax variable has generally been found to be uncorrelated with other independent variables, and their coefficients are quite insensitive to changes in other independent variables, we have excluded that from our equation. It may be noted that the D.-W. values in Table 2 are much better than those obtained by Eckstein and Brinner [1972], whose dependent variable was in the form of four quarter changes.

7. A fuller development of the rationale for UFK as an exogenous variable in the price equation can be found in deMenil [1974].

8. The role of actual inflation in addition to expected prices has been emphasized by Kuh [1964] and Gordon [1971]. Cukierman [1974] also included P_t in his wage equation and argues that Eckstein-Brinner's [1972] index of inflation severity essentially catches this marginal revenue product effect.

9. Carlson [1977a, p. 29] presents a good illustration: "... late in 1957 the CPI stood at 121.1 in both September and October. The average of the forecasts when they came in was 121.2 for June, 1958. In effect, the forecast was for no change, or a very slight change. But when the CPI was released for November, it was 121.6 or 0.5 over the figure given in Livingston's questionnaire when it was sent out. This posed a problem. As a journalist, Livingston wanted to include the latest figure. But, with no adjustments, this would indicate that economists were predicting deflation: a decline from 121.6 to 121.2. He reasoned that this was contrary to their real expectations. Consequently, in presenting the data for publication, he revised the consensus upward by an average of 0.5, or by the amount of the change in the CPI from October (and September) to November. Thus, he showed a November index of 121.6 and a June 1958 forecast of 121.7."

10. To compute the FIML estimates we have used LISREL-III, developed by Joreskog and Sörbom [1976]. It is a general computer algorithm where the variables in the equation system can be either observed or latent variables and there may be multiple indicators or causes of each latent variable. Thus, the so-called MIMIC models of Goldberger and Joreskog [1975] can be estimated as special cases. Since LISREL-III can not handle more than 15 exogenous variables, we have implemented the rational expectations models with conventional instrumental variable procedure. However, in Section IV, we have estimated the RE models with LISREL-III, where the estimates were independent of the auxiliary regressions.

11. Since the application of instrumental variable methods generally bring in additional sampling variability, it is advisable to conduct these tests of errors-in-observations, particularly when there is substantial multicollinearity. An example follows: Frankel [1979] developed a theory of exchange rate movements in which the spot rate (specifically the Deutsche mark/Dollar rate) is expressed as a function of the relative money supply, relative income level, the nominal interest differential (with one sign hypothesized negative), and the expected long-run inflation differential (with the sign hypothesized positive). Since the last variable is unobserved, he took the long-term government bond differential as the proxy for it and applied the IV procedure to obtain expected results. The ordinary least squares estimates, however, did not yield these results. Thus, a very crucial issue here is whether the observational error associated with the proxy is sufficiently "noisy" to warrant the application of IV procedure. It is interesting to note that the Hausman test did not indicate that the measurement errors were significant enough to warrant the application of IV techniques See Lahiri and Gold [1980].

12. Sims [1980] has presented some evidence which also suggests that unemployment is not important in the wage equation. However, in his experiment, unemployment together with money, GNP, and import price index did not pass a joint exogeneity test against the hypothesis that only wage and price variables could be treated as endogenous. The treatment of U_t^{-1} as an exogenous variable has been justified (cf. Gordon [1976b]) by saying that the wage-price subsystem forms only a block in a block-recursive structural model. To see if treating U_t^{-1} as an endogenous variable can help to reinstate it in the wage equation with REH, we assumed the following autoregressive scheme for U_t^{-1}:

$$U_t^{-1} = \sum_{i=1}^{n} U_{t-i}^{-1} + \varepsilon_2 \ . \qquad (3.16')$$

Now, equations (3.12), (3.13), (3.15) and (3.16') constitute our model. In order to take care of the endogeneity of U_t^{-1}, we obtained $\hat{U}_t^{-1}$ by regressing U_t^{-1} on all the exogenous variables of the system including the lagged values of U_t^{-1}. Then we applied the IV method with $\hat{U}_t^{-1}$ as the instrument for U_t to the wage equation. The results were almost the same. Holmes and Smyth [1979] have surveyed labor market models in which the relationship between unemployment and excess demand for labor plays a key role and have found that none of them provide an adequate basis for the conventional Phillips curve.

13. The different options under REH had the following $\bar{R}^2$:

	Option I	Option II	Option III	Partly Rational with Six Lags in Prices	Partly Rational With Six Lags in Prices & Money Supply
$\bar{R}^2$:	.427	.556	.524	.353	.550

14. Feige and Pearce [1976] develop the concept of "econometrically rational expectations" which explicitly considers the trade-off between benefits and costs of added information when forecasting future inflation rates. It is interesting that they found that the autoregressive model may well represent economically rational expectations. Pesando [1976] reviews the properties of RE in the context of autogressive forecasting. See also McCallum [1976b].

15. See Goldberger [1972b, 1974].

16. We used LISREL-III to estimate the model. Note that this is a very general version of the REH, in the sense that the informational content of the rational price forecasts are quite general.

17. MG_t in the wage equation was, however, found out to be statistically insignificant - indicating that the real balance effect has possibly been relatively unimportant over our sample period.

18. The estimated equation was:

$$U = \underset{(.018)}{.046} + \underset{(.149)}{1.54}\ U_{-1} - \underset{(.220)}{1.28}\ U_{-2} + \underset{(.214)}{.812}\ U_{-3} - \underset{(.123)}{.287}\ U_{-4};\ \bar{R}^2 = .79$$

Standard errors are in the brackets. Durgin's h = .06.

19. Fama [1975, p. 279] noted, "The only hint of evidence against the model is in the estimates of (21) for five- and six-month bills in Table 9. As predicted by the model, the values of a_1 and a_2 for one- to four-month bills are close to 1.0 and 0.0 and the residual autocorrelations are close to 0.0. For the five- and six-month bills, however, the values of a_1 are rather far from 1.0 and the values of a_2 are rather far from 0.0."

20. See, for example, Levi and Makin [1978, 1979], Elliott [1978] and Turnovsky [1974].

21. Note that under the assumption that conditional expectation in (5.2) is linear, (5.3) should in fact be non-stochastic. The random disturbance η_t was still included because we do not believe that we can as yet model expectations exactly over diverse time-periods. However, imposing $\eta_t = 0$ on the estimation procedure did not change out estimates in Table 5.1 indicating that the variance of η_t may indeed be small.

22. For an explicit analysis of the Instrumental Variable technique in Rational Expectations Models, see McCallum [1976a].

23. However, following Fama [1975], we also estimated all the models with R_t, defined as the treasury bill rates for June and December and $P_t = (CPI_t/CPI_{t-1})^2 - 1) \times 100$. Also, the April and October surveys were related to bill rates for June and December respectively. The results were very similar.

24. See Hendershott and van Horne [1973, Fn. 14] and Carlson [1979].

25. Gandolphi [1976] has developed a simple model of saving and capital accumulation where he has demonstrated that the "Fisher effect" will be a close approximation to reality if the partial derivative of investment with respect to the real interest rate is very large and/or the effect on saving is very small. On the basis of this result he concluded that "the relative success of the "Fisher effect" in explaining post-war movements in U.S. nominal rates suggest that this may well be the case."

26. The variables were constructed following Sargent [1969]. See Appendix C.

27. It can be argued that in (5.21), the loanable funds variables should also be treated as endogenous. To check whether this possibility should make any difference, we used the estimated values of all the right-hand side variables in (5.21) in our second-stage regressions, where each variable was regressed on P, P_{-1}, P_{-2}, percentage change in monetary base, and contemporaneous values of all exogenous variables that appeared in Chapter 3. Our results using $\bar{P}_t^e$ and P_{t+1} as two different proxies for P_t^e, indicate that possible endogeneity in RGNP, ΔRGNP, and RMG does not lead to rejection of the hypothesis that real rates were constant over our sample period.

28. There are more serious problems with the Levi-Makin [1979] estimates. First, their use of $\dot{y}_t$ as an exogenous variable is indefensible. The use of level or rate of growth of real output in the interest rate equation have produced very conflicting results. See, for example, Pyle [1972], Cargill [1976], Feldstein and Eckstein [1970], Sargent [1969] and Yohe and Karnosky [1969]. As a result, their estimates are very sensitive to the sample period chosen. In a recent paper, Bomberger and Frazer [1980] have demonstrated that $\dot{y}_t$ and σ_t become statistically insiginificant when the model is estimated over 1952-70. Secondly, their use of sample standard deviation of individual respondent's forecasts as a measure of the market's uncertainty about future inflation has dubious value. The former, at least in part, will be determined by the changing nature of Livingston's surveys over years. When we tried to use this series in the errors-in-the-variables framework estimates of all the coefficients became statistically insignificant.

29. Note that a non-zero $\mathrm{Cov}(p^e,v)$ does not affect our estimates of α_1 and β.

30. The two <u>indicators</u> for the unobserved price expectations variable are the nominal interest rate and the actual rate of inflation.

31. Hendershott and van Horne [1973] concluded that during the 1960's the Livingston's data systematically underestimated the true price expectations implied by their interest rate equation.

32. It may be noted that Nelson and Schwert [1977] analyzed the first order autocorrelation coefficient for r_t which is consistent also with higher order autoregressive processes. They, however, explicitly considered the first-order autoregressive process and their σ_w^2-estimates were computed under such an assumption (see Nelson and Schwert 1977, p. 480). We should emphasize that our procedure can also be generalized to handle a higher order autoregressive scheme for i_t, subject to the availability of an adequate number of instrumental variables. In the present context, the structure (6.1) - (6.2) was, however, found to be adequate for our purpose. More on this type of models can be found in Maddala [1977].

33. In all the experiments, the correlation between the ranks and $\hat{u}_t$ was zero up to three decimal places. See also footnote 36.

34. Arithmetic average of the six-month treasury bill rates for the appropriate periods were used as the nominal interest series and the basic inflation variable was defined as the annual percentage change in the C.P.I. during the six-month period from t to (t+1).

35. Note that over the period 1959/2 - 1971/2, σ_ε^2 and σ_i^2 together accounts for nearly 90% of the total variation in the EPRR. The relatively small covariance term (to the order of nearly -.05) between the EARR and ε is consistent with market efficiency. During the latter sample periods though, the covariance term became significantly positive.

36. It may be pointed out that with high correlation between r_t and r_{t-1}, r_{t-2} can now be used as the instrumental variable. Over 1959/2 - 1973/2, the IV estimates utilizing r_{t-2} as the instrument were very similar to those reported in Table 1. This indicates that the instrumental variable we used is appropriate.

37. The additional assumption is that the covariance between $(\hat{P}_t - P_{t-1})$ and i_t is the same as that between $(p_t^e - P_{t-1})$ and i_t, where $\hat{p}$ is a ARIMA time series predictor for p_t^e. Since $\hat{P}_t = p_t^e - a_t$, where a_t can be interpreted as the information available to market beyond past inflation rates, $Cov(\hat{P}_t, i_t) = Cov(\hat{p}_t^e - a_t, i_t) = Cov(p_t^e, i_t) - Cov(a_t, i_t)$. Therefore, their assumption basically implies: $\sigma_{ia} = 0$.

38. Since the Livingston's data, cf. Carlson [1977a], represents expectations held at specific points of time (viz. April and October), we approximated the expectation held during the half year "t" by taking the mean of the expectation held right before "t" and the expectation held at the latter part of "t". See Appendix C.

39. Note that a non-zero (positive) correlation between η_t and p_t^e will mean that our $\hat{\beta}$ is overestimated, and the magnitude of bias will be given by $Cov(\eta_t, p_t^e)/S_{21}$. Since S_{12} is relatively large, the bias, if at all, is expected to be very small. Also, an autocorrelated η_t would have no immediate effect on the parameter estimates.

40. For instance, in Yohe and Karnosky's [1969, p. 38] regression of short-term rate of interest on past inflation rates, the constant term was 2.41 (with a t-ratio of 25.90). They attributed the whole of 2.41 to the real interest rate.

41. cf. Hess and Bicksler [1975] and Shiller [1978].

REFERENCES

Anderson, P.A. (1979). Rational expectations forecasts from non-rational models, Journal of Monetary Economics, V(January).

Anderson, T.W. and Hurwich, L. (1949). Errors and shocks in economic relationships, Econometrica, XVII(July).

Arrow, K.J. (1978). The future and the present in economic life, Economic Inquiry, XVI(April).

Auernheimer, L. (1979). Adaptive - regressive expectations and the price level: a reformulation, Journal of Monetary Economics, V(January).

Barro, R.J. (1976). Rational expectations and the role of monetary policy, Journal of Monetary Economics, II(January).

Barro, R.J. and Fischer, S. (1976). Recent developments in monetary theory, Journal of Monetary Economics, II(April).

Barro, R.J. (1977). Long term contracting, sticky prices, and monetary policy, Journal of Monetary Economics, III(July).

Bomberger, W.A. and Frazer, Jr., W.J. (1980). Interest rates, inflation and uncertainy: uses of the Livingston data, Journal of Finance, forthcoming.

Brown, B.W. and Maital, S. (1981). What do economists know? An empirical study of experts' expectations, Econometrica, IL(forthcoming).

Brunner, K. and Meltzer, A. (1972). Money, debt and economic activity, Journal of Political Economy, LXXX(September).

Cagan, P. (1956). The Monetary dynamics of hyperinflation. In: Friedman, M. (ed.), Studies in the Quantity Theory of Money (Chicago: University of Chicago Press).

Cargill, T.F. (1976). Anticipated price changes and nominal interest rates in the 1950's, Review of Economics and Statistics, LVIII (August).

Carlson, J. and Parkin M. (1975a). Inflationary expectations, Economica, XLII(May).

Carlson, J.A. (1975b). Are price expectations normally distributed? Journal of the American Statistical Association, LXX(December).

Carlson, J.A. (1977a). A study of price forecasts, Annals of Economic and Social Measurement, VI(Winter).

Carlson, J.A. (1977b). Short-term interest rates as predictors of inflation: comment, American Economic Review, LXVII(June).

Carlson, J.A. (1979). Expected inflation and interest rates, Economic Inquiry, XVII(October).

Chow, G.C. (1974). A family of estimators for simultaneous equations systems, International Economic Review, XV(October).

Cukierman, A. (1974). A test of the 'no trade-off in the long run' hypothesis, Econometrica, XLII(November).

Cukierman, A. and Wachtel, P. (1979). Differential inflationary expectations and the variability of the rate of inflation: Some theory and evidence, American Economic Review, LXVIV(September).

Darby, M.R. (1975). The financial and tax effects of monetary policy on interest rates, Economics Inquiry, XIII(June).

de Menil, G. and Enzler, J.J. (1972). Prices and wages in the FRB-MIT-Penn econometric model, In: Eckstein, O. (ed.), The Econometrics of Price Determination (Washington: Board of Governors of the Federal Reserve System).

de Menil, G. (1973). Rationality in popular price expectations, mimeographed, Princeton University.

de Menil, G. (1974). Aggregate price dynamics, Review of Economics and Statistics, LVI(May).

de Menil, G. and Bhalla, S. (1975). Direct measurement of popular price expectations, American Economic Review, LXV(March).

Dhrymes, P.J. (1970). Econometrics: Statistical Foundations and Applications, (New York: Harper and Row).

Durbin, J. (1954). Errors in variables, Review of the International Statistical Institute, XXII(January).

Durbin, J. (1970). Testing for serial correlation in least squares regression when some of the regressors are lagged dependent variables, Econometrica, XXXVIII(May).

Eckstein, O. and Brinner, R. (1972). The inflation process in the U.S., a study prepared for the use of the Joint Economic Committee, 92 Congress, 2nd Session.

Elliott, J.W. (1977). Measuring the expected real rate of interest, American Economic Review, LXVII(June).

Equations in the M.I.T.-Penn-SSRC Econometric Model of the United States (MPS), 1975 (January). Available from the Board of Governors of the Federal Reserve System.

Fair, R.C. (1979). An analysis of a macro-econometric model with rational expectations in the bond and stock markets, American Economic Review, LXVIV(September).

Fair, R.C. (1974, 1976). A Model of Macroeconomic Activity. (Mass: Ballinger).

Fama, E.F. (1975). Short-term interest rates as predictors of inflation, American Economic Review, LXV(June).

Fama, E.F. (1976). Foundations of Finance, Portfolio Decisions and Securities Prices, (New York: Basic Books).

Fama, E.F. (1977). Interest rates and inflation: the message in the entrails, American Economic Review, LXVII(June).

Feige, E.L. and Pearce, D.K. (1976). Economically rational expectations: are innovations in the rate of inflation independent of innovations in measures of monetary and fiscal policy? Journal of Political Economy, LXXXIV(June).

Feldstein, M. (1975). Inflation, income taxes, and the rate of interest: a theoretical analysis. American Economic Review, LXXVI(December).

Feldstein, M. and Eckstein, O. (1970). The fundamental determinants of the interest rate, Review of Economics and Statistics, LII(November).

Feldstein, M. and Summers, L. (1979). Inflation, tax rules and the long-term interest rate, Brookings Papers on Economic Activity, X(No. 1).

Ferber, R. (1953). The Railroad Shippers' Forecasts. (Urbana: Bureau of Economic Research, University of Illinois).

Fischer, S. (1977). Long-term contracts, rational expectations and the optimal money supply rule, Journal of Political Economy, LXXV(February).

Fishe, R.P.H. and Lahiri, K. (1981). Models of expectations based on qualitative survey data, Annals of Econometrics, supplement to Journal of Econometrics (April).

Fisher, R. (1972). Comment on paper by R. Lucas. In: Eckstein, O. (Ed.), The Econometrics of Price Determination (Washington, D.C.: Board of Governors, Federal Reserve System).

Fisher, I. (1930). The Theory of Interest, (New York: A.M. Kelly 1965 reprinted).

Frankel, J. (1979). On the mark: a theory of floating exchange rates based on real interest differentials, American Economic Review, LXVIV(September).

Frenkel, J.A. (1975). Inflation and the formation of expectations, Journal of Monetary Economics, I(December).

Frenkel, J.A. (1976). Inflationary expectations and some dynamic aspects of the welfare cost. In: Parkin, M. and Zis, G. (Eds.), Inflation in the World Economy (Manchester: Manchester University Press).

Frenkel, J.A. (1977). The forward exchange rate, expectations and the demand for money: the German hyper-inflation, American Economic Review, LXVII (December).

Frenkel, J.A. (1978). Further evidence on expectations and the demand for money during the German hyperinflation, Journal of Monetary Economics, V(January).

Frazer, W.J., Jr. (L978). Evolutionary economics, rational expectations and monetary policy, Journal of Economics Issues, XII(June).

Friedman, B. (1979). Optimal expectations and the extreme information assumptions of 'rational expectations' macro models, Journal of Monetary Economics, V(January).

Friedman, M. (1968). The role of monetary policy, American Economic Review, LVII(January).

Friedman, M. (1977). Nobel Lecture: Inflation and unemployment. Journal of Political Economy, LXXXIV(June).

Gandolphi, A.E. (1976). Taxation and the Fisher effect, Journal of Finance, XXXI(December).

Gelfand, J., Lahiri, K. and Osborne, T. (1981). Government policy dynamics in structural and reduced form estimation, Empirical Economics, forthcoming.

Geraci, V.J. (1976). Identification of simultaneous equation models with measurement errors, Journal of Econometrics, IV(August).

Gibson, W. (1970). Price expectations effects on interest rates, Journal of Finance, XXV(March).

Gibson, W. (1972). Interest rates and inflationary expectations: new evidence, American Economic Review, LXII(December).

Goldberger, A.S. (1972a). Maximum likelihood estimation of regressions containing unobservable independent variables, International Economic Review, XIII(February).

Goldberger, A.S. (1972b). Structural equation methods in the social sciences, Econometrica, XL(November).

Goldberger, A.S. (1974). Unobservable variables in econometrics, In: Zarembka, P. (Ed.), Frontiers in Econometrics (New York: Academic Press).

Goldberger, A.S. and Joreskog, K.G. (1975). Estimation of a model with multiple indicators and multiple causes of a single latent variable, Journal of the American Statistical Association, LXX(September).

Gordon, R.J. (1971). Inflation in recession and recovery, Brookings Papers on Economic Activity, III(No. 1).

Gordon, R.J. (1972). Wage-price controls and the shifting Phillips curve, Brookings Papers on Economic Activity, IV(No. 2).

Gordon, R.J. (1973). Interest rates and prices in the long-run: a comment, Journal of Money, Credit and Banking, V(February).

Gordon, R.J. (1976a). Recent developments in the theory of inflation and unemployment, Journal of Monetary Economics, II(April).

Gordon, R.J. (1976b). Comment on paper by W. Oi, In: Brunner, K. and Meltzer, A. (Eds.), The Economics of Price and Wage Controls, (Amsterdam: North-Holland).

Granger, C.W.J. (1969). Investigating causal relations by econometric models and cross-spectral methods, Econometrica, XXXVII(July).

Griliches, Z. (1974). Errors in variables and other unobservables, Econometrica, LXII(November).

Hamburger, M.J. and Platt, E.N. (1975). The expectations hypothesis and efficiency of the treasury bill market, Review of Economics and Statistics, LVII(May).

Hausman, J.A. (1975). Full information instrumental variable estimation of simultaneous equation models, Econometrica, XLIII(July).

Hausman, J.A. (1977). Errors in variables in simultaneous equation models, Journal of Econometrics, V(May).

Hausman, J.A. (1978). Specification tests in econometrics, Econometrica, XLVI(November).

Hendershott, P.H. and van Horne, J.C. (1973). Expected inflation implied by capital market rates, Journal of Finance, XXVII(May).

Hendry, D.F. (1976). The structure of simultaneous equations estimators, Journal of Econometrics, IV(February).

Hess, P. and Bicksler, J. (1975). Capital asset prices versus time-series models as predictors of inflation, Journal of Financial Economics, II(December).

Hirsch, A.A. and Lovell, M.C. (1969). Sales Anticipations and Inventory Behavior, (New York: John Wiley and Sons, Inc.).

Hoffman, D.L. and Schmidt, P. (1978). Testing the restrictions implied by the rational expectations hypothesis, Econometrics Workshop Paper No. 7804, Michigan State University, October.

Holmes, J.M. and Smyth, D.J. (1979). Excess demand for labor, unemployment, and theories of the Phillips curve, Journal of Macroeconomics, I(Fall).

Hsiao, C. (1976). Identification and estimation of simultaneous equation models with measurement errors, International Economic Review, XVII (April).

Joreskog, J.M. and Sorbom, D. (1979). Lisrel IV - Estimation of Linear Structural Equation System by Maximum Likelihood Methods, (Chicago: National Education Resources, Inc.).

Juster, T. (1973). Savings behavior, uncertainty and price expectations, In: Strumple, et.at. (Eds.), Surveys of Consumers: 1972-1973 (Ann Arbor: Institute for Social Research, University of Michigan).

Juster, T. and Comment, R. (1978). A note on the measurement of price expectations. Mimeographed, University of Michigan, Ann Arbor.

Kantor, B. (1979). Rational expectations and economic thought, The Journal of Economic Literature, XVII(December).

Kmenta, J. and Gilbert, R.F. (1968). Small sample properties of alternative estimators of seemingly unrelated regressions, Journal of the American Statistical Association, LXII(December).

Koopmans, T.C., Rubin, H. and Leipnik, R.B. (1950). Measuring the equation systems of dynamic economics. In: Koopmans, T.C. (Ed.), Statistical Inference in Dynamic Economic Models (New York: Wiley).

Koopmans, T.C. (1957). The State of Economic Science (New York: McGraw-Hill).

Kuh, E. (1967). A productivity theory of wage levels - an alternative to the Phillips curve, Review of Economics Studies, (October).

Lahiri, K. (1976). Inflationary expectations: their formation and interest rate effects, American Economic Review, LXVI(March).

Lahiri, K. (1977). A joint study on expectations formation and the shifting Phillips curve, Journal of Monetary Economics, III(July).

Lahiri, K. and Schmidt, P. (1978). On the estimation of triangular structural systems, Econometrica, LXVI(October).

Lahiri, K. (1979). On the constancy of real interest rates, Economics Letters, III(No. 3).

Lahiri, K. and Gold, K. (1980). On the mark: a theory of floating exchange rates based on real interest differentials: comment, mimeo., State University of New York. (January)

Laidler, D.E. and Parkin, M.J. (1975). Inflation: a survey, Economic Journal LXXXV(December).

Land, K.C. (1973). Identification, parameter estimation and hypothesis testing in recursive sociological models. In: Goldberger, A.S. and Duncan, O.D. (Eds.), Structural Equation Models in the Social Sciences (New York: Seminar Press).

Levi, M.D. and Makin, J.H. (1978). Anticipated inflation and interest rates: further interpretation of findings on the Fisher equation, American Economic Review, LXVIII(March).

Levi, M.D. and Makin, J.H. (1979). Fisher, Phillips, Friedman and the measured impact of inflation on interest, Journal of Finance, XXXIV (March).

Levi, M. and Makin, J. (1980). Inflation uncertainty and the Phillips curve: some empirical evidence, American Economic Review, LXX(December).

Lipesy, R.G. and Parkin, J.M. (1970). Incomes policy: a reappraisal, Economica, XXXVII(May).

Lucas, R.E., Jr. and Rapping, L.A. (1969). Real wages, employment and inflation, Journal of Political Economy, LXXVII(Sept./Oct.).

Lucas, R.E., Jr. (1973). Some international evidence on output-inflation trade-offs, American Economic Review, LXIII(June).

Lucas, R.E., Jr. (1975). An equilibrium model of the business cycle, Journal of Political Economy, LXXXIII(December).

Lucas, R.E., Jr. (1976). Econometric policy evaluation: a critique. In: Brunner, K. and Meltzer, A.H. (Eds.), The Phillips Curve and Labor Markets (Amsterdam: North-Holland).

Maccini, L.J. (1978). The impact of demand and price expectations on the behavior of prices, American Economic Review, LXVII(March).

Maddala, G.S. (1977). Econometrics (New York: McGraw-Hill).

McCallum, B.T. (1976a). Rational expectations and the natural rate hypothesis: some consistent estimates, Econometrica, LXIV(January).

McCallum, B.T. (1976b). Rational expectations and the estimation of econometric models: an alternative procedure, International Economic Review, XVII(June).

McCallum, B.T. (1977). Price-level stickiness and the feasibility of monetary stabilization policy with rational expectations, Journal of Political Economy, LXXXV(June).

McCallum, B.T. (1979). On the observational inequivalence of classical and Keynesian models, Journal of Political Economy, LXXXVII(April).

McGuire, T. (1976a). Price change expectations and the Phillips curve. In: Brunner, K. and Meltzer, A. (Eds.), The Economics of Price and Wage Controls (Amsterdam: North-Holland).

McGuire, T. (1976b). On estimating the effects of controls. In: Brunner, K. and Meltzer, A. (Eds.) The Economics of Price and Wage Controls (Amsterdam: North-Holland).

Miller, M.H. and Modigliani, F. (1966). Some estimates of the cost of capital to electric utility industry, 1954-57, American Economic Review, LVI(June).

Modigliani, F. and Shiller, R.J. (1973). Inflation, rational expectations, and the term structure of interest rates, Economica, XL(February).

Mortenson, D.T. (1970). A theory of wage and employment dynamics. In: Phelps, E.S., et. al. (Eds.), Microeconomic Foundations of Employment and Inflation Theory (New York: Norton).

Mullineaux, D.J. (1978). On testing for rationality: another look at the Livingston price expectations data, Journal of Political Economy, LXXXVI(April).

Mullineaux, D.J. (1980). Inflation expectations and money growth in the United States, American Economic Review, LVV(March).

Mundel, R. (1963). Inflation and real interest, Journal of Political Economy, LXXI(June).

Mussa, M. (1975). Adaptive and regressive expectations in a rational model of the inflationary process, Journal of Monetary Economics, I(December).

Muth, J.F. (1960). Optimal properties of exponentially weighted forecasts, Journal of American Statistical Association, LV(June).

Muth, J.F. (1961). Rational expectations and the theory of price movements, Econometrica, XXVIV(July).

Nelson, C.R. and Schwert, G.W. (1977). On testing the hypothesis that real rate of interest is constant, American Economic Review, LXVII(June).

Nelson, C.R. (1979). Granger causality and the natural rate hypothesis, Journal of Political Economy, LXXXVII(April).

Nerlove, M. (1958). The Dynamics of Supply: Estimation of Farmers' Response to Price, (Baltimore: The Johns Hopkins Press).

Oi, W.Y. (1976). On measuring the impact of wage-price controls: a critical appraisal. In: Brunner, K. and Meltzer, A. (Eds.), The Economics of Price and Wage Controls (Amsterdam: North-Holland).

Pearce, D.K. (1979). Comparing survey and rational measures of expected inflation, Journal of Money, Credit and Banking, XI(November).

Perry, G.L. (1967). Wages and guideposts, American Economic Review, LVII(September).

Perry, G.L. (1969). Wages and guideposts: reply, American Economic Review, LVIV(June).

Perry, G.L. (1970). Changing labor markets and inflation, Brookings Papers on Economic Activity, II(No. 3).

Pesando, J.E. (1975). A note on the rationality of Livingston price expectations, Journal of Political Economy, LXXXIII(August).

Pesando, J.E. (1976). Rational expectations and disbuted lag expectations proxy, Journal of the American Statistical Association, LXXI(March).

Phelps, E.S. (1967). Phillips curves, expectations of inflation and optimal unemployment over time, Economica, XXXIV(August).

Phelps, E.S. and Taylor, J.B. (1977). Stabilizing powers of monetary policy under rational expectations, Journal of Political Economy, LXXXV(February).

Poole, W. (1976). Rational expectations in the macro model, Brookings Papers on Economic Activity, VII(No. 2).

Pyle, D.H. (1972). Observed price expectations and interest rates, Review of Economics and Statistics, LIV(August).

Revankar, N.S. (1980). Testing of the rational expectations hypothesis, Econometrica, XLVIII(September).

Roll, R. (1972). Interest rates on monetary assets and price index changes, Journal of Finance: Papers and Proceedings, XXVII(May).

Rutledge, J. (1974). A Monetary Model of Inflation Expectations, (Lexington: Lexington Books).

Santomero, A.M. and Seater, J.J. (1978). The inflation - unemployment trade-off: a critique of the literature. Journal of Economic Literature, XVI(June).

Sargan, J.D. (1958). The estimation of economic relationships using instrumental variables, Econometrica, XXVI(July).

Sargent, T.J. (1969). Commodity price expectations and the interest rate, Quarterly Journal of Economics, LXXXIII(February).

Sargent, T.J. (1971). A note on the accelerationist' controvery, Journal of Money, Credit and Banking, 3(August).

Sargent, T.J. (1973). Rational expectations, the real rate of interest and the natural rate of unemployment, Brookings Papers on Economic Activity, V(No. 3).

Sargent, T.J. (1976). A classical macroeconomic model for the United States, Journal of Political Economy, LXXXIV(April).

Sargent, T.J. and Wallace, N. (1975). Rational expectations, the optimal monetary instrument and the optimal money supply rule, Journal of Political Economy, LXXXIII(April).

Sargent, T.J. and Wallace, N. (1976). Rational expectations and the theory of economic policy, Journal of Monetary Economics, II(April).

Sheahan, J. (1967). The Wage-Price Guideposts, (Washington, D.C.: The Brookings Institution).

Shiller, R.S. (1978). Rational expectations and the dynamic structure of macroeconomic models, Journal of Monetary Economics, IV(January).

Shuford, H.L. (1970). Subjective variables in economic analysis: a study of consumers' expectations, Ph.D. dissertation, Yale University, New Haven.

Sims, C. (1980). Macroeconomics and reality, Econometrica, XLVIV(January).

Solow, R.M. (1969). Price Expectations and the Behavior of the Price Level. Manchester: Manchester University Press).

Taylor, J.B. (1975). Monetary policy during a transition to rational expectations, Journal of Political Economy, LXXXIII(October).

Tanzi, V. (1980). Inflationary expectations, economic activity, taxes, and interest rates, American Economic Review, LVV(March).

Tintner, G. (1952). Econometrics. (New York: Wiley).

Turnovsky, S.J. (1970). Some empirical evidence on the formation of price expectations, Journal of the American Statistical Association, LXV(December).

Turnovsky, S.J. (1974). On the role of inflationary expectations in a short-run macro-economic model, Economic Journal, LXXXIV(June).

Turnovsky, S.J. (1979). Inflationary expectations in a two-sector model of wage price determination, Oxford Economic Papers, XXXI(March).

Turnovsky, S.J. and Wachter, M.L. (1972). A test of the 'expectations hypothesis' using directly observed wage and price expectations, Review of Economics and Statistics, LIV(February).

Visco, J. (1975). Inflation and the rate of interest, Quarterly Journal of Economy, LXXXXIX(May).

Wallis, K.F. (1980). Econometric implications of the rational expectations hypothesis, Econometrica, XLVIV(January).

Wachtel, P. (1977). Survey measures of expected inflation and their potential usefulness. In: Pokin J. (Ed.), Analysis of Inflation, (Cambridge: Ballinger Publishing Co.).

Wachter, M.L. (1976). The changing cyclical responsiveness of wage inflation, Brookings Papers on Economic Activity, VIII(No. 1).

Wickens, M.R. (1969). The consistency and efficiency of generalized least squares in simultaneous equation systems with auto-correlated errors, Econometrica, XXXVII(October).

Wold, H. (1963). Forecasting by the chain principle. In: Rosenblatt, M. (Ed.), Proceedings of the Symposium on Time Series Analysis, (New York: Wiley).

Wu, D.M. (1973). Alternative tests of independence between stochastic regressors and disturbances, Econometrica, XLI(July).

Yohe, W.P. and Karnosky, D.S. (1969). Interest rates, and the price level changes, Federal Reserve Bank of St. Louis Review, LI(December).

Zellner, A. (1962). An efficient method of estimating seemingly unrelated regressions and tests for aggregation bias, Journal of the American Statistical Association, LVII(June).

Zellner, A. (1970). Estimation of regression relationships containing unobservable independent variables, International Economic Review, XI(October).

Zellner, A. (1971). An Introduction to Bayesian Inference in Econometrics (New York: Wiley).

INDEX

Accelerationist hypothesis, 2, 11, 61, 169
Anderson, P.A., 22, 50, 60, 69
Anderson, T.W., 20
Anticipated inflation, 149 see also: Expectations
Arrow, K,J., 48
Auernheimer, L., 170, 213
Autocorrelation, 145, 147
Autoregressive process, 71, 84
Auxiliary regression, 28, 31, 33, 62, 66

Barro, R.J., 48, 63, 175
Bhalla, S., 188, 193, 197
Biased proxy, 150, 175
Bicksler, J., 218
Bomberger, W.A., 217
Brinner, R., 1, 8, 20, 213
Brown, B.W., 197
Brunner, K. , 66
Business Conditions Digest, 203

Cagan, P., 4
Capital market, 119
Carlson, J.A., 22, 34-35, 49, 121, 129, 145, 152, 159, 189, 196, 216
Chow, G.C., 178
Chow test, 36, 40, 112
Comment, R., 193
Compensation per manhour, 7, 130
Conditioning variables, 67
Consensus forecast, 34-35, 130
Consistency property, 49, 152
Consumer Price Index, 106
Counter-cyclical policy, 63
Cukierman, A., 19-20, 22, 34-35, 49, 121, 129, 145, 152, 159, 189, 196, 216

Darby, M., 120, 129
de Menil, G., 56, 188, 192-193, 197, 213
Depreciation, 129
Dhrymes, P.J., 30
Directional question, 189
Distributed lag of past prices, 2
Dummy variables, 78, 112
Durbin, J., 9, 20, 148
Durbin-Watson statistic, 9, 32, 58, 73

Eckstein, O., 1, 8, 20, 213
Econometric artifact, 60
Efficiency property, 48, 152, 183
Efficient market model, 149
Elliott, J.W., 146, 156, 158, 174, 216
Equilibrium theory, 73
Equity-debt ratio, 129
Enzler, J.J., 56
Error-adjustment, 2
Errors of measurement, 2, 4, 11, 20, 26, 33, 109, 129, 169
Error-variance, 11
Estimation:
- empirical results, 9, 31, 54, 107, 128
- maximum-likelihood, 51-53, 68, 77, 122, 177, 183, 194
- non-linear, 18, 85
- three-stage least squares, 27-29, 76, 109, 184
- two-stage least squares, 8, 10

Expectations:
- adaptive, 2, 5, 9, 106, 170
- catch-up term, 10
- distributed lag, 4, 18, 106
- extrapolative, 2, 5, 32, 106
- long term, 9, 107
- partly rational, 59, 66, 75, 123
- rational, 48, 58, 64, 66
- regressive, 2, 5, 9, 106, 170
- twelve-month, 7

Exploitable Phillips curve, 69
Extended reduced form, 71, 81

Fair, R.C. , 50, 69
Fama, E., 119, 145, 149, 158, 216
Feedback effects, 62
Feldstein, M., 120, 129
Feige, E.L., 215
Fischer, S., 48, 175
Fishe, R.P.H., 193
Fisher effect, 2, 119, 122, 135
Fisher equation, 19, 103, 157, 173
Fisher, F., 48
Fixed-weight wage index, 7
Follow-up question, 189
Forecasting error, 145
FRB-MIT-PENN model, 22
Frankel, J., 214
Frazer, Jr., W.J., 217
Frenkel, J.A., 5-6, 9-10, 13, 106-107, 170
Friedman, B., 48-49, 66
Friedman, M., 22, 200, 213

Gandolphi, A.E., 216
Gelfand, J., 77
Generalized least squares, 178

Geraci, V.J., 30
Gibson, W., 2, 35, 104-105, 109, 156
Gilbert, R.F., 187
GNP gap, 133
Gold, K., 214
Goldberger, A.S., 20, 23, 28, 122, 214-215
Gordon, R.J., 1-3, 7, 10, 12, 19-20, 22, 36, 38-40, 50, 58, 103, 215
Government spending, 74
Granger causality, 64
Growth model, 129
Guideposts, Kennedy-Johnson period, 8-10

Hamburger, M.J., 120
Hausman, J.A., 20, 34, 57, 178
Hendershott, P.H., 121, 133, 216
Hendry, D.A., 183
Hess, P., 218
Heteroskedasticity, 32, 152
Hirsch, A.A., 5
Hoffman, D.L., 69, 72
Holmes, J.M., 215
Hsiao, C., 20
Hurwich, L., 20

Identification condition in EVM model, 30
Identifying restrictions, 65, 135 see also: Overidentifying restrictions

Inflation:
- cost-push, 21,
- demand-pull, 21
- sustained, 1
- unanticipated, 41, 49, 60, 62, 86
- uncertainty in, 132, 188
- welfare cost of, 7

Inflationary expectations, 1, 8, 103 see also: Expectations
Information availability assumption, 64, 66, 99, 172
Instrumental variables, 8, 11, 28, 34, 54, 60, 75, 148, 183, 216, 218
Interest rate:
- nominal, 103, 160, 173
- real, 49, 103, 119, 130, 145, 149, 155

Internal instrument, 54
IS-LM model, 74

Jöreskog, J.M., 77, 135, 214
Juster, T., 189, 193

Kantor, B., 67
Karnowsky, D.S., 111, 146, 156
Keynesian policy, 50
Kmenta, J., 187
Knowledge surrogates, 67
Koopmans, T.C., 30, 67
Kuh, E., 213

Labor market disequilibrium, 21
Lahiri, K., 9, 77, 193, 214
Laidler, D.E., 213
Land, K.C., 178
Leipnik, R.B., 30
Levi, M., 132, 200, 216
Lipsey, R.G., 1
Liquidity Preference, 130
Livingston's survey data, 2, 9-10, 19, 39, 49, 57, 105, 129, 149, 189
Loanable Fund theory, 130
Log-likelihood function, 73, 85, 184, 195
Lovell, M.C., 5
Lucas, R.E., 22, 37, 48, 171, 213

Maccini, L.J., 23, 33
Macro models, 48, 132
Maddala, G.S., 217
Maital, S., 197
Makin, J., 132, 200, 216
Marginal tax rate, 129
Market efficiency, 119
Maximum likelihood estimater, 8, 9, 56, 66, see also: Estimation
McCallum, B.T., 32, 50, 54, 56, 63, 65, 73, 75, 175, 215, 218
McGuire, T., 19, 36, 39, 170
Meltzer, A., 66
Model:
  structural, 20
  unobservable-variable, 12
Modligliani, F., 182
Monetarist Phillips curve, 62
Monetary policy, 62
Money supply, 5, 32, 67
Mortensen, D.T., 213
MPS model, 65
Mullineaux, D.J., 152
Mundell, R., 120, 145, 149, 151, 174
Mussa, M., 213
Muth, J.F., 48-49, 58

Natural rate hypothesis, 18, 33, 36, 40, 49, 60, 75, 78, 181
Nelson, C.R., 64, 145, 147, 158, 174
Nerlove, M., 4
Neutrality of real variables, 56
Newton's method, 178
Normal distribution, 193
Normalization, 69, 137

Osborne, T., 77
Overidentification, 20, 22
Overidentifying restriction, 24-26, 37, 40, 72, 82, 170
Overtime rates, 39

Path analysis, 178
Pay board, 39
Pearce, D.K., 153, 212
Peasando, J.E., 152, 215
Perfect forecast, 62
Perry, G.L., 1, 7-8, 13, 20
Phelps, E.S., 115, 213
Philadephia Inquirer, 2
Phillips curve, 1, 11, 41, 48-49, 54, 60, 76, 171, 188
Platt, E.N., 120
Policy evaluation, 22, 171
Policy mix, 64
Policy neutrality, 66
Poole, W., 48, 61
Potential output, 74
Predictive efficiency, 159
Price forecast, 188
Productivity, 21
Proxy variable, 27, 103, 122, 130
Pyle, D.H., 2, 35, 105, 109, 130

Random walk model, 120
Rapping, L.A., 213
Rational expectations hypothesis, 48-49, 53-54, 119, 130, 135, 152
Rationality of survey data, 154
Real effects, 61
Recessions, 159
Recursive model, 177
Reduced form equations, 18, 35, 38
Revankar, N.S., 69
Roll, E., 120
Rubin, H., 30
Rutledge, J., 56, 59, 66

Sample survey, 20
Sampling error, 150
Santemero, A.M., 213
Sargan, J.D., 20
Sargent, T.J., 1, 48, 61, 63, 66, 130, 216
Schmidt, P., 9, 69, 72
Schwert, W., 145, 147, 158, 174
Seasonal adjustment, 74
Seater, J.J., 213
Seemingly unrelated regression, 38
Sheahan, T., 8
Shiller, R.J., 152, 218
Shufford, H.L., 192
Sims, C., 215
Simultaneous equations, 8
Smyth, D., 215
Solow, R.J., 20
Sörbom, D., 77, 135, 214
Specification test, 37

Spurious promotion, 39
Stabilization policy, 48, 54, 62
St. Louis model, 22, 69
Structural change, 111, 170
Structural model, 2-3, 108, 147
Subcontracting of work, 39
Summers, L., 129
Supplementary surveys, 189
Survey of Current Business, 202
Survey Research Center, 188

Tanzi, V., 129, 132
Tax deductions, 129
Taylor, J.B., 63, 175
Technical progress, 32
Tests for:
- errors-in-variables, 20, 33, 57 see also: Errors in measurement
- rational expectations, 69, 73, 86, 154, 171

Three-indicator models, 133
Tintner, G., 23
Treasury bills, 106, 119, 132, 145, 173
Trend productivity, 130

Unemployment:
- dispersion index, 7, 10, 169
- disguised, 7, 10
- natural rate, 18, 48
- official rate, 3, 7, 48, 60
- total rate, 59, 62

Unfilled orders to capacity, 21, 130
Unobservable variables, 64
Unobservable-variable model, 122, 169

van Horne, J.C., 121, 133, 216

Wachter, M.L., 2-3, 10-12, 35, 56, 103
Wage equation, 20, 67
Wage inflation, 18
Wage-Price Controls, 36-38, 40, 171
Wage-price model:
- inflexibility of, 48
- instability of, 8, 36
- simultaneity in, 18, 21, 24, 33, 49, 54, 66, 170

Wallace, N., 48-49, 63, 66
Wallis, K.F., 69, 76-77, 172
Watchel, P., 175, 192, 196
Wickens, M.R., 32
Wold, H., 153
Wu, D.M., 34

Yohe, W.P., 111, 146, 156

Zellner, A., 38, 122, 124, 178, 183